# ISLANDS UNDER SIEGE

# DEVELOPMENT OF WESTERN RESOURCES

The Development of Western Resources is an interdisciplinary series focusing on the use and misuse of resources in the American West. Written for a broad readership of humanists, social scientists, and resource specialists, the books in this series emphasize both historical and contemporary perspectives as they explore the interplay between resource exploitation and economic, social, and political experiences.

John G. Clark, University of Kansas, General Editor

# ISLANDS
# UNDER SIEGE

## National Parks
## and the Politics
## of External Threats

John C. Freemuth

 University Press of Kansas

Published by the University Press of Kansas (Lawrence, Kansas
66045), which was organized by the Kansas Board of Regents and is
operated and funded by Emporia State University, Fort Hays State
University, Kansas State University, Pittsburg State University,
the University of Kansas, and Wichita State University

Library of Congress Cataloging-in-Publication Data

Freemuth, John C. (John Carter)
    Islands under siege : national parks and the politics of external
threats / John C. Freemuth.
        p.    cm. — (Development of western resources)
    Includes bibliographical references and index.
    ISBN 0-7006-0434-0 (alk. paper)
    1. National parks and reserves—Government policy—United States.
2. United States. National Park Service. 3. National parks and
reserves—West (U.S.)—Management. 4. Transboundary pollution—West
(U.S.) 5. National parks and reserves—Law and legislation—United
States. 6. Environmental policy—United States.   I. Title.
II. Series.
SB482.A4F74    1991
333.78'3'0973—dc20                                              90-43742
                                                                    CIP

British Library Cataloguing in Publication Data is available.

Printed in the United States of America
10 9 8 7 6 5 4 3 2 1

The paper used in this publication meets the minimum requirements of the American
National Standard for Permanence of Paper for Printed Library Materials Z39.48-1984.

To my father, John Lincoln Freemuth,
and in memory of my mother,
Doris Mae Ashmore Freemuth . . .

And to our first trip West

But ever since I was old enough to be cynical I have been visiting national parks, and they are a cure for cynicism, an exhilarating rest from the competitive avarice we call the American Way. They were cooked up in the same alembic as other land laws—the Homestead Act, Preemption Act, Timber and Stone Act, Mining Act of 1872—but they came out as something different. Absolutely American, absolutely democratic, they reflect us at our best rather than our worst. Without them, millions of American lives, including mine, would have been poorer. The world would have been poorer.

—*Wallace Stegner*

# CONTENTS

# ILLUSTRATIONS

# PREFACE

In January 1987, an article appeared in the magazine *Nature*. That article probably passed unnoticed by readers outside the scientific community, but its topic dealt with an issue that may be increasingly familiar to the many visitors to our national parks. The title of the article, "A Land-Bridge Island Perspective on Mammalian Extinctions in Western North American Parks," may sound academic, but the topic is not. The author, William Newmark, examined a hypothesis developed to explain the rate of extinction of species on "land-bridge islands" (islands once connected to a mainland) and applied the hypothesis to mammalian species in selected national parks in the western United States and Canada. His conclusion was that the species loss he found "indicates that virtually all western North American national parks were too small to maintain the mammalian faunal assemblage found at [the] time of park establishment."[1] Any future loss, said Newmark, "will most probably require that the mammalian fauna within the parks be more actively managed and that the parks be 'enlarged' either through the acquisition or the cooperative management of lands adjacent to the parks."

The article was not any sort of landmark, as it did not highlight a new problem. But it did bring some clear and important scientific information to an issue that was gaining a lot of attention both within and outside the National Park Service: the increasing impacts on park resources and values from activities outside the boundaries of the national parks. These activities have come to be known as "external threats."

Consider one recent example—oil and gas extraction near the boundaries of Glacier National Park in Montana. In 1980, the Park Service identified this "crown jewel" park as the park in the western United States with the most threats. Oil and gas development figured prominently as one of the most serious threats. Later, in 1987, the Wilderness Society named Glacier as one of the ten parks in the United States most threatened by adjacent development, once again listing oil development as a major problem. Yet in 1989, Montana's Board of Oil and Gas Conservation approved more oil drilling next to the park. As one might expect, environmentalists were outraged, saying that there were areas of the earth "where dangerous development, where any kind of industrialization doesn't belong."[2] Developers promised to be careful while wondering what all the fuss was about, noting that "there are producing wells on college campuses, downtown business districts, in back yards. They can be made almost totally compatible with almost any environment."[3] The Park Service, with no regulatory control over development outside Glacier's boundaries, expressed hope that industry would invest in enough mitigation to make it a "good neighbor."[4] Other drilling was also planned, approved by "sister" federal land management agencies, the Forest Service and the Bureau of Land Management (BLM).

Although this case is particularly illustrative of the issue, the problem of external threats is not confined to Glacier. It is a problem throughout the park system. It is also not the type of problem that the National Park Service is used to dealing with, as most park management issues have traditionally been within the boundaries of a park system unit. Nor is it often something the Park Service has any clear legal authority to act on. Yet today, it is increasingly easy to argue that the national parks, an American idea Wallace Stegner once called the "best we ever had," are islands surrounded by a rising tide of civilization.[5] How we ultimately manage and deal with this problem may tell us whether these parks will remain for future generations throughout the world to enjoy.

# ACKNOWLEDGMENTS

Over the course of writing this book, I was fortunate to have the help and encouragement of a large number of people. This book was originally my dissertation. The faculty with whom I worked at Colorado State University—Phil Foss, Henry Caulfield, Norm Wengert, Wayne Peak, Bob Dudley, and Burnell Held—kept me focused on the politics of external threats when I often would get bogged down in details. They made writing an experience that was positive, and I thank them for that.

A special note is in order regarding Phil Foss. His guidance, comments, and criticisms were essential to my work on the external threats issue. My writing improved remarkably during the process, because he took the time to insure that it did. Readers who are familiar with Foss's work know his contribution to political science in general and to natural resource policy in particular. He was the key to establishing a doctoral program at Colorado State that emphasized natural resource policy. His book *Politics and Grass* (Seattle: University of Washington Press, 1960) was one of the first to identify the "iron triangle" relationship. He applied it to the Bureau of Land Management, the ranchers and grazing boards, and western congressmen. However, he called the relationship "a private government." Academe being what it is, that term didn't catch on, but iron triangle did.

Roderick Nash has kindly followed my activities since our first visit ten years ago. He has encouraged me to pursue my studies in this area and was of great help on this manuscript. He also suggested the title for this book.

I completed this work while I was at Boise State University (BSU), which is in a state that has mountain wilderness, an infrequently visited canyon country, and no national parks. I want to thank my colleagues at BSU who created the environment necessary for a new professor to write and flourish, thereby adding perhaps to the claim that Idaho "is what America was." Special thanks go to Will Overgaard, my first chair; Gary Moncrief, my second chair; and Jim Weatherby, director of the Master of Public Affairs Program. Greg Raymond, our most accomplished scholar, also took the time to be encouraging and supportive, even during his own active research efforts.

I would also like to draw attention to the numerous natural resource professionals who helped with this study. It has become more than fashionable to criticize the public bureaucracy. That criticism is sometimes justified, but not in this case. The people I worked with, who helped me with documents, read drafts of chapters for technical accuracy, and took the time to be interviewed, represent the best of the public service. Thanks go to Tom Slater and Ronald Bolander of the state office of the BLM, Salt Lake City, for their help with the BLM perspective on the tar sands case. There were also many people in the Park Service who shared invaluable insights about the agency and its problems, the parks, and park policy. They include Larry Belli, Chuck Wood, Jim Holland, Vic Vieira, David Joseph, Brian Mitchell, Bill Malm, and Bill Paleck. Chuck Wood read the tar sands chapter for factual accuracy. David Joseph and Brian Mitchell went to special lengths to read the visibility chapter, which could not have been written without their help. I am particularly grateful to two people in the Park Service who followed this work from the outset. Bill Supernaugh has been a good source of insight on the Park Service since I first met him in 1979 while I was a ranger at Glen Canyon. The late Tom Lucke spent more than a few afternoons in Fort Collins pointing me in the right direction as I struggled with making sense out of the threats problem. The National Park Service lost someone irreplaceable when he passed away.

The people at the University Press of Kansas are also to be thanked for making my work on this manuscript easier, and a much better product as a result.

Finally, and most important, I must acknowledge the support of my family during what must have seemed to them an endless and bewildering ordeal. My mother and father were probably a bit worried when I headed off to graduate school at the age of thirty-two; I hope this book rewards their patience. I regret that I couldn't have figured it all out earlier so that my mother could have seen my work in print. My sister, Anne Brown, provided a computer and laser printer when they were most needed. My father-in-law, Ken Zumwalt, inspired me when his own book on the *Stars and Stripes* was recently published to great reviews. The support of my wife, Sheri, has been the most crucial. She more than anyone had to bear the stress and complaining. Without her encouragement, I could not have finished this book. I now plan to start worrying about the next one.

# CHAPTER ONE

# Studying the
# External Threats Problem

The national park system of the United States is one of the best-known and most-admired examples of natural resource protection in the world. In 1916, Congress created the National Park Service (NPS) and at the same time gave that agency statutory direction on how to manage the parks under its care. The Park Service Organic Act (1916) stated in a now familiar passage that

> the service thus established shall promote and regulate the use of the Federal areas known as national parks, monuments and reservations . . . by such means and measures as conform to the fundamental purpose of the said parks, which purpose is to conserve the scenery and the natural and historic objects and the wildlife therein and to provide for the enjoyment of the same in such manner and by such means as will leave them unimpaired for the enjoyment of future generations.[1]

This section of the act created what has come to be known as the "use versus preservation" policy debate, a debate carried on both within and outside the Park Service. It centers on whether the national parks should be managed more for human visitation and "enjoyment" (hence use) or more for "unimpaired" resource protection (hence preservation).

For example, Ronald Foresta, a scholar of national park policy, claims: "A park is anthropocentric, its special quality comes from its appeal to humans." Perhaps it is appropriate to have a lodge in a park, then. On the other hand, a coalition of environmental interest groups recently argued that "any activity which degrades [the parks'] pristine quality is contrary to the purpose for which they were established." That same lodge may no longer belong in a national park.[2] Historically, the debate has raged over Park Service management policies *within* the boundaries of a park unit.[3] An example familiar to many would be the extent of automobile access to be permitted in parks such as Yosemite or Grand Canyon. Visitors who have ridden shuttle buses during peak summer visitation months at either of these parks have experienced Park Service attempts to manage for both use and preservation.

Today, however, the Park Service is faced with a new and growing man-

1

agement problem that affects both aspects of the agency's mission. The parks are increasingly seen as islands surrounded by the rising tide of civilization. In one sense, being threatened by aspects of civilization is nothing new for the park system. Historically, parks were created to avoid being exploited, primarily by commercial development, because of their scenic attractiveness. Today, however, energy development, urban encroachment, and air and water pollution are the newest manifestations of civilization. At the Grand Canyon, a visitor's ability to see across that mighty chasm may well be affected by pollutants from as far away as the Los Angeles basin. These same pollutants may also affect some of the park's flora and fauna. More and more, it seems, the Park Service faces a resource management problem that stems from outside the boundaries of the parks themselves.

In most cases, the agency does not have the authority to act on these outside problems, or "external threats," so any resolution of the external threats problem must often rely on consultation and cooperation with other federal agencies, as well as with state and local governments and agencies. As the Park Service noted:

> Because neighbors of federal lands [including other federal neighbors such as the Forest Service] often have different land-use objectives and expectations, conflicts can be formidable. Service actions to protect and preserve the irreplaceable park resources of national significance must be forged in the crucible of the political process as attempts are made to determine the appropriate relationship between park lands and lands of neighbors.[4]

The external threats issue is thus fundamentally a political problem—and a rather large one. A Park Service study conducted in 1980 identified over two thousand outside activities affecting various units of the national park system.[5] In addition, there is, as has been mentioned, often no clear direction given on or authority speaking to the external threats problem. Where there is some statutory direction, it is often focused on one type of threat (or threatened resource), such as air pollution or water pollution, or on a specific park. Yet this piecemeal approach to the external threats problem also contains vital lessons that can help us understand the politics of the threats issue. A careful examination of selected case studies can offer the opportunity to generalize about the potential to resolve the larger problems of external threats throughout the park system.

CASE STUDIES

Perhaps the most useful criterion for determining which external threats issues to study is the seriousness of the threat. Fortunately, different authorities seem to agree on which threats are the most serious. William Everhart, a former assistant to the director for policy in the Park Service, as well as historian of the agency, noted that "air pollution, principally from the burning of fossil fuels, poses the greatest threat to the parks."[6] J. Douglas Wellman, another park policy expert, pointed out that the coal-fired power plants near Farmington, New Mexico, created a plume that was the only visible sign of human activity seen by the Gemini III astronauts in orbit around the earth.[7] These power plants are close to the many national parks and monuments of the Colorado Plateau region of the Southwest, including Grand Canyon, Mesa Verde, Zion, Bryce, and Arches national parks.

Wellman's next most serious threat was what he termed "energy-related" activity. Ronald Foresta echoed this observation in slightly different language when he stated that

it was perhaps in connection with the parks of southern Utah that these external development threats were most severe. . . . [T]he impressive vistas they offer and the feeling of grandeur they evoke depend on the vast empty spaces of the southern Colorado Plateau which surrounds them. . . . [H]owever, the last few years have seen mineral extraction and energy development threaten the matrix in which the parks are set, and consequently the views from the parks and sometimes the air quality within the parks.[8]

Air pollution and mineral extraction and development thus are likely to be two of the most serious external activities threatening parks. As Foresta noted, they are often intertwined.

Another concern is where to study the external threats problem. Over two hundred fifty units of the park system have reported some type of external threat. Yet there is strong consensus that the large natural-area parks of the western United States constitute the core of the park system. According to Foresta, "If there is one charge wholly unquestioned by Park Service personnel or the agency's critics, it is agency responsibility for the management of America's great natural areas, the several dozen national parks commonly referred to as the 'crown jewels' of the National Park System."[9] Protection of these crown jewels would seem a priority. They are the core of the park system and are symbols to many people of the national park ideal.

A further narrowing can be made by considering the parks of the Colorado Plateau (see Map 1.1). This so-called golden circle of parklands may be the most concentrated grouping of nationally known park units in the American system. More important, the parks of this region also

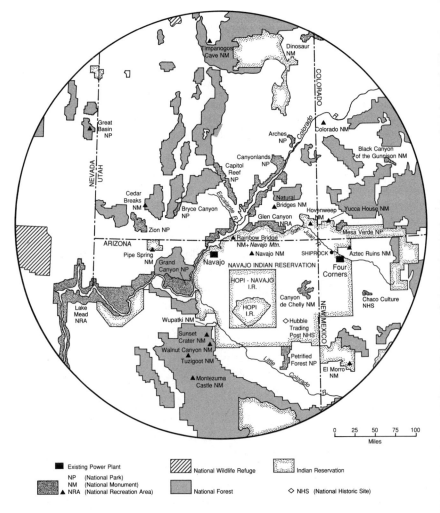

Map 1.1. The Golden Circle of Parklands

appear to be severely affected by the two activities that pose the worst threats—the production of fossil fuels and mineral extraction and development. Foresta made mention of this fact in his study, and there is other abundant evidence.

Park Service visibility studies have identified the Colorado Plateau region as having the second clearest air in the lower forty-eight states, the first being an area of southern Idaho, northern Utah, and eastern Nevada that currently contains only four units of the park system.[10] A study commissioned by the Park Service on mineral activity around and inside the national parks found that the Rocky Mountain, western, and southwestern administrative regions (all of which have jurisdiction over some part of the Plateau region) had the highest number of mineral development activities.[11] Finally, the presence of coalfields and tar sands in Utah and Colorado; the Overthrust Belt (Rocky Mountain area in Idaho, Wyoming, and Utah); the power plants at Page, Arizona, and Farmington, New Mexico; and air pollution problems created by the urban areas of Denver and Los Angeles all suggest that the external threats issue is of particular relevance to the parks of the Colorado Plateau.

A strong case can be made that the parklands of Alaska are unquestionably of crown jewel status. However, I chose to exclude these parks from this study for two reasons. First, many of Alaska's national parks, with adjoining national preserves (which allow hunting, fishing, and some mineral extraction), were only recently formed in 1980. The Park Service has had difficulty establishing a presence there because of Alaskan resistance to the idea of national parks and because of the remoteness and size of many Alaskan units.[12] Gates of the Arctic, for example, encompasses seven million acres.

Second, and more important, Alaska does not reflect as intensely the value conflict over preservation and development witnessed in the lower forty-eight states. The large western parks are now accepted and admired examples of preservation management; however, energy needs, pollution, and encroaching development represent other legitimate uses increasingly brought to bear on these parks. The use versus preservation conflict is not quite so severe in Alaska, although the problem is growing if the debate over oil development in the Alaska Wildlife Refuge or the Exxon oil spill are indications.

My decision to focus on adjacent mining and air pollution necessarily precluded a third aspect of the threats problem—adjacent activities controlled by local governments. There is no question that these activities are worth study. Yet they, by their very nature, are difficult to generalize about. As the Park Service put it in an analysis of its various park protection authorities: "Participation in these types of state and local proceedings [land use decisions] is fundamental to the effective use of such state and local authorities. This can only be done on a park by park, jurisdiction by jurisdiction basis."[13] Many threat activities have their origin in either locally controlled or locally regulated land use. Examples that might be familiar to many readers are impacts caused by "gateway" communities outside national parks, such as Estes Park near Rocky Mountain National Park, or the observation tower outside of Gettysburg National Military Park.

Yet, it is unrealistic to expect a consistent national public policy on these external activities. As the Conservation Foundation stated in a study of the parks and the Park Service:

> At the heart of opposition to park service power over nonfederal land are respect for private property rights and resistance to federal intrusion into what are generally perceived to be purely local affairs. These values . . . can provoke hostility when the service raises its voice against a project.
>
> To address these concerns as well as park needs, protective measures need to be tailor-made accommodating the diversity of parks and their local jurisdictions.[14]

Thus, solutions to locally regulated external activities appear to be driven by a case-by-case approach. Although I will not be addressing this type of external threat, it is a fruitful area for further research, especially if a comparative framework can be developed for understanding solutions to locally regulated threats.

*Tar Sands Development*

In the first case study—adjacent mineral extraction—I examine the proposed development of tar sands in south-central Utah. Tar sands are oil-impregnated rocks that must be heated in order for the oil to flow so it can be pumped to the earth's surface for recovery. These tar sands are located near Canyonlands National Park and adjacent to and in Glen Canyon National Recreation Area (GCNRA). The proposed tar sands development presents several interesting aspects that make it worthy of study. First, it was a proposed development that has yet to become an existing threat to nearby park resources and values. External threats can obviously be one of two types: those already in existence and those proposed. As will be seen in more detail in the next chapter, a great deal of attention has been given to providing the Park Service with more authority to prevent potentially harmful activities from occurring. The tar sands development case is an example of such an activity.

Second, the tar sands issue involves Park Service interaction with another agency in the Department of the Interior, the Bureau of Land

Management (BLM). Many of the national parks of the western United States were carved out of public lands and thus often find themselves with BLM–administered lands as neighbors. Since the BLM is in charge of mineral leasing on federally owned public lands, it is likely that a great deal of energy-related activities that might threaten parks would be under the jurisdiction of the bureau. The BLM has what is popularly known as a "multiple-use" land management mission, and so mineral leasing and development, under proper regulation, is something the agency is supposed to allow. The tar sands leasing issue thus represents a common NPS-BLM external threats dilemma.

A third reason for studying the tar sands leasing case ties directly into Park Service relations with the BLM. The early 1980s saw several attempts to pass legislation that would structure decision making on external threat activities. That legislation focused on federally controlled activities, such as those under the administration of the BLM or the Forest Service. The 1983 Park Protection Act (see chapter 3) provided for the secretary of the Interior to review his/her leasing authority to insure that proposed leasing and resultant extraction activities would not have "adverse effects" on adjacent parkland values. This review process would be contained within the structure of the National Environmental Policy Act (NEPA) of 1969, but it was designed to draw more attention to potential impacts on park resources and values.

The 1981 Combined Hydrocarbon Leasing Act (CHLA) and resultant federal regulations required the secretary of the Interior to first determine whether tar sands leasing within Glen Canyon National Recreation Area could adversely affect the recreation area or "contiguous" park units before he or she could allow the leasing to occur. The secretary delegated this responsibility to the Park Service. Under the provisions of the CHLA, the Park Service could object to tar sands lease conversion and development on its own land if the proposed development had the potential to harm the resources of the GCNRA or adjacent parks. The actual determination would stem from information gleaned from an environmental impact statement (EIS) prepared on lease conversion proposals as structured by the NEPA process. Thus the tar sands case leasing process is similar to the proposed Park Protection Act and offers some basis for predicting how such legislation might work in practice should it pass the Congress. It is rare that such prediction of policy implementation is available to students and practitioners interested in natural resource policy. In summary, the tar sands leasing case study provides an example of a *proposed* activity with "external threat" implications; an example of NPS-BLM interaction on a threat issue; and possible signposts on how a more generic statute governing external threats might work in practice.

*Visibility Impairment*

The second case study focuses on visibility and provides opportunities not found in the tar sands case. Visibility was addressed in a specific act of Congress: the Clean Air Act Amendments of 1977. Section 169A mandated the protection of visibility in what were termed "federal Class I areas." These areas include many western national parks. Both existing visibility impairment and possible impairment from new sources of pollution were covered by the law. The Park Service was given the "affirmative responsibility" to protect "air quality related values," including visibility. This law also stated that air-quality control was, to a great extent, a state responsibility, thus placing the Park Service into close working relations with state environmental protection officials. In addition, the Environmental Protection Agency (EPA) was given important oversight and policy responsibilities concerning state enforcement of the Clean Air Act and its amendments. Much of the environmental legislation passed in the 1970s is structured somewhat like the Clean Air Act, parceling out authority to different levels of government as well as different agencies. For example, the Clean Water Act of 1977 and the Resource Conservation and Recovery (hazardous waste) Act of 1976 have similar qualities. This second case study provides an example of an *existing* threat activity; and an example of the use of an intergovernmentally structured environmental statute of the 1970s that addresses a specific external threat.

During recent attempts to pass legislation on the external threats problem, the Reagan administration took the position that no new legislation was needed to protect parks from external threats (see chapter 3). Both Interior Secretary William Clark and his successor, Donald Hodel, argued that existing legislation was adequate to protect the parks. Presumably, then, both case studies provide a test of this claim of the Reagan administration. Are the Clean Air Act Amendments, NEPA, and CHLA adequate to protect certain parks from tar sands development and visibility impairment? If they are, were these statutes used to the extent necessary to protect parks from certain threat activities? The two case studies will help to answer these questions.

# CHAPTER TWO

# The Emergence of External Threats as a Policy and Management Issue

The external threats issue is a relatively new one. It was not something that either the pre-Park Service parks or the early Park Service faced. Rather, it evolved with time, biological science, and the urbanization of much of the United States.

## THE PARKS BEFORE THE PARK SERVICE

As is well known by now, the national park system was born out of a concern for the protection of areas of scenic grandeur from the ravages of commercial exploitation and out of a belief that these areas had a beneficial impact on those who visited them. Credit is generally given to the artist George Catlin for first conceptualizing the idea of a national park. In 1834, while visiting the Great Plains, he wrote: "What a beautiful and thrilling specimen for America to preserve and hold up to the view of her refined citizens and the world, in future ages. A nation's Park, containing man and beast, in all the wild[ness] and freshness of their nature's beauty."[1] A careful reading of Catlin, however, suggests a park that would resemble something approaching a living history museum (complete with Indians), which was simply not feasible.

Scholars, as well as popular writers, have had a minor field day arguing about which park received the first legislative acknowledgment of the park idea. Some opt for Yosemite, pointing out that the 1864 congressional grant of the valley floor and nearby peaks to California for both public use and resource protection was enough to give that unit the honor.[2] H. Duane Hampton and Aubrey Haines, on the other hand, interpret the legislative action somewhat more narrowly, arguing that the Yosemite grant was not conceived of as a *national* park; rather, the honor of that conceptual first should belong to Yellowstone.[3] What is perhaps more interesting is the intent of Congress in establishing Yellowstone and granting Yosemite to California, because it can help clarify the early purposes of the national parks.

Exploration of western North America revealed a landscape unlike any that had been confronted before. Yet closely following exploration came exploitation, creating an awareness that the excitement over the

9

discovery of scenic beauty might soon give way to lamentation over its destruction for either resource or commercial needs. As startling as it might appear to us today, the discovery of the giant Sierra redwoods led to one of them being shipped to New York and later London as proof of the phenomenal tree's existence.[4] Americans also had to look no farther than Niagara Falls to see what unchecked commercialization might do to the new western discoveries.[5]

Despoliation aside, it was the pure scenic attractiveness of places like Yosemite and Yellowstone that led to the concept of a national park. It has been suggested that this was due to two factors. First, by the mid- to late nineteenth century, Americans had begun to shed their understandable fear of wilderness for a more appreciative point of view.[6] Second, Americans were beginning to see in these scenic landscapes a treasure that could rival the centuries of civilized achievement of the European Continent.[7] At last there was something that Americans could point to that was uniquely theirs.

These influences can be seen in the 1872 act that established Yellowstone National Park. The park was "dedicated and set aside as a public park or pleasuring-ground for the benefit and enjoyment of the people."[8] The secretary of the Interior was to provide rules and regulations for "the preservation from injury or spoilation of all timber, mineral deposits, natural curiosities, or wonders . . . and their retention in their natural condition."[9] This included the protection of fauna from "wanton destruction," especially destruction for a profit.[10]

The early years of park history in the United States were chaotic. The establishment of other parks followed Yellowstone, notably Mount Rainier, Crater Lake, Sequoia, and General Grant (Kings Canyon). Robert Shankland described the early efforts at administration:

> The attention . . . Congress gave to any particular work depended upon the influence of that park's special friends. The concessioners operated under widely variant regulations from park to park. The division of authority among the parks, and even, inside a single park, came close to chaos. In Yellowstone all improvements and their appropriations were managed by an officer of the Army Corps of Engineers, who answered to neither the Interior Department nor the park superintendent; the superintendent was himself an Army officer, appointed by the Secretary of War; and exclusive control [supposedly] rested with the Secretary of the Interior.[11]

The administrative situation was further exacerbated by the 1906 Antiquities Act. This act, sponsored by one of the great conservationists in congressional history, John Lacey, was a response to the widespread vandalism that was visited upon many of the archaeological sites of the American Southwest. The act did several things. First, it provided penalties for unauthorized excavations and injury to ruins and objects of antiquity. Second, it allowed the president to "declare by public proclamation historic landmarks, historic and prehistoric structures . . . to be national monuments and may reserve as a part thereof parcels of land, the limits of which in all cases shall be confined to the smallest area compatible with the proper care and management of the objects to be protected."[12] This act has been liberally used by various presidents to set aside well-known areas such as the Grand Canyon and large tracts of land in Alaska until Congress decided to make them national parks. The Antiquities Act led, however, to an administrative problem, because some of the monuments proclaimed in the early twentieth century were maintained by the Forest Service in the Department of Agriculture, others by the War Department, and still others by Interior.

Besides the administrative chaos that came about from the decentralized nature of management, administrators faced the need to establish the importance of parks in the minds of Americans and to protect the various units from those who resisted the parks' preservation focus. Much of the responsibility for protecting the large natural areas was given to the army, because Congress failed to pass adequate protection authority or appropriate sufficient funds so that the civilian administration of Yellowstone could carry out protection duties. The secretary of the Interior was able to call on the secretary of the army to provide troops to protect game and other park resources. The success of the army in managing Yellowstone led to its authority being extended to Yosemite, Sequoia, and General Grant.[13] Hampton described in detail the role the army played in protecting the new parks from poaching, vandalism, and squatting.[14] The army was "able to convince a skeptical public that preservation of the Parks was in the public interest and not an unwelcome invasion of property rights."[15] One specific legacy of the army's protection was the establishment of parks as game refuges, something not clearly provided for in the enabling legislation of many pre–Park Service parks.[16] Thus the early years of park management were those in which preservation was established as a legitimate way to manage certain public lands. Or, to put it another way, this was the period during which the parks began to be seen as "islands" to be protected from resource exploitation.

## THE CREATION OF THE NATIONAL PARK SERVICE

By the first years of the twentieth century, the administrative decentralization of the parklands had stirred calls for the creation of a single bu-

reau to oversee the parks. A coalition of influential private citizens, legis-
lators, and key administrators in the executive branch—led by J. Horace
McFarland, president of the American Civic Association—began lobby-
ing the White House to support the formation of a national parks
agency.[17] The group was able to get several bills before Congress as early
as 1900, but no action was taken. Then two important events occurred.
First, San Francisco proposed building a dam in the Hetch Hetchy valley
of Yosemite, further mobilizing the parks lobby. And although the
group, and other friends of the park, eventually lost this fight, their efforts drew greater attention to the plight of the various parks already in
existence.[18]

Second, the appointment of Stephen Mather as assistant secretary of
the Interior in charge of parks brought an energetic promoter and friend
of the parks into a position of authority. Mather launched a nationwide
publicity campaign urging Americans to spend their vacations at home
in the parks rather than abroad.[19] He also courted those in Washington
who had the power to make the park bureau a reality. As a result of his
two-week tour of the Yosemite area, during which he was accompanied
by influentials both in and out of government, Mather built an impressive coalition that helped realize the eventual passage of legislation creating the National Park Service.[20]

In 1916, the time was finally ripe for resolution of the management
problem. Again, an influential group of public and private citizens was
instrumental in drafting the bill that eventually became law. Frederick
Law Olmsted, Jr., proposed the section that set forth the new agency's
management charge and that became the core of the Park Service's Organic Act (see chapter 1).[21]

## EARLY POLICY DIRECTIONS

The first twenty years of the new agency were focused on promotion,
both of the parks and the Park Service. The first report of the director of
the Park Service provides an excellent example of this promotion. Inter-
preting the functions of the new agency under its 1916 enabling legislation, acting director Horace Albright noted: "What a brilliant statement
of constructive conservation policy is this. . . . What benefits for the
people of our time and for posterity in the direction of safeguarding
health and providing recreational facilities are promised. What splendid
recognition is given to the economic and educational value of our wonderful playgrounds."[22] Pointing out that a substantial increase in world-
wide tourism could be expected after the end of World War I, Albright
urged funding for a "systematic campaign of education" to encourage

park visitation.[23] He went on to note the efforts at promotion already under way, including the first picture book of the parks called *National Parks Portfolio,* automobile guide maps, and films and other promotional efforts by the railroads (for example, offering the addresses of companies providing rail access to the parks). On the projected increase in automobile travel to the parks, Albright was effusive in his boosterism, supporting a national highway system connecting the parks that "would stand for all time as the greatest scenic highway in the world."[24]

Albright ended with: "Our national parks need no world's fairs to lure the American people to their neighborhoods; it was clear that the movement begun here in Washington the year before to make known to America its own scenic grandeur had proved successful. Even more gratifying is the revelation of public sentiment made by the spectacular increase in national parks patronage during the season of 1917 and 1918."[25] Thus one could conclude as Donald Swain did:

> Mather held that the parks were "for the people." To deny them good roads or comfortable lodgings, he argued, was both unwise and unreasonable. The political facts of life in 1915 and 1916 simply demanded that the parks be "used." Unless and until the American people started flocking to the national park reservations, Congress would refuse to appropriate adequate funds for the administration and protection of the parks.[26]

The administrative interpretation of the 1916 Organic Act was stated in a letter from Secretary of the Interior Franklin Lane to Mather. Actually, this letter was not written by Lane but by Mather and his assistant Albright for Secretary Lane's signature. Right before he died, Horace Albright claimed credit for authoring the letter.[27] There were three directives in it: "First, that the national parks must be maintained in absolutely unimpaired form for the use of future generations as well as those of our own time; second, that they are set apart for the use, observation, health and pleasure of the people; and third, that the national interest must dictate decisions affecting public or private enterprise in the parks."[28]

It seemed that on the use versus preservation question, Mather and Albright thought the two could be reconciled. They noted that all service activities were subordinate to the Organic Act's charge to "preserve the parks for posterity in essentially their natural state. . . . [But] every opportunity should be afforded the public, wherever possible, to enjoy the national parks in the manner that best satisfies the individual taste. Automobiles and motorcycles will be permitted in all of the national parks; in fact, the parks will be kept accessible by any means practicable."[29] Lodges and similar facilities could also be used commercially for the "accommodation and entertainment of visitors."[30] Mather and Albright pursued the expansion of the number of parks, pushing for the inclusion of other important natural areas within the system.

Mather and Albright continued to enlist the backing of influential elites who had given political support to the parks in the past. These included important conservation groups such as the Sierra Club and the National Parks Association (founded by Mather and others to support Park Service activities and later renamed the National Parks and Conservation Association [NPCA]) and powerful individuals such as John D. Rockefeller, Sr. Mather and Albright also courted parts of the private sector by pointing out the financial attractiveness of tourism in and near the parklands.[31]

Both men, while promoting public use of the parks, nevertheless adhered to a policy of protection when it came to physical use of park resources. There were pressures to open parks to resource exploitation after the United States entered World War I (pressures that also occurred during World War II), but acting director Albright stressed that resources in the parks should continue to be protected unless the war was going badly.[32] In a different vein, Mather, in an action still recalled fondly by some in the Park Service, once dynamited a particularly ugly sawmill built by the Great Northern Railroad in Glacier National Park.[33]

Resource use within the parks, however, is often something the Park Service can do nothing about. Congress, in writing the Organic Act, originally permitted grazing in all existing parks except Yellowstone.[34] Congress also expressly allowed, and continues to allow, mining in national park units under certain conditions.[35] One of those units is Glen Canyon National Recreation Area, a park unit of the first case study.

## EXTERNAL THREATS: EARLY WARNING SIGNALS

By the early 1930s, the first inkling of a new management problem surfaced. In 1933, the Park Service issued the first in a series of reports on wildlife issues within the national parks. The authors of this seminal report, George Wright, Joseph Dixon, and Ben Thompson, looked at several biological problems facing wildlife administrators in the national parks. In one section, they addressed problems caused by geographical shortcomings. Basically, they contended that the major cause of unfavorable wildlife conditions stemmed from the "insufficiency of park areas as self-contained biological units."[36] In a prophetic statement that previewed the arguments of ecologists and environmentalists in the 1960s and 1970s, the authors noted: "Our natural heritage is richer than just scenic features; the realization is coming that perhaps our greatest national heritage is nature itself, with all its complexity and its abundance of life."[37] This observation was an indication that the parks were being viewed as more than the playgrounds outlined by Albright.

The report was a plea for parks with more natural boundaries and thus more complete habitats where feasible. As an example of problems caused by artificial boundaries, the report pointed to the destruction of carnivores outside of park boundaries, which protected the animals within the park. The report made four recommendations: inclusion of year-round habitat, enough habitat to maintain minimum reproductive populations, natural faunal boundaries, and complete faunal surveys for new parks.[38] Thus came official recognition that park boundaries could be permeable and might not be able to keep out all external influences.

Interestingly, the authors were quite realistic in their assessment of what actually could be accomplished: "Man can restore a needed range to a park provided he is willing to do it, but there is absolutely no way he can keep every unfavorable influence out of that park—not so long as boundaries are artificial, and some of them must always be that."[39] This is important and worth more discussion. Today, there are those, such as historian Alfred Runte, who argue that national parks will not be complete until they move from their current status of having "political boundaries" to that of encompassing full ecological units. The blame for inadequate boundaries lies with Congress. And praise should go to Wright and his colleagues, says Runte, for pointing out the inadequacy of existing park boundaries.[40]

It seems that George Wright understood the limits as well as the virtues of the "ecosystem" argument. Although certainly an appealing idea to those with environmental sensibilities, complete ecosystem parks are much more difficult to authorize, in many cases because of competing demands on resources within the ecosystems. By Runte's own standard, for example, full protection of Everglades National Park, which was created more for its biological than its scenic importance, would require a park *four* times the present unit's size.[41] One can imagine the reaction such a proposal would engender in Florida. Arguing for ecological integrity, therefore, tends to divert attention from the fact that park management will more often have to deal with problems in a much more politically complicated and messy way, because ecologically based boundaries for large natural-area parks appear to be politically infeasible. If such parks are ever created, it would be only because they have overcome the obstacles any new idea must confront in working through our political process. Ecosystem management may hold some potential. For example, the condition of grizzly bear populations around the Yellowstone area has been a catalyst for discussion about the need for more coordinated management around the park (discussed later in this chapter).

Finally, some Park Service officials closely involved with resource management and trained as biologists make the point that Wright and his colleagues were ahead of their time. Wright's recommendations for trained resource specialists, inventories of park resources, and resource planning are being adopted today, fifty years after Wright first advocated them.[42] Wright died tragically in an automobile accident in 1936, and his innovative visions temporarily receded from view as the nation became obsessed with other concerns.

## THE 1960s ✳

The next important milestone in the identification of external impacts as a policy issue occurred in the 1960s. Two reports were issued by independent panels studying various aspects of problems facing park management. The first report, issued in 1963, dealt with wildlife management problems. The panel, chaired by A. Starker Leopold, reaffirmed that most parks were simply not large enough to be considered full ecological units and thus were vulnerable to the effects of neighboring activities.[43] Citing a bighorn sheep management problem in the Sierras, the report noted that grazing on adjacent forest land might adversely affect the sheep: "The National Park Service might well take the lead in studying this problem and in formulating cooperative management plans with other agencies even though the management problem lies outside the park boundary."[44] The report called for more research on potentially threatened wildlife and for all wildlife management activity to be placed under the jurisdiction of "biologically trained personnel."[45] Finally, it noted that at least in the case of predators, some type of buffer zone to protect these animals from control activities might be a good idea.[46]

The second report dealt with research in the national parks. It was also issued in 1963 by a special committee under the auspices of the National Academy of Sciences (NAS). Pointing out that a well-defined research program in various aspects of natural history would do much to help the Park Service fulfill the protection part of its mandate, the report asserted that the agency's research efforts had lacked "continuity, coordination, and depth," as well as suffered from "expediency rather than 'long-term' considerations."[47] In its summary recommendations, the committee urged that "research should include specific attention to significant changes in land-use, in other natural resource use, or in economic activities on areas adjacent to national parks likely to affect the parks."[48]

Finally, the committee took an in-depth look at the problems of the Everglades, established in 1934 (acquisition 1947) as a national park. As stated earlier, it was the first national park created for biological rather than scenic attributes (unless one believes that biological resources can attract visitors in the same way that scenery does).[49] Sufficient water was the key resource necessary for the preservation of the park's biological communities, and the report summarized the ongoing activities of several cities and conservation districts that might have future impacts on the park's water resources.

One should not overestimate the actual policy importance of these two documents on the Park Service's attitude toward impacts on park resources caused by external activities. In 1964, George Hartzog, then director of the National Park Service, mentioned the two reports in his testimony to the House Subcommittee on National Parks. His emphasis was more on the increasing impact of visitation, but he did call attention to the possibility of urban encroachment on some parks.[50] He asserted that two policy actions influenced by the reports were the coordination of all natural history research under a single assistant director and the exploration of joint public-use planning with the Forest Service near Mount Rainier and Yellowstone.[51]

Furthermore, both reports had served as catalysts for later recognition of the seriousness of the adjacent lands and outside activities problems. Wildlife management was beginning to reveal the ecologic shortcomings of gerrymandered park boundaries, and the research that did get done in the parks could serve as a baseline for later comparisons on the extent of resource degradation.[52] Thus some Park Service officials view these two documents as vital to encouraging the growth of resource management within the agency as well as suggesting research as an essential component of the Park Service mission. In addition, some officials in the Park Service believe that the Leopold and NAS reports may have put the agency's lack of awareness concerning its own resources on the preservationists' agenda.[53]

Interestingly, perhaps the most influential report on recreation, the Outdoor Recreation Resources Review Commission (ORRRC) report (1962), did not have much to say about the adjacency issue. Foss, writing for the ORRRC report about jurisdictional problems facing the Park Service, noted: "According to the Forest Service, when an area is set aside for exclusive recreational use, it tends to disrupt other activities in the surrounding area. . . . Furthermore, recreationists expect that uses of adjacent lands will complement the recreational objectives of the park."[54] Evidently, the Forest Service viewed new parks as the source of adjacency conflicts, which is not surprising given the different mandate of that agency.

## THE 1970s

It was not until the 1970s that the policy problem of external threats to park resources finally found a place on the political agenda. Two conservation organizations, the growing environmental movement, and lingering questions about Park Service management philosophy were the prime movers during this period. The Park Service was still adjusting to the results of its Mission 66 program, an ambitious ten-year effort (from 1956 to 1966) to modernize park facilities to cope with the increasing pressures of post–World War II visitation. For example, the visitor center, familiar to those who visit large parks today, had its genesis in the Mission 66 years.[55]

Yet at the same time that Mission 66 seemed to be a success for the Park Service, it had apparently driven the agency and its traditional conservation supporters apart. One criticism was that the program had increased visitation while doing "little for the plants and animals."[56] As Foresta pointed out:

> To them [the preservationists] Mission 66 was the essence of those things they detested; it was the sacrifice of preservation to mass use; it was catering to the lowest common denominator of park taste; it was the submergence of the unique qualities of the individual parks under the weight of seemingly interchangeable, undistinguished development plans. If Mission 66 was a cure for that which ailed the system, it was worse than the disease.[57]

Granted, those sentiments could have been expressed by certain preservationists of the Mather-Albright era. But there was another reason for this renewed concern. "With increasing environmental awareness in the 1960's and 1970's, and a shift in ecological thought among environmentalists and the public at large, the major national parks came to be valued both as important parts of the global ecosystem and as unique, distinct areas where nature-altering human activities must not be allowed to take place."[58] This new perception of parks as ecosystems worth protection led to an increasing awareness of all aspects of human use and activities that might cause harm to the ecosystem.

By the late 1970s, this awareness had grown into a major concern about activities on land outside the parks that appeared to have an impact on park resources and traditional functions. In 1979, the National Parks and Conservation Association published its adjacent-lands survey.[59] The organization asked a large number of park superintendents about the various problems their respective units faced. The threats, or "incompatible activities," came from a variety of sources, including residential development, energy extraction, and industrial development. The survey noted that nearly 50 percent of the respondents thought they had inadequate authority to deal with the threats.[60] Actions taken by superintendents tended to be along informal lines—for example, "working with" various levels of government and private individuals as well as doing some monitoring and research.[61]

The NPCA made a series of policy recommendations, which included hiring specialized personnel in areas such as urban planning and developing stronger ties with other agencies. The group also called for new legislation that would accomplish two things: "stop federal grants, loans, and loan guarantees that can support incompatible development harmful to the parks";[62] and give the Park Service activity-specific zoning and acquisition authority on private land adjacent to the parks to stop incompatible activity where necessary.

At almost the same time as the NPCA survey, the Conservation Foundation conducted its own survey, which was somewhat wider in scope.[63] It involved not only the Park Service but also the Forest Service, the BLM, the Fish and Wildlife Service, the Heritage Conservation and Recreation Service, and the Council on Environmental Quality. The survey was designed to cover the multiplicity of relations among federal land managers and between those managers and their nonfederal neighbors. Wilderness designation, for example, was a federal activity that local citizens and governments could view as harmful from an economic development point of view. The results of the survey, as well as policy and research suggestions, are too lengthy to summarize here; however, there were several pertinent conclusions.

Scenic impact appeared to be the most important general activity of concern for visitors to national parks.[64] This is significant in itself because it suggests that contrary to some preservationists, the parks are still important to a majority of users because of their scenic attractiveness.[65] Air and water degradation were also cited as negative consequences of activities on lands adjacent to the parks.[66]

Interestingly, the report found that traditional land-use controls, notably acquisition and exchange, had limited utility.[67] Rather, "the challenge is to link federal agency action with the actions of state and local government. . . . [I]f federal agencies are to be able to perform as working partners in such cooperative efforts, field-level staff will require direction, training and the assistance of experts in such fields as urban dynamics, economics, and the law."[68] The Conservation Foundation believed that most federal administrators were not well prepared in the political intricacies of intergovernmental relations, but interestingly, no mention was made in the report for training land managers.[69]

The National Environmental Policy Act proved helpful in guiding intergovernmental relations, but the resolution of agency conflict lacked overall statutory direction, and other statutory provisions relating to adjacency problems were found to be unorganized at the time of the report.[70] This led the group to call for more congressional action to clarify the priorities that should govern the resolution of interagency conflict.[71]

Finally, the report highlighted areas where research was needed on both federal agency policy implementation and coordination of federal policy with other levels of government. Specifically, the study called for an examination of acquisition and exchange programs, research on development in environmentally sensitive areas, and the use of both cooperative agreements and intergovernmental coordinating mechanisms.[72]

## Congress, the Environment, and Threats to National Parks

Congress was active during the late 1960s and 1970s, passing a series of environmental laws, perhaps the most notable of which was NEPA.[73] Many of the other environmental laws of this period fit into what Michael Reagan calls "intergovernmental mandates."[74] The Clean Air Act Amendments of 1977 are an example. These amendments were written in such a way as to require intergovernmental cooperation. That is, the states were given primary responsibility for air-quality protection, but federal involvement was also mandated.[75] Thus, in the case of visibility, the states, the EPA, and the Park Service all have some responsibility for the protection and regulation of air quality related to visibility.

Another example of an intergovernmental mandate is the Surface Mining Control and Reclamation Act (SMCRA) of 1977. Once again, Congress gave primary responsibility for the regulation of surface coal mining to the states, because of variations in the mining environment, and at the same time provided for national standards. Section 522 prohibits mining if such activity would have adverse effects on nearby parks. The adverse effects determination is subject to a joint decision by the regulatory agency (usually the state) and the Park Service.[76]

There are many other statutes that speak indirectly to the external threats problem—so many, in fact, that the Park Service compiled guidelines so agency decision makers could familiarize themselves with the complexities of this area. As the first draft of those guidelines so aptly states: "No uniform decisionmaking process has been provided to resolve the conflicts that inevitably occur."[77]

Therefore, it was not surprising that the Park Service would become more involved with threats to park resources. In the late 1970s, two former Park Service employees, then working for the National Parks Subcommittee of the House Interior Committee, spurred Congress and through it the Park Service into doing its own survey of possible threats to park resources.[78] The survey was based on responses to a questionnaire that was sent to each of the more than three hundred units of the park system on threats to park resources and values. The park system consists not only of the better known natural-area parks in the West but also of much smaller single-purpose historic sites, Civil War battlefields, and large urban recreation areas.[79] The survey attempted to do two things. First, it sought data about the nature of each of the purported threats to park resources—were they documented by research, were they located internally or externally, and were they documented in the unit's resource management plan? Second, the survey sought to identify specific threats in categories such as air and water pollution, encroachment by exotic plants, and aesthetic degradation.[80]

The results were sobering. In the executive summary, the agency concluded:

> More than 50 percent of the reported threats were attributed to sources or activities located *external* to the parks. The most frequently identified external threats included: Industrial and commercial development projects on adjacent lands; air pollutant emissions, often associated with facilities located considerable distances from the affected parks; urban encroachment; and roads and railroads.[81]

The agency went on to note: "We must pay additional attention to those threats which are associated with sources and activities located external to the parks. These threats today pose unique problems because of the Service's *limited ability to deal directly* and effectively with such outside influences" (emphasis mine).

In the two largest threat categories—aesthetic degradation and air pollution—the external nature of the threat was even more pronounced. In the first category (which included such varied activities as mineral surveys, urban encroachment, and trespassing cattle), 61 percent of the reported threats came from external sources. In the next largest category, over 88 percent of the reported threats came from external sources.[82]

The Park Service attempted to get some sense of the validity of its own survey by examining the documentation level of the reported threat. Thus, 33 percent of reported threats were "suspect, and need[ed] documentation," 42 percent were "known, but need[ed] further documentation," and 25 percent were "adequately documented by research, and data [were] available." The aesthetic degradation category came closest to adequate documentation, but over 58 percent of the threats were still inadequately documented.[83] It is important to understand that the survey was based on the *impressions* of field employees in each of the park units rather than on conclusive scientific information.

The agency ended its report with several policy recommendations.[84] First, it noted that its personnel and budget commitments in natural and cultural science programs were, in its view, underfunded, with 2 percent of monies and 1 percent of personnel given to baseline research. The connection between research and adequate knowledge and understanding of threat activities was obvious. Second, it stated that the amount of agency attention given to field resource management was also inadequate. Resource management was slowly but increasingly becoming a "specialist" position within the agency, much like visitor protection and law enforcement and interpretation. Counting all personnel that devoted at least some of their time to resource management, the agency found about 2 percent of employees involved. Thus the Park Service made a plea to Congress for more resources that could be devoted to these personnel areas.[85]

Several years later, respected environmental writer Robert Cahn reviewed the progress made since the Park Service survey and recommendations were published. He found little reason for optimism—the baseline data had still not been accumulated, and personnel levels remained about where they had been.[86] Actually, about thirty resource management specialist trainees were hired by the agency shortly after Cahn wrote his article. This increase was supposed to be part of a general mitigation response by the Park Service to the *State of the Parks* report.[87] That plan involved the following strategies: (1) identification and ranking of the most significant resource problems; (2) development of resource management plans for all units of the system; (3) resource management training, including the hiring of thirty new midlevel (GS 9–11) resource management specialists each year to increase the number of these specialists in the field; (4) further expansion of prevention and mitigation activities for threats of internal origin; and (5) more appropriations from Congress.[88]

The Park Service mitigation plan acknowledged that external threats were much harder problems to deal with. Mitigation, the report said, "will require a substantially expanded program within the service augmented in many instances by favorable zoning, land use, and regulatory control actions on the part of local and state governments."[89] The plan made no specific mention of external threats caused by activities on federal lands except to note that in the case of air and water pollution, cooperation with other agencies would be essential.[90]

Cahn reported that the new Reagan administration had apparently stressed that the burden of proof regarding resource impacts was now to be placed on the Park Service, thereby rendering mitigation efforts much more problematic.[91] As an example, he cited Park Service policy made in 1980 terminating commercial fishing in the Everglades over a five-year period because it was not in the park's best interest. The policy was backed by then secretary Cecil Andrus. But, Cahn claimed, under the new administration Reagan appointees Assistant Secretary Ray Arnett and his assistant Rick Davidge were now requiring the Park Service to prove that commercial fishing was indeed harmful. Until the agency could do that, the fishing was allowed to continue.[92]

Shortly following the publication of Cahn's article, the National Parks and Conservation Association testified to Congress that then secretary James Watt had ignored most of the threats presented in the *State of the Parks* report and refused to implement the Park Service's proposed mitigation plan, including personnel and budget increases: "Regretfully, this mandate has been ignored and in some cases deliberately frustrated by the Reagan administration through the action or inaction of . . . Watt and his appointees."[93] As far as external impacts were concerned, the NPCA charged that Watt "told Director of the Park Service Russ Dickenson, 'You're on your own,' with regard to policy action to mitigate external threats."

## CONGRESS ATTEMPTS TO ACT ON EXTERNAL THREATS

Because the Park Service, as well as its preservationist supporters, continued to claim that it did not have enough authority to deal with externally caused impacts on park resources and values, Congress made several attempts to address this deficiency. In 1982, the House passed a bill (HR 5162) designed to protect the parks from nearby resource development, overvisitation, and the actions of other governmental agencies.[94] The bill passed 319 to 84 and was referred to the Senate Committee on Energy and Natural Resources, where no further action was taken.

In 1983, another attempt was made in the House. This bill, which was similar to that of 1982, was sponsored by John F. Seiberling (D-Ohio), again as a response to the 1980 *State of the Parks* report. The bill, as reported by the House Interior and Insular Affairs Committee, had numerous important provisions relating to the external threats issue. For areas that were within a unit of the park system (section 10), where the secretary of the Interior had the authority to lease, permit use and development of, or use or dispose of lands, waters, and materials, the secretary could exercise that authority only after determining that no "significant adverse effect" would occur to the values for which the unit was established. The determination could be made only after notice and a hearing on the record. Existing planning procedures such as NEPA were to be used, but the secretary had to publish the adverse effect determination separately from the NEPA documentation.

For areas adjacent to a park unit (also section 10), where the secretary of the Interior had the same authority as he/she had for areas within the park unit, the same adverse effect determination had to be made. In this case, the proposed action could occur if the public interest in proceeding with the activity outweighed the value of the park unit. The secretary's decision to proceed was to be published in the *Federal Register* and notification given to the Senate Committee on Energy and Natural Resources and the House Committee on Interior and Insular Affairs. This notification would initiate a thirty-day implementation delay while both committees reviewed the decision.

Regarding federal actions (projects, grants, or loans to a public body) within or adjacent to a park unit that were not under the jurisdiction of the Department of the Interior (section 11), the agency in charge of the activity or resource was to consider whether the action might degrade the natural or cultural resources of the unit in question. If so, the agency head was to notify the secretary in writing. He/she in turn was to respond within sixty days with an evaluation of the proposed action's impact and a recommendation for changes. If the secretary learned of a proposed action, he/she could initiate the above sequence of events. The secretary was to consider all adopted city, county, and federal plans and, if requested by a local government, hold a hearing on a contemplated negative response to a proposed action.

Regarding federal actions on federal lands within a park, the secretary's recommendations were to be adhered to. In the case of federal actions on nonfederal lands within a park, the acting agency was to consider the secretary's recommendations, balancing them with the public interest. The acting agency's decision was to be published in the *Federal Register* and the above two congressional committees notified, with the thirty-day delay again occurring. In the case of adjacent areas, the secretary's recommendations were to be considered by the acting agency. Disagreement between the two, stemming from the acting agency's response to the recommendations, again required congressional notification and implementation delay. Section 11 also provided that any court action under the act was to be brought in the district court where the park unit was located.[95]

The definition of the word "adjacent" was crucial to understanding the bill's intent. The committee intentionally used vague language in its report. It noted that a "rule of reason" should apply based on the nature of the proposed action and its potential impacts. Thus, it said, the proposal to site a nuclear waste dump next to Canyonlands National Park would be an adjacent activity, as would proposed leases for geothermal energy about ten miles from Yellowstone. But a proposed federal building two blocks from Ford's Theatre in Washington would not be considered adjacent to that theater.[96] The committee also noted that the review done by the secretary was to be concurrent with other agencies' normal decision-making processes.[97] Thus, the committee concluded, the bill "merely establishes a review and coordination mechanism to assure that all aspects of any federal action's impact on national park resources are fully considered."[98]

The Reagan administration opposed the bill. This put Russell Dickenson, then director of the Park Service, in the interesting position of having to testify against the legislation.[99] The administration's position is represented by the testimony of J. Craig Potter, assistant secretary of the Interior, who said that the proposed law "is unnecessary, duplicates existing laws and administrative programs, creates more red tape, and imposes inflexible requirements on resource management efforts that should remain flexible enough to apply available staff and funds to changing needs. It attempts to impose statutory mandates on what are properly discretionary administrative functions."[100] By this time, Reagan park policy had become clear. The Park Service under James Watt did fairly well when it came to infrastructure repairs that were needed in many of the system's units. But cuts in Land and Water Conservation Fund money, growing concessionaire influence, and inattention to internal and external resource degradation seemed to belie Potter's assertions.[101]

The floor debate in the House on October 4, 1983, focused on a rewritten section of the bill. In the floor proceedings, the original bill was replaced by one from Morris Udall (D-Ariz.), which in turn was amended by Seiberling. Except, perhaps, for removing the lawsuit provision, these amendments did not notably change the committee's bill. Seiberling explained the original intent of section 11 by stating that the section would have "little effect on agencies fully complying with . . . NEPA. . . . NEPA already requires the kind of notice and comment required by section 11 wherever a national park would be adversely affected to a significant degree."[102]

During the floor debate, Cong. James Hansen from Utah attempted to alter section 10 of the bill by removing the provision mandating secretarial review of activities on adjacent lands under his/her jurisdiction.[103] Curiously, Hansen did not attempt to alter section 11 of the bill. His stated concern was over what an "overzealous" secretary of the Interior might attempt to accomplish under the bill's provisions in the name of park protection.

Seiberling responded with his own example of overzealousness—James Watt, the current Interior secretary.

> The gentleman talked about zealous Secretaries of Interior. Certainly none is more zealous than the present incumbent. What his zeal is directed to is another question.
> Certainly it is not directed to protecting the natural and cultural values in the national parks to the same degree as it is directed toward developing certain other types of resources, regardless of the consequences on the national parks or on other natural values.[104]

Extraction industries also opposed HR 2379, arguing that the bill created de facto "buffer zones" around the parks.[105] Such zones would, they thought, preclude development on multiple-use lands. There was also a great deal of congressional debate about whether the bill would create de facto buffer zones around many national parks, as extraction industries had charged. Opponents of the bill referred to a Congressional Research Service (CRS) study that claimed that the bill would "effectively" create buffers, even though the language of the bill was not specific.[106] Seiberling argued that the creation of buffers was not the intent of his bill and noted that even the CRS had been forced to conclude there was no language in the bill that was explicit in that regard. Seiberling's bill passed the House 321 to 82. The Senate took no action on it when it failed to clear the Senate committee.

An analysis of Seiberling's bill reveals several important points. First, the bill appeared to take a case-by-case approach to the threats issue. Each activity that could potentially affect a specific park was to be reviewed independently. Moreover, park protection was not institutionalized as an overarching value, with resource development activities subordinated to it. Park protection was highlighted, but existing decision rules were not changed. It might be argued that the burden of proof regarding an external development activity still remained with the affected park and not with the proposed activity.

There was a notable exception to the scope of HR 2379. Local activities were left out of its focus unless federal money was involved. The question of federal involvement in local land-use decisions is very controversial, which probably explains its exclusion from the bill. At present, the relation of parks to local land use is structured very much on a case-by-case basis. Recent additions to the park system allow for Park Service participation in zoning decisions.[107] In other cases, the Park Service is encouraged to participate in negotiation with local authorities.[108] In still other cases, the agency has been given the authority to initiate nuisance claims or condemn land.[109] Also, the Park Service, through congressional legislation, has occasionally utilized partial ownership (easements, for example) and greenline (mixed landownership) parks.[110]

Recently, Saguaro National Monument in Arizona has been the focus of an interesting attempt to deal with a local land-use issue: the growth of the city of Tucson on the borders of the desert park. The Pima County Board of Supervisors and the Pima County Planning and Zoning Commission considered a "buffer overlay zone." The commission's draft ordinance defines the purpose of the zone as permitting "the reasonable use of lands while at the same time preserving and protecting the open space characteristics of those lands in the vicinity of the public preserves [including Saguaro]."[111] The draft ordinance was structured to create mechanisms to provide an "ecologically sound" transition between the preserves and urban development. The park's superintendent, William Paleck, presented the concerns of the park to the county commission and was an active participant in the planning process.[112] A last-minute campaign organized in opposition to the zone prevented it from being adopted as an ordinance.[113]

Caution is in order regarding any generalizations about what does happen near Saguaro, because of variabilities in state and local land-use laws and the resulting range of regulatory processes. What is perhaps most notable about this example is the active role taken by the park superintendent in the local governmental planning processes. This behavior is unusual for many superintendents, as they often are not trained in planning and other aspects of public administration. Yet it may soon become necessary for superintendents to be more involved as adjacent growth becomes a problem for increasing numbers of parks. The Conservation Foundation has also recently prepared a guide for park managers on dealing with local land use. What seems most useful, perhaps, is for the Park Service to familiarize itself with this issue and to begin to acquire knowledge regarding policy successes and failures in this area of the external threats problem.[114]

Finally, a point needs to made about buffer zones. The idea of creating buffer zones around certain national parks is not a new one and seems to resurface with some regularity. In 1975, during congressional action to expand the boundaries of Grand Canyon National Park, Barry Goldwater of Arizona introduced legislation that included a buffer zone, or "zone of influence," around the park. The zone would be administratively created and adjusted by the secretary of the Interior. Mining was not permitted on any federal lands within the designated zone, and the secretary was permitted to purchase, exchange, or acquire land through donation.[115] The original version of the park enlargement bill had been drafted by Goldwater with environmentalists' help—help that included developing the zone of influence concept. Yet the environmentalists re-pudiated the zone concept in later debate on the bill because they thought the lands that would be included in the original zone should ac-tually be in the park. Goldwater was furious. Speaking on the floor of the Senate, he said that the zone

> originated under a different name with the leadership of the Sierra Club. . . . [T]he club now attacks this provision as fostering eco-nomic exploitation of the Canyon and its surrounding areas. This is the interpretation which Club members are giving to the Club's op-position to this provision and it is one of the most ridiculous innu-endos which the Club is making about my bill. Strangely enough, the very economic interests whom the Club infers will benefit from the "Zone of Influence" are the people, who, with the Club, have ex-pressed the most vocal opposition to this provision at the Senate hearings on the bill.
>
> Actually, the provision . . . was a good conservationist idea that could have stood as a landmark precedent for the protection of other areas of the National Park system, but it apparently has been shot down as a viable idea in Congress because it was opposed even by the conservation groups which fathered it.[116]

In 1988, environmentalists found themselves opposed to possible ura-nium mining near the Grand Canyon.[117] One can only speculate about how useful the zone of influence could have been in preventing mining from taking place near the Grand Canyon or other parks had the zone of influence become law.

THE CHAFFEE BILL

In late February 1986, Sen. John Chaffee of Rhode Island introduced an-other bill that focused on the threats issue. His bill, S 2092, prohibited federal spending within parks or in "contiguous federally managed ar-eas" unless the secretary of the Interior determined that the expenditure "will not degrade or destroy the natural or cultural resources within any unit of the National Park System."[118] The secretary was also allowed to designate "park resource protection areas" on contiguous federally man-aged land. Once an area had been so designated, the expenditure prohi-bition would not apply. Instead, each federal agency had to insure, in consultation with the secretary, that new federal actions within such ar-eas would not degrade park resources.[119] The Park Service was to be noti-fied of proposed activities through the NEPA process.

The bill contained other interesting features. First, it required the Park Service to prepare a biennial report for Congress on the condition of park units.[120] One section of the report would be an assessment of ongoing and proposed federal programs having detrimental effects on any Park Service units and an assessment of laws and regulations that could help mitigate the reported activities.[121] Such a report might be viewed as similiar to the *State of the Parks* report. Second, the legislation mandated the establishment of a special division within the Park Service to be devoted to "mission-related" research.[122]

Third, Chaffee's bill drew special attention to Park Service units that are either United Nations–designated Biosphere Reserves or World Heritage Sites. The Biosphere Reserves are Big Bend, Channel Islands, Denali, Everglades, Great Smoky Mountains, Noatak, Olympic, Organ Pipe, Rocky Mountain, Sequoia–Kings Canyon, Virgin Islands, Yellowstone, Isle Royal, Big Thicket, and Glacier. World Heritage Sites are Everglades, Grand Canyon, Great Smoky Mountains, Mammoth Cave, Mesa Verde, Olympic, Redwood Wrangell–St. Elias, Yellowstone, and Yosemite national parks, as well as several historic sites, such as San Juan and the Statue of Liberty.[123] The Biosphere Reserves were to be studied for possible boundary adjustments to protect the core of the reserve, the national park.[124]

Chaffee's bill appeared to somewhat reverse the balance of proof regarding external activities affecting park units. Seiberling's bill required the secretary of the Interior to determine the likelihood of an activity's having an adverse effect and then to weigh the value of the proposed activity against the park's value. Chaffee's bill, by contrast, prohibited a proposed activity unless it was shown that the activity would not harm relevant park values and resources.

## RECENT EVENTS AND THEMES

### Ecosystems

Legislative attempts to deal with the threats problem have occupied much but not all of the attention on the issue. Two other themes related to the threats problem have also emerged. One has to do with defining some of the big western parks as parts of larger ecosystems. The other has to do with legal remedies for external threats. The ecosystem approach will be examined first. Considering parks as parts of larger ecosystems probably has its intellectual roots in several sources. First, the research of George Wright in the 1930s was oriented toward wildlife and other problems not neatly constrained and defined by park boundaries.

Second, Alfred Runte's history of the national park idea argued that these parks would not be conceptually complete until they were redrawn to encompass entire ecosystems. The ecosystem approach has progressed furthest at Yellowstone, due in large part to the problem of declining grizzly bear populations. The bear population problem has drawn attention to the fact that the grizzly habitat ranges beyond the boundaries of Yellowstone.

In 1985, the House Interior Subcommittee on National Parks and Recreation held hearings on what was termed the "greater Yellowstone ecosystem." That area, according to Cong. John Seiberling, "refers to the area within the States of Montana, Wyoming and Idaho which contains not only the Yellowstone and Grand Teton National Parks, but also the Red Rock Lakes National Wildlife Refuge, the National Elk Refuge, and portions of the Gallatin, Custer, Shoshone, Bridger-Teton, Caribou, Targee and Beaverhead National Forests, and various wilderness areas designated therein."[125] Concern for the Yellowstone ecosystem is not about enlarging Yellowstone National Park but rather about coordinating land management decisions to better protect key resources in the Yellowstone area.

Coordination is a proper-sounding term that no one can disagree with. Yet coordination also implies shared values. As Harold Seidman pointed out, "If agencies are to work together harmoniously, they must share at least some community of interests about basic goals."[126] Since the BLM and the Forest Service are multiple-use management agencies, and the Park Service is a resource preservation agency, there is doubt whether coordination will result easily in solutions that some may wish for. Bob Barbee, Yellowstone's superintendent, stated the problem succinctly: "There have to be sovereign conditions in the ecosystem that we can all agree to—that go beyond our agency missions and mandates—in order to insure this [ecosystem] integrity."[127] Coordination may have utility, but it is hard to see how it can resolve fundamental value conflicts between resource use and resource preservation unless resource preservation in the Yellowstone area is given priority through Barbee's "sovereign conditions." Or as George Hartzog, a former Park Service director, said, the missions of the Park Service and the Forest Service are "incompatible and adversarial," once again rendering coordination problematic.[128]

Scientific understanding also complicates the goal of ecosystem management. During the 1985 hearings, the following exchange took place between Cong. Larry Craig (R-Idaho) and Park Service Director William Penn Mott:

> *Mr. Craig:* Is it possible to say, that an ecosystem is in the eye of the beholder? His or her interpretation of it?

*Mr. Barbee:* I would in a sense agree with that.

*Mr. Craig:* Mr. Mott, would you agree with that?

*Mr. Mott:* Technically, it seems to me we have to recognize that in applying the word "ecosystem" it should be applied to a specific subject. We know what the ecosystem is of the grizzly, for example. We can define that. But when we use it as a general term as I indicated, we are using it incorrectly scientifically. We should be calling it a biogeographical—

*Mr. Craig:* But that may not get people's emotions flying.

*Mr. Mott:* That is right.

*Mr. Craig:* If you get too scientifically technical, but you are right, it isn't the buzzword so it doesn't engender the emotion that an endangered ecosystem does, is that correct?

*Mr. Mott:* That is probably correct.[129]

Craig's point appears to be that the term "endangered ecosystem" might have the same appeal as did the famous Sierra Club ads alerting people to possible dams in the Grand Canyon. Those ads asked people if they would want the Sistine Chapel dammed so visitors could view the ceiling up close. The above exchange also implies that there may not really be something called the Yellowstone ecosystem but rather a series of systems that appear to be dependent on the range of various biological resources within each system, such as the bear.

Glacier National Park has also been the focus of the ecosystem protection debate. Joseph Carlton, chairman of the Committee of the Bob Marshall Ecosystem, favors "managing the giant area on an ecology first, economics second basis. Referring to the wildlife-rich area as the 'Serengeti plains of North America,' Carlton says that the Glacier–Bob Marshall country is ecologically intact. . . . He blames fragmented agency management and what he says is Forest Service reluctance to recognize the area as more important for wildlife than development."[130]

The ecosystems approach to the external threats problem seems to view parks as integral parts of larger systems. Most of those favoring this approach do not argue for expanded park boundaries but rather some type of integrated land management approach. Yet what remains problematic about this approach is that the decisions concerning development still appear to remain focused on a specific resource that might be threatened by an activity rather than on an entire system. Thus in the Yellowstone ecosystem, it is really the grizzly bear that is threatened, not the system. Or as another example, the geysers of the park would be threatened by geothermal development, not the ecosystem. Indeed, even in the case of threats to *park* resources, it is usually a specific park resource that is threatened, not the entire park. Perhaps a threatened park resource that is wide ranging might be the visitor experience of an affected park. The ecosystem approach does have utility, however. It has begun to nudge decision makers toward thinking more broadly when considering development decisions—a step ecosystems advocates must think is promising.

### The Public Trust Doctrine

Another approach that has arisen regarding the external threats problem is legal in scope and based on what is called the public trust doctrine. As the General Accounting Office (GAO) summarized:

> The Public Trust Doctrine is derived from the general statutory obligations imposed on the Secretary of the Interior by the [Park Service] Organic Act of 1916 and reaffirmed in a 1978 statute, 16 USC 1a-1, Public Law 95-250. . . . [O]ne characterization of the Doctrine is that the Department [of the Interior] holds park resources in trust for the public and therefore has the duties and obligations of a trustee to protect the trust property on behalf of the beneficiaries.[131]

There is a variety of opinions about what the public trust doctrine means in terms of action on the part of the secretary of the Interior. Some legal scholars have contended that the secretary has a duty to protect parks from adjacent activity, while others have disputed that claim.[132] The debate centers on section 1a-1 of the amended Park Service Organic Act. This section was added in 1978 in response to problems that the Park Service was having at Redwoods National Park. That unit was experiencing logging adjacent to park boundaries that was causing erosion and siltation inside the park. Section 1a-1 states that

> the authorization of activities shall be construed and the protection, management, and administration of these areas shall be conducted in light of the high public value and integrity of the National Park System and shall not be exercised in derogation of the values and purposes for which these various areas have been established, except as may have been or shall be directly and specifically provided by Congress.[133]

There are two points of disagreement. The first is whether this section means external as well as internal threats when it speaks to park "protection." The second concerns the "exception" clause and whether the multiple-use missions of the BLM and Forest Service are thus exceptions.

Law professor Robert Keiter stated how the issue stands today by using Forest Service activities as an example:

> The Secretary might argue that, with its 1978 amendments, the Or-
> ganic Act reflects Congress' intent to protect the parks, and that it
> would, therefore, be unreasonable for the Forest Service to permit
> incompatible activities that jeopardize park resource values. Unless
> the Organic Act trumps the Forest Service's organic legislation—a
> view that has not yet been endorsed by any court—the Secretary will
> probably be forced either to rely upon the goodwill and cooperation
> of the Forest Service or to invoke other federal environmental con-
> trol statutes, such as the National Environmental Protection [Policy]
> Act or the Endangered Species Act, as a means of limiting threaten-
> ing activities in the national forests.[134]

What appears necessary, then, is one of three actions: The Interior
secretary brings suit to enjoin an adjacent activity not under his/her control; the secretary stops an activity under his/her authority; or an outside
party sues the secretary for failing to take action. None of these situa-
tions has arisen or appears likely in the near future. Once again, the
multiple-use mission of other federal agencies is something "specifically" provided by Congress and thus not obvious grounds for invoking
the public trust doctrine. As far as local or private activities are concerned, it is doubtful whether the federal government wants to intervene
in the manner suggested by the public trust doctrine for fear of appearing overzealous and overreaching, because of the long legal tradition of
deferring to local control over land-use decisions.

*Environmentalist Responses*

Environmentalist groups concerned with national park policy have also
entered the fray over external threats. In the spring of 1988, the NPCA issued its eleven-volume *National Park Plan*. One volume of the plan focused on external threat activities. The NPCA recommended that a
"zone of concern" around the natural-area units of the park system be
created in close consultation and cooperation with other levels of government and with private landowners.[135] The association stated that

> if other agencies controlling adjacent federal lands . . . are willing to
> take the needs of adjacent park resources into account in their deci-
> sion making, then simple cooperative agreements between these

agencies and the NPS would suffice. On adjacent private lands, NPS should have the necessary tools, funds and expertise to assist local governments in developing zoning codes that are compatible with park resource protection.[136]

There may be quite a lot of wishful thinking in that statement. Whether federal agencies will want to take Park Service concerns into much account in their own land management is doubtful. So too is the likelihood that sufficient Park Service funding and expertise will be available to help local governments. Yet the NPCA probably realized these problems and was simply trying to set a park policy agenda for the next presidential election and thus speaking in general terms.

Finally, the Park Service remained on record opposing new park protection legislation. Director Mott, in an interview with *Federal Parks and Recreation* in 1986, again stated that no new park protection legislation was necessary.[137] The Reagan administration's position was that "coordination" and "cooperation" were the best way to solve the external threats issue.

In 1984, the Department of the Interior convened a task force to work on the issue of park protection. In 1985, that group issued its recommendations, which relied heavily on implementing internal agency procedures to "improve the anticipation, avoidance, and resolution of resource conflicts."[138] In 1987, a GAO report noted that no agency had yet done so.[139] What is more, Park Service attempts to formulate the agency's response to the recommendations were stopped by Assistant Secretary William Horn. The Park Service wanted to begin documenting harmful adjacent activities as part of its action plan in response to the working group's recommendations. But Horn objected and told the agency to remove that action from its proposed response.[140]

## CONCLUSION

A new policy and management problem for the National Park Service has entered the political arena. The agency is faced with impacts on park resources and functions that require cooperation with other agencies. In some cases, statutory authority structures the cooperation and provides some power to the Park Service. In other cases, all the agency can do is provide comments on proposed actions. Thus the specificity of statutory authority may be one variable that influences resolution of the threats issue.

In addition, the unity of the two traditional park constituencies—the users and the preservationists—may also be essential for successful resolution of the various adjacency problems. We have seen that the preservationists' recent stress on ecological integrity has served as a policy catalyst on the threats issue. But that emphasis may also have driven the preservationists and the more-traditional users of the parks apart because of the former group's implied opposition to much use within the parks. The threats issue may serve as a way to bring these two constituencies together, because both use and preservation can be viewed as threatened by external activities.

Those concerned with the external threats problem still seem to be searching for a conceptual way to deal with it. Two possible approaches—the ecosystem concept and the public trust doctrine—seem fraught with difficulty. It is hard to imagine the ecosystem approach working in more than a handful of parks. Yet at the same time, it is also hard to imagine other land managers voluntarily subscribing to the ecosystem management concept if use of that concept restricts their traditional management tasks and orientation. What is possible, however, is to identify key parks and ecosystems where such an approach might be worth a try. Perhaps a good place to start would be the designated World Biosphere Reserves. Still, it is equally doubtful that an approach will work through any other mechanism than congressional recognition of key parks as worthy of special attention by land managers.

Use of the public trust doctrine also poses problems. The Reagan administration was not sympathetic to the resolution of the threats problem, and it is unlikely that an administration such as that would use the solicitor's office in Interior to initiate a suit based on the public trust doctrine. Moreover, there are strong legal arguments that this doctrine is simply not very clear and instructive when it comes to the problem of external threats. If a flagrant threat does become highly visible, it might be possible that one of the environmental groups would initiate a test of the doctrine in court, but this has not yet occurred. It also seems a rather cumbersome way to address the threats problem.

Probably the best way to approach and deal with the threats problem is through new legislation. The key question such legislation would have to address is where the burden of proof should fall when determining whether an activity is harmful to park resources and values. Should Seiberling's or Chaffee's bill be the model? Seiberling's approach is more likely to be politically acceptable, because it requires park values to be weighed with other societal values. Chaffee's approach would probably find favor with environmentalists, because it resembles an ecosystem approach to the threats problem. The resolution of the threats issue may finally and rightfully depend on the willingness of Congress and the president to confront the issue. We have seen that the Reagan administration did not view the threats issue as an important problem. We have also seen that Congress has not often been able to pass legislation that might make some of the adjacency issues easier to resolve. One must remember that the external threats issue is, at its core, a conflict over values that are not easy to reconcile. The national parks represent our belief that certain lands are more valuable to us in their preserved state. We have always acknowledged, though, that activities not allowed in the parks were more than allowable and even encouraged elsewhere. Only recently have we seen that these same activities may threaten the parks we thought were preserved for all time. If the external threats problem is ever to be resolved, Congress and the president must confront this difficult issue.

# CHAPTER THREE

# The Creation of Glen Canyon National Recreation Area

The tar sands leasing issue takes place in a region of the United States that has become synonymous with public policy battles over the preservation and use of our nation's resources. The region is the Colorado Plateau, and it contains the so-called golden circle of America's parklands: Grand Canyon, Capitol Reef, Zion, Bryce, Arches, and Canyonlands. The Plateau is also the location of one of the largest man-made lakes in the world, Lake Powell, whose primary existence is to provide water and electricity to California and Arizona. Near the lake is the coal-fired Navajo power plant, which burns the region's abundant coal deposits to supply energy to far-off western cities. To fully understand the policy battles over the tar sands resource, one must have an understanding of the context within which the issue developed.

## PRESERVATION AND DEVELOPMENT ON THE COLORADO PLATEAU

The Colorado Plateau contains an abundance of national parks ranging from internationally known large natural areas (Grand Canyon and Zion) and archaeological parks (Chaco Canyon and Mesa Verde), to smaller units that preserve scenic attractions (Rainbow Bridge National Monument), to archaeological (Wupatki National Monument) and historic sites (Pipe Spring). Lying in the geographic heart of the Plateau is Lake Powell surrounded by the Glen Canyon National Recreation Area.

In the 1930s, the Department of the Interior and the Park Service studied for inclusion in the U.S. park system part of what was to become the GCNRA. The study area was given the name Escalante National Monument and would have stretched from near the confluence of the Green and Colorado rivers to the Arizona-Utah state line along the course of the Colorado.[1] The 1939 report of the secretary of the Interior mentioned the need to reconcile the proposal with power development interests before the monument could be authorized; certainly, the entry of the United States into World War II was also an important factor. Indeed, during the war the Park Service was moved to Chicago with other agencies not essential to the war effort.[2] In 1964, the Park Service, in its

*Parks for America* study, suggested that park status be given to three hundred thousand acres near Rainbow Bridge National Monument.[3] The agency's objective in raising this possibility is unclear: The area to the south of Rainbow Bridge is part of the Navajo Indian Reservation, and the area to the immediate north was being administered as a recreation area by the Park Service through a cooperative agreement with the Bureau of Reclamation because it was soon to become Lake Powell.

Lake Powell is evidence of the other facet of natural resource policy on the Colorado Plateau: development. Since 1916 when E. C. Larue of the U.S. Geological Survey undertook a comprehensive study of water resource development possibilities in the Colorado River basin, the damming of the river and its tributaries had been a distinct possibility. By the 1920s, the growth of southern California and Arizona had led to a partitioning of the Colorado's waters to protect the water resources of the upriver states through the Colorado River Compact.[4] The compact divided the flow of the river in half, giving 7.5 million acre-feet to the lower basin states of California, Arizona, and Nevada and the same amount to the upper basin states of Utah, New Mexico, Wyoming, and Colorado.[5] The latter states needed to insure that the lower basin states got their share of the water guaranteed by the compact. Thus a new dam was necessary on the Colorado. But this dam would serve other purposes as well. As Helen Ingram noted: "Western interests perceive water projects as the vehicle through which they get their fair slice of a much larger national subsidies pie that is distributed across the country."[6] This subsidy could be used to promote economic development of the region.[7]

The dam that was originally proposed was to be at Echo Park, near Dinosaur National Monument. Preservationists, in what may be called their first major victory over resource development, were able to prevent the construction of the Echo Park Dam. Instead, a site was found farther downriver in Glen Canyon. The irony was that Glen Canyon was worthy of park status but because it was still relatively unknown, it was not protected.[8] Perhaps if World War II had not intervened, Escalante National Monument would have been established and thereby precluded the development of Glen Canyon. Lake Powell is the storage reservoir that now stands behind the Glen Canyon Dam.

Water resource development points to a fundamental economic fact about the Colorado Plateau. Much of the area is resource rich but economically poor. This was graphically illustrated by a 1981 report issued by Resources for the Future, *The Southwest under Stress*. The area that contains the tar sands resource is in the middle of what the report calls the "Southwest poverty diagonal." Ranging northwest from northern New Mexico through northeastern Arizona and southeastern Utah, the region is rich in natural resources but low in income and education levels and poor in economic development.[9] Residents of Utah, including those living in the diagonal, were found to favor development more than those of the other Four Corners states.[10] The energy shocks of the 1970s drew national attention to the natural resources of the intermountain West and the Colorado Plateau; naturally, calls for development of these resources were viewed sympathetically if not hopefully by the residents of southeastern Utah.

It is important to recognize the uniqueness of the region where the tar sands development issue takes place. It is one of the most scenically attractive areas of the United States; its parklands are world famous. Yet it is also an economically poor region, a region that, from the testimony of local residents, should have more natural resource development. This tension has been in existence for a long time—almost every park boundary in the region resulted from compromises engendered by the preservation-development conflict. Indeed, these two aspects of natural resource policy are mixed throughout the history of the Plateau, and one must be aware of the tension between them to understand the politics of the tar sands issue. In turn, the politics of the issue exacerbates the tension.

## THE TAR SANDS RESOURCE

Tar sand, as defined by the Bureau of Land Management, is "sedimentary rock containing bitumens [residuals of lighter crude oils]."[11] Although "oil-impregnated rock" is probably a more accurate term than "tar sand," the latter appears to be the one generally accepted.[12] Tar sands deposits have been found on all continents except Australia and Antarctica. On our own continent, the largest and best known are the Athabasca deposits of Alberta, Canada.[13] Although twenty-four American states have known deposits of tar sands, 95 percent of these deposits are in Utah.[14] In Utah, tar sands deposits occur in two major areas, one around the Uinta Basin in the northeast and the other in the southeast in what has come to be known as the "tar sands triangle."[15] Utah contains about 26 billion barrels of in-place bitumen, with over half the known deposits occurring in the tar sands triangle.[16] The first concerted effort to locate and map Utah's tar sands began in 1964.[17]

During the course of the tar sands leasing debate, estimates of the size of the tar sands triangle deposits were revised to about 6.3 billion barrels of recoverable oil. The amount within leased units was about 1.75 billion barrels (or four months of U.S. oil consumption), because the units did not include the entire tar sands triangle.

Bitumen within the tar sands can be extracted either by surface mining (where deposits are near the surface) or by in-situ extraction (where the deposits are deeper in the earth).[18] The tar sands triangle is subject to in-situ recovery, which involves heating the bitumen to allow it to move through and be recovered from the tar sands deposits.[19] The efficiency of recovery is estimated to be 30-40 percent of the known bitumen.[20] I will discuss the recovery process in more detail later in this chapter.

The same year that research was begun on the tar sands deposits of Utah, Canyonlands National Park was established near what was later to be designated the tar sands triangle. No evidence can be found in the public record that this park's boundaries were drawn with knowledge of the tar sands resource. This was not the case, however, with the establishment of Glen Canyon National Recreation Area.

## PRELUDE: THE NATIONAL RECREATION AREA CONCEPT AND GLEN CANYON

There is often confusion about the status of a national recreation area within the U.S. park system.[21] In the Park Service's words: "Originally, national recreation areas in the Park System were units surrounding reservoirs impounded by dams built by other federal agencies. . . . The concept of recreational areas has grown to encompass other lands and water set aside for recreational use by acts of Congress and now includes major areas in urban centers."[22]

The origins of the national recreation area concept can be found in the 1930s. Then secretary of the Interior Harold Ickes saw the recreation area as a means to increase the jurisdiction of the Park Service, and thus Interior, over more federal lands. The Park Service had already noted, by this time, that the traditional view of national parks as "unmodified territory" made it difficult to establish new areas within the park system.[23] Ickes hoped to make the recreation area idea acceptable so that the Park Service might be able to compete with the Forest Service as a multiple-use management agency.[24] He stated that "people are more and more reluctant to give us prospecting and hunting rights. They can both prospect and hunt in national forest areas . . . there will be a loud outcry [if a traditional national park is created]. If we take them over as national recreation areas, there ought not to be so much opposition. This will be outflanking the Forest Service."[25]

Today, in a national recreation area designated by Congress, the Park Service is supposed to stress recreation more than resource protection, and stress it more than in a national park. Many national recreation areas also allow grazing and mineral extraction. In addition, the Forest Service administers two recreation areas that are almost indistinguishable from national parks: the Sawtooth in Idaho and Hell's Canyon in Idaho and Oregon. This further confuses understanding of the purpose of a national recreation area.

GCNRA was established in 1972. The Senate, in 1970 and again in 1971, was the first to consider authorizing the new recreation area. It held hearings on four bills that set up the recreation area, changed two national monuments to national parks (Arches and Capitol Reef), and altered the boundaries of Canyonlands National Park. The tar sands resource was discussed several times at these hearings.

In 1971, during a discussion of a boundary variation between the Park Service recommendations for Canyonlands and those within the Senate bill, Sen. Frank Moss of Utah made the following observation:

There are three sections the department recommends go [in the park] . . . that I have left off. Now, I left them off deliberately because they have tar-sands deposits and the state geological and mineralogical survey was quite concerned that these sections be available for exploration, and I have included them, therefore, in the National Recreation Area, where mineral exploration and production is permissible, and taken them out of the national park.[26]

The Interior Department, the Park Service, and the Sierra Club and Friends of the Earth supported the inclusion of the land in Canyonlands National Park. A major condition of the preservationists' support for an enlarged park was that vehicle access to park overlooks be provided.[27]

Thus the Senate hearings appear to assert that the recreation area would be available for mineral exploration under certain conditions. This, however, was not all the Senate intended for parts of the recreation area. During the hearings, Moss's bill was revised and new land added to the recreation area so it included the scenically spectacular Orange Cliffs, which bordered Canyonlands on the west. Senator Moss had this to say about the inclusion: "The reason for including that section in the recreation area in the northern part is to give the Park Service jurisdiction in building overlooks over the park and camp sites. It also provides as a buffer zone and protection for the park and yet still permits grazing in that area where there is some grazing."[28] This area also contains most of the Park Service section of the tar sands resource.

In the Senate report on the recreation area bill, the Interior committee again stressed why it had excluded certain lands from Canyonlands:

The committee does not accept the proposal of the Department of the Interior to exclude 1,920 acres from the recreation area immedi-

The Orange Cliffs (by the author)

ately adjacent to the southwest boundary of Canyonlands National Park. This area is known to contain tar sands deposits and therefore the committee concluded it properly belongs to the recreation area where mineral exploration and development may be conducted if energy demands make such development economically feasible and desirable.[29]

The acreage of what would later be called the tar sands triangle is much larger than the acreage given by the Interior committee; what is important is the *intent* of Congress in establishing the recreation area. In the language of the Senate report, "these deposits [the tar sands deposits] could not be developed if the acreage was included within the boundaries of a national park. It is proposed . . . that this area be included within the Glen Canyon National Recreation Area, where mineral exploration and development is permissible, under careful supervision to protect scenic and recreational values."[30] Both the Canyonlands

The Orange Cliffs—a view down Millard Canyon (by the author)

enlargement and Glen Canyon enablement bills were passed without debate by the Senate on June 21, 1971.

The House held its hearings on Glen Canyon's establishment as a recreation area a year later. Interest in the proposed legislation appears to have increased a great deal during this period. The amount of public involvement as measured by appearances before the House Subcommittee on National Parks and Recreation, as well as letters to that committee, mushroomed. The primary reason for this heightened interest had to do, not with the tar sands, but with a road proposal that involved a relatively pristine area of the proposed recreation area in the Escalante Canyon.

The proposed legislation had become more complicated as well. Three bills were introduced to the subcommittee, one by Sherman Lloyd of Utah (HR 13550), one by Gunn McKay of Utah (HR 8214), and the already passed Senate version of the bill (S 27). Lloyd's bill was perhaps the most complex. Its version of the new recreation area was about one-third the size of the Senate bill's. In addition, Lloyd introduced a new concept: the Canyon Country National Conservation Area. This area would be administered by the BLM and would encompass much of the land in the recreation area created by the Senate. This, according to

Lloyd, was done to give the BLM the "authority, tools and funds it needs for managing this area of unique and significant value."[31] Lloyd's proposal would also have permitted wilderness zoning by the BLM within the conservation area. The other bills were less complex than Lloyd's. HR 8214 was identical to the original bill considered by the Senate. S 27 was the amended version of that bill passed by the Senate the previous year.

During the hearings in the House, several issues emerged that are germane to this study. Lloyd's bill had excluded the northern portion of the proposed recreation area. Lloyd said, "May I call the subcommittee's attention to the fact that there is strong exception to the inclusion of an area in the northeastern portion known as the Orange Cliffs, which overlooks Canyonland[s] National Park. . . . I suggest particular evaluation of the grazing and mineral potential of that area for possible exclusion from the boundaries of the bill."[32] The strong exception he referred to came from the state of Utah. Gordon Harmston, executive director of the Utah Department of Natural Resources, made the dissatisfaction clear. Pointing to the exclusion from Canyonlands of three sections of land (the 1,920 acres) because they blocked access to the large tar sands deposits, he stated: "We do not think it proper at this time to include that area [the tar sands] in the national recreation area."[33]

This objection on the part of Utah led to the citing of a letter from Park Service director George Hartzog to Senator Moss during the Senate hearings on the bill. About mining the area, Hartzog had said, "Prospecting and the extraction of minerals, sand gravel, and rock, administered by the Bureau of Land Management would continue after the enactment of S 27 if the specific activity is compatible with and does not significantly impair public recreation and the conservation of scenic, scientific, historic and other values contributing to public enjoyment."[34] Calvin Rampton, then governor of Utah, accepted Hartzog's letter and declared: "If this intent of the Park Service to continue BLM administration of mineral leases can be incorporated into the language of the Bill, the state of Utah would withdraw its objection to the proposed boundaries in the Orange Cliffs area where there are deposits of bituminous tar sands."[35] Assistant Secretary of the Interior Nathaniel Reed confirmed that although the Park Service would prefer to administer mining in the recreation area itself, the agency had "no problems" with BLM management.[36] The provision giving the BLM leasing authority was included in the bill that was eventually passed by the House, at which point Utah dropped its objection.[37] Thus Orange Cliffs became part of the recreation area.

Senator Moss, in testimony during the House hearings, again stressed the buffer aspects of the Orange Cliffs: "New lands are added to

The Maze area in western Canyonlands (by the author)

the recreation area to provide a buffer zone for the Maze area of Canyonlands National Park."[38] The Maze area of Canyonlands, west of the Colorado River, is accessible only by four-wheel-drive vehicles or walking. It is also an area celebrated by Edward Abbey in his well-known *Desert Solitaire*. Several weeks later, Moss noted that a recreation area permitted both mining and grazing.[39] Cong. Roy Taylor of North Carolina added to this definition, saying that grazing and mining were permitted so long as they did not interfere with the dominant use of a recreation area—recreation.[40]

Preservationists involved with the Glen Canyon legislation focused their attention on opposition to a proposed road that would cross the Escalante drainage. The Escalante is a side canyon and tributary of the Colorado, which for much of its course preserves landscape that has been in existence since before the creation of Lake Powell. However, both the Sierra Club and the National Parks and Conservation Association had comments about the tar sands. Their position favored inclusion of the Orange Cliffs in Canyonlands, but they did not actively pursue the issue.[41] Instead, they argued that the Park Service should regulate mining to protect parklike qualities and scenic views while also noting that technology did not currently exist to extract the resource.[42] The NPCA also argued that tar sands development would never be economical and thus the Orange Cliffs should be included in Canyonlands.[43]

Two other aspects of the House hearings are important. The first has to do with local attitudes toward federal land management and tourism. Although certainly not held by all participants from local communities, these views were probably indicative of predominant attitudes. It has already been described how local interests, including the state of Utah, favored the exclusion of the tar sands resource from Canyonlands and only accepted its inclusion in the recreation area so long as the BLM would continue to administer mineral leases. One could sum up this position by saying that many local Utah interests supported access and development of natural resources and the exclusion of these resources from parks. This, of course, is similar to a century-long attitude of some Americans that national parks should only be "economically worthless" lands.[44]

But local interests in Utah are not completely opposed to national parks; they appear to support parks that are accessible to a majority of the public. Consider the testimony of Calvin Black, San Juan County (Utah) commissioner: "I do not believe that area [the recreation area] should be able to be seen by only the people that can backpack, that have the special equipment, that are young enough to do it, or have the money to rent a boat or buy a boat or charter an airplane or own an airplane."[45] The reason Black and others supported access is simple: It would bring in tourists and tourist dollars that, they were told, would offset the loss of resource development revenue.[46] Thus local Utah interests support developed parks and recreation areas, but not what they perceive as inaccessible wilderness parks. One can conclude that if local interests had their way politically, they would first support resource development. If this was not obtainable, they would then support parks and recreation areas if public access was provided.

The second aspect of the hearings worth noting concerns Park Service and Department of the Interior attitudes toward the various bills under consideration. During his testimony, Nathaniel Reed, assistant secretary of the Interior for Fish, Wildlife, and Parks, said: "While the Department recommends enactment of HR 8214, with suggested amendments, we do not object to S 27 as passed by the Senate, including amendments adopted by the Senate."[47] HR 8214 did not include the Orange Cliffs region in the recreation area; S 27 as amended did. Apparently, the Department of the Interior supported the House bill because it kept more acreage in Canyonlands; therefore, it did not pay much attention to the Orange Cliffs addition.[48]

The House reported its version of the recreation area on September 26, 1972. It was HR 15716, an amended version of the previous bills. The Orange Cliffs region was included in this legislation, but no mention was made of either tar sands or the buffer zone concept. The Canyon

Country Conservation Area was dropped from the bill. Administration of mineral leasing remained with the BLM. The committee stressed the recreational aspects of the area (because it promoted more access to the region) but did not make any statement about its multiple-use aspects.[49]

During the floor debate on the legislation, McKay contrasted a recreation area with a national park by noting that a recreation area provided more access to its lands than a park.[50] He made this point in defense of the proposed road into the Escalante, but it does stress the difference between the two types of park units, at least in McKay's mind. Certain congressional members who were traditional supporters of the national parks—for example, Udall of Arizona and Seiberling of Ohio—were not pleased by the Escalante road proposal but supported the bill in the hope that a later amendment would alter it.[51] There was no mention of multiple use, tar sands, or the Orange Cliffs as a buffer zone.

The bill the House passed was different from the Senate's. The day before passage, September 25, Moss voiced displeasure with the House's delay. He commented that the House had split off consideration of Glen Canyon from the other three bills having to do with nearby parklands. Moss questioned why it had taken the House so long to consider and report the Glen Canyon bill, adding that it might not even get considered during that session of Congress.[52] Once the House did pass the bill, Lloyd reacted strongly to Moss's criticisms. He asserted that the need to hold hearings in Utah and a large congressional work load explained the delay.[53]

The House and Senate were able to come to agreement over the differences between the two bills the next day. The only point of contention had to do with road-building. The final bill authorized a study of a proposed route between Glen Canyon City and Bullfrog Marina but did not grant an easement to Utah to build the road. The road has yet to be built.[54]

## THE CREATION OF GLEN CANYON
## NATIONAL RECREATION AREA

There are several sections of the law that established Glen Canyon that bear closer examination because they are important to later events. All sections of the law are drawn from the U.S. Code Title 16 (1982). Section 460dd is the statement of purpose for the recreation area. There are two purposes established by law: "(1) to provide for public outdoor recreation use and enjoyment of Lake Powell and lands adjacent"; and "(2) to preserve scenic, scientific, and historic features contributing to public enjoyment of the area."[55]

Language for other recreation areas varies, so there is no logical way to assume a uniform "purpose" for all recreation areas. This is especially true considering 16 U.S.C. 1(c)(b), which states that "each area within the national park system shall be administered in accordance with the provisions of its enabling act."[56] This section thus places the administration of Glen Canyon under the two stated purposes of section 460dd, which stress recreation more than the 1916 Organic Act that established the National Park Service. But section 460dd(3) places Glen Canyon under the provisions of sections 1 and 2–4 of Title 16, the general statutory authority for the Park Service, including the codified Organic Act, plus any other statutory authority given the secretary of the Interior, providing that that authority furthers the purposes of the recreation area.[57] Thus the management objectives, or the "politics" of Park Service management, would seem to revolve around how closely a recreation area resembles a national park. Or, put another way, does the placement of the recreation area under the general statutory authority that governs the Park Service at all modify the two purposes of the recreation area and thus allow the agency to manage the area more like a national park?

Perhaps the key section of the legislation establishing Glen Canyon is section 460dd(2), which states that the secretary

> shall permit the removal of leasable minerals from lands or interests in lands within the recreation area in accordance with [here follows a list of statutes relating to minerals] if he finds that such disposition would not have *significant adverse impacts* [emphasis mine] on the Glen Canyon project [the dam and reservoir] or on the administration of the national recreation area pursuant to this subchapter.[58]

It should already be apparent that mineral leasing was an intended activity in the recreation area. But what is one to make of the "significant adverse impacts" phrase? This phrase was included in S 27, HR 8214, and HR 15716, but there was next to nothing said about it in the hearings, reports, and floor debates. The key appears to lie with Utah governor Rampton's letter to Roy Taylor of the House Subcommittee on National Parks and Recreation, in which Utah promised to drop its opposition to the inclusion of the Orange Cliffs if some provision was made about BLM management of leasing. Utah relied on Park Service director Hartzog's own letter, which asserted that the BLM would administer leases on mineral activities if the activities were compatible with and did not significantly impair recreation and other conservation values contributing to public enjoyment.[59]

The provision giving the BLM administrative leasing authority was included in the bill (section 460dd[5]) but was subject to other provisions of the act. One of those provisions, 460dd(3), is the administrative "charge" to the Park Service. The other provision is the adverse impacts section. Thus one can only conclude from the correspondence and the final statutory language that "significant adverse impacts" had something to do with impact on the recreational purposes of the area. But in reality, what does that mean and how should it be interpreted? How should the secretary assess the impact of a mineral activity: What if mineral extraction harmed a segment of the Orange Cliffs piñon-juniper forest that was not near the area where most of the recreation would take place? Since most of the recreation would probably occur on Lake Powell, would a majority of those using the area object to mineral activity off the lake? Would any of these impacts be considered adverse to a visitor's enjoyment of the area? The dilemmas raised by questions such as these would receive a great deal of additional discussion and debate.

There are several points to make in conclusion. First, it is obvious that both the political process and chance played a much larger role in this issue than rational land-use planning. Chance is important because the outbreak of World War II probably prevented further consideration of the region as a national park or monument. After the war, it appears that the battle over water allocation dictated that Lake Powell would take the place of Escalante National Monument. Ironically, it was the isolation and unknown quality of undammed Glen Canyon that helped bring about the lake. Preservationists won their first major antidevelopment victory with the Echo Park controversy, but even they did not know enough about Glen Canyon to prevent the dam. The Sierra Club's lavish publication lamenting the dam, *The Place No One Knew*, is testimony to that ignorance.

The politics surrounding the establishment of the recreation area reveals congressional attention to the conflicting demands of preservation and development that clashed during the area's establishment. Development advocates would probably have preferred that the tar sands resource, or what was known of it, be kept out of the recreation area. Instead they accepted what must have appeared to them a reasonable compromise: Put the tar sands in the recreation area, but leave the area open to mineral leasing administered by the BLM.

Preservationists were not quite as clear as development advocates on the tar sands issue, focusing their attention instead on possible road development in the Escalante River drainage. Their own testimony reveals that they did not want tar sands development and thought it economically infeasible. Although they wanted the Orange Cliffs region in Canyonlands, they accepted its inclusion in Glen Canyon National Recreation Area. Moss's emphasis on the buffer qualities of the area probably influenced their decision. As will be seen later, the Park Service came to stress this buffer aspect as well.[60]

In summary, Congress appears to have attempted a political weighing of the demands of the various interests involved in the recreation area's establishment. Victory by the development forces would have meant a much smaller recreation area; victory by preservationists would have meant a much larger Canyonlands and no tar sands development. Mineral leasing in the recreation area might appear to be a victory by development proponents, but the adverse impacts clause seems to indicate that Congress meant what it said about recreation as the dominant use of the area, with mineral use subordinated to it.


THE PARK SERVICE TAKES OVER

The passage of legislation simply moves the policy process into a new phase—implementation. In the case of Glen Canyon, implementation revolves around Park Service management of the area as articulated through the agency's planning process and the general management plan (GMP). Public Law 94-458 (the Park Service General Authorities Act) requires that each unit of the national park system have a general management plan.[61] The Park Service stated that the management plan for the recreation area, written in 1979, "provides for the realization of the park's purpose in consonance with applicable legislative management policies and park management objectives."[62] Each management plan contains a statement of the unit's purpose and management objectives, a zoning of land and water within the unit, and "subplans" for resource management, interpretation (campfire talks, guided walks, displays, handouts, and so on) and visitor use, and future recreational development of the unit.[63]

The recreation area management plan stated that the purpose of the unit was "to provide for public outdoor recreation use and enjoyment . . . and to preserve scenic, scientific, and historic features contributing to public enjoyment of the area."[64] This, of course, is simply a restatement of the enabling act's relevant language. The Park Service then noted several legislative constraints on its management, such as the agency's authority to permit mining only if it led to no significant adverse impacts and the BLM's authority to lease. Finally, the Park Service listed five levels of management objectives. The three most important were management for maximal recreational enjoyment; acknowledgment of the constraints imposed by Congress; and minerals management "in accordance with the preservation of scenic, scientific, and historic features contributing to public enjoyment of the area."[65]

All of these objectives needed to be translated into concrete land-use decisions. This was done through a proposed division of the recreation area into four management zones (common throughout the park system)—"natural," "cultural," "development," and "recreation and resource utilization." The natural zone had 668,670 acres; the recreation and resource utilization (RRU) zone had 557,890 acres and constituted all but 19,745 acres of the recreation area. The natural zone emphasized natural processes, could be considered for wilderness, and allowed some grazing but prohibited mining. The recreation and resource utilization zone allowed mineral extraction and grazing.

Accompanying the management plan in 1979 was a final environmental impact statement on the plan, which presented two other zoning proposals developed by the Park Service. The first, alternative A, contained over 1 million acres in the natural zone. The second proposal, alternative B, contained only 164,000 acres. A final zoning proposal was chosen over these two alternatives. The management plan and final EIS also supplied comments from public agencies and interested groups and individuals involved during earlier stages of the planning process (to be discussed later).

The two most important zones obviously are the natural and the recreation and resource utilization zones. The Park Service used the zoning concept to analyze the potential impacts of developing the tar sands resource. First, the agency noted that about 18 percent of the total tar sands resource was in the natural zone, thus closing it to mineral activity, although mining could legally take place. This was not really a problem, the Park Service said, because this area was of insufficient thickness to allow any type of in-situ mining process to be used.[66] The rest of the deposit within the recreation area was in the RRU zone and thus theoretically accessible for recovery. The key, as the Park Service had pointed out, was that tar sands were then "a subeconomic resource in the submarginal category requiring new technology before economic recovery is feasible."[67] That is, it appeared unclear whether the resource could be developed within the near future.

It is not difficult to imagine the conflict that arose over the various zoning proposals included in the Park Service's general management plan. The agency was criticized by both preservationists and those who favored a more accessible and multiple-use recreation area. Governor Scott Matheson of Utah was not pleased with the Park Service's recommended alternative; rather, he favored, by way of compromise, a reduced natural zone as manifested in the Park Service's alternative B: "Many of our citizens question the propriety of any wilderness designation [the natural zone] within a national recreation area. However, to meet the concerns of the National Park Service, Utah citizens have reached this compromise recommendation and it should be recognized as such. The recommendation is a sincere attempt at accommodating a true multiple-use concept."[68] The Southeastern Utah Association of Governments was of a similar opinion as Matheson: "This proposal obviously and blatantly ignores the legislative intent, in that the four zone designations emphasize restrictive uses and ignore multiple-purpose uses."[69]

Park Service response to these comments is illustrative of the logic behind its management plan. To the state of Utah, the agency asserted that the recreation area was not a "classic" multiple-use area because Congress had subordinated resource use to the Glen Canyon project and to recreation.[70] To the southern Utahans, the Park Service response was even broader. The agency first asserted that the enabling act for the recreation area had withdrawn lands within the boundary of the park unit from the public lands where the concept of multiple use was practiced. Then, perhaps stretching its logic a bit, the Park Service said Congress had placed the recreation area under the Organic Act, an act that made no mention of multiple use. Finally, the 1972 enabling legislation made the purposes of the recreation area recreation and preservation that enhanced public enjoyment. Mining (multiple use) was allowed if there were no significant adverse impacts on the administration of the recreation area (for recreation and enjoyment) or the storage project.[71] This made it clear that the Park Service did not rank mineral extraction on the same level as recreation. Certainly, there was statutory evidence for the Park Service's position, but perhaps too the agency was uncomfortable with a nontraditional use of lands under its administration.

The BLM also questioned the Park Service's interpretation of its mineral management function through the zoning decisions. Again, the argument revolved around the attitude of Park Service management toward mineral extraction.[72] The BLM pointed out that the Park Service had yet to show any adverse effects brought on by mining activity.[73] The Park Service responded as it had to the state of Utah.[74]

It is interesting, and essential, to contrast the Park Service's response to Utah's and the BLM's criticisms of its management plan with its response to the preservationists. Preservationists were strongly opposed to the Park Service zoning of the Orange Cliffs. The Park Service had placed part of the area east of the Orange Cliffs within the natural zone and the rest within the RRU zone. This did not suit the preservationist community. The Sierra Club thought that the area west of the Orange Cliffs (which has a flat, mesalike appearance) should be zoned natural and ultimately designated as wilderness by Congress.[75] Furthermore, the club did not like the fact that a *dirt* road would be kept open to one of the overlooks in the area, Panorama Point.[76] Apparently, the group believed that access to an area it thought was "one of the most beautiful places God had created" was only for those who could walk.[77] This was the same area that the Sierra Club had once spoken of as very favorable to automobile access. Other preservation organizations made similar points.[78] The Park Service response explained that the area west of the Orange Cliffs was zoned RRU because it had mineral resources that could be developed, and thus the zoning decision was fulfillment of congressional intent.[79]

Interestingly, one mineral extraction company that commented on the zoning decision was in agreement with the Park Service regarding the Orange Cliffs.[80] The Oil Development Company of Utah (which later became the Santa Fe Energy Company) had proposed the pilot project discussed above. Since the area east of the Orange Cliffs would require strip mining to recover the tar sands resource, the company likely foresaw the political difficulties in getting approval of extraction by that method.

Another issue relating to the area's tar sands emerged during this time and was mentioned in the general management plan. The Oil Development Company of Utah had proposed to recover commercial quantities of oil from part of the tar sands area. This proposal first involved a test project (Project Fireflood Development) that would inject a combustible material down wells where it would be ignited. The resulting heat would lower the viscosity of the oil and allow it to be pumped out of the wells. Before this project could be undertaken, however, the Department of the Interior issued several letters asserting that the tar sands resource could only be leased under section 21 of the Mineral Leasing Act of 1920. This meant that Interior had declared the tar sands resource *not* leasable for oil and gas. The Oil Development Company of Utah, however, had a lease that *was* for oil and gas (section 17 of the same law). The company was unable to begin its test project until Interior lifted the leasing moratorium on tar sands in 1981 and Congress passed the Combined Hydrocarbon Leasing Act (to be discussed later) the following year.

The general management plan had promised further clarification of minerals management within the recreation area. This clarification came about in 1980 with the minerals management plan (MMP), the first such document ever prepared by the Park Service. The MMP sought to identify areas within the RRU zone that would be open to mineral development as mandated by the enabling act for the recreation area. The plan reasserted the zoning decision set forth in the GMP—that the tar sands deposit east of the Orange Cliffs was in the natural zone and not open to mineral development. The MMP pointed out that the extent of the tar sands deposit was based on projection and inference, and thus it was not clear how much of the resource was in the recreation area and how much in the natural zone.[81] The MMP also updated the status of the proposed Project Fireflood Development, noting that no development had yet occurred because of the continuing debate over the leasability of tar sands under the various sections of the Mineral Leasing Act.

One can make several observations about the general management plan for the recreation area. First, it is clear that the Park Service tried to fit the plan into a management philosophy with which the agency was comfortable. The Park Service's contention that the recreation area fell under the agency's Organic Act is proof of this. Francis Rourke pointed out that agencies have a vested interest in their own survival and thus will search for missions that necessitate the allocation of more resources to the agency, thereby preserving it.[82] Ronald Foresta argued that recreation areas fulfill the criterion of an appropriate mission for the Park Service.[83] But the administration of mineral extraction *in* a recreation area is apparently something that does not fit well with Rourke's description of the search for an appropriate mission.

One must remember that the Park Service's original mission was to promote both resource preservation and visitor use of the areas under its charge. Thus a recreation area was an appropriate management unit for the Park Service—it corresponded to the recreational aspects of the agency's original mission. It meant more land to manage and more resources to carry out that management. But minerals management was different—it did not fit well into the traditional mission of the agency and indeed may have contradicted it. The Park Service was apparently not comfortable with this new charge from Congress (some other parks do allow mining) but was politically astute enough to accept it. But with the acceptance came an interpretation of its management task that was as close to the original mission of the agency as possible. That interpretation emphasized placing minerals management under the 1916 Organic Act. To some extent, this was what Congress had said the agency could do. But Congress had also stressed the recreational aspects of the new unit, not the natural aspects. Thus, for example, it is certainly unclear whether many of the visitors that use the area, primarily the lake, would find mineral extraction off the lake that much of a problem. Most of these visitors are boating enthusiasts who may not visit the area primarily for its natural aspects. But if the recreation area was really more like a park, then the area's managers would certainly see extraction as a potential problem.

The reason that the Park Service was able to interpret its mineral task the way it did is not difficult to see: Congress was vague as well as contradictory in its enabling legislation charge. It is significant that some local interests actually foresaw what eventually happened. They had wanted exclusion of known mineral resources from the recreation area, or barring that, the BLM to manage mineral leasing within the recreation area. They had not wanted Park Service management of the unit because, after all, the Park Service manages parks, not multiple-use areas. If the agency was to manage land under the concept of multiple use, it would manage it as much as possible like a park—or so the local interests seemed to think. When Congress is vague in its statutory language, it is partly to render itself less vulnerable politically.[84] But this caution in effect gives the enforcing or implementing agency the discretion to interpret the law as it pleases. It is hardly surprising, then, that the agency in question will interpret the law to correspond to that agency's norms and values.

This question of interpretation can be applied to other interests in the Glen Canyon struggle. Preservationist interests saw the recreation area in even more parklike terms than the Park Service. Their support for the designation of over 85 percent of the land in the recreation area as natural and ultimately wilderness can be seen in this light. It suggests a common preservationist strategy of supporting the least-intensive use possible—for example, supporting Park Service administration over that of the BLM, a natural zone over an RRU zone, and wilderness over vehicular access. The rhetoric to support such land-use decisions often sounds noble—the "sacredness" of the land, "ecological integrity," and so on. Other interests perceive a hollowness to the rhetoric, however. It still seems to provide for use, but use that caters to a small group to the exclusion of many others. The contrast between the preservationists' opposition to a road to Panorama Point (or North Point) in the Orange Cliffs because the area was "sacred" and their support of a road providing access to wilderness in Canyonlands National Park might illustrate why local interests sometimes feel the way they do about preservationists.[85]

Initially, local interests did not try to urge a more development-oriented interpretation of the recreation area; they simply opposed it or wanted it kept small. But once they had come to accept the area, they saw the Park Service's task as being similar to BLM's: They were both charged with multiple use. Thus it seems that there is no easy answer to the question of what Glen Canyon National Recreation Area was supposed to be except to say somewhat bemusedly, "Why, it's anything folks wanted it to be!" Yet the law that created the area apparently left the last word with the Park Service. The energy crisis, its later "demise," and the election of Ronald Reagan would render that last word problematic.

# CHAPTER FOUR

# The Tar Sands
# Leasing Controversy

The Park Service minerals management plan for Glen Canyon was written in 1980, which would prove to be an eventful year for natural resource policy in the United States. That year would see the election of Ronald Reagan and the implementation of policies affecting both resource development and protection that were drastically different from those of previous administrations. Oil prices would skyrocket to over $30 a barrel, for a time making resources like tar sands look somewhat more attractive for development. The influence of these events will become clear as this chapter proceeds. We begin with the passage of a law that appeared to perform a housekeeping function but ended up encouraging threats to parks.

## THE COMBINED HYDROCARBON LEASING ACT
## OF 1981

The major "stated" purpose of the Combined Hydrocarbon Leasing Act (CHLA) of 1981 was to resolve confusion about the definition of tar sands. This confusion had been graphically illustrated by the refusal of the Department of the Interior to issue any federal leases having to do with tar sands. David Russell of the Interior Department stated the problem this way:

> Under present law, tar sand is leased under section 21 of the Mineral Leasing Act and oil and gas under section 17 of the same act. Leases under section 17 and 21 are mutually exclusive. A lease granted under section 17 gives no rights to deposits of native asphalt, bitumen and bituminous rock, including tar sand, and a section 21 lease carries no rights to deposits of oil and gas. Because of the difficulty in distinguishing between tar sand and conventional oil prior to well completion, tar sand has not been leased since 1965. If a tar sand lease were issued under section 21 of the Act, the lessee might begin exploratory drilling and discover oil to which he would have no

rights. . . . A combined hydrocarbon lease would eliminate the need for the Department of the Interior to distinguish between deposits of tar sand by permitting the development of both resources under a single lease.[1]

The Interior Department decided to lift its leasing moratorium as Congress began hearings on the 1981 act. Apparently, this decision was based on Interior's hope that Congress would create a combined hydrocarbon lease, which was needed because only about 30 percent of the known tar sands resource could be leased; the rest was already leased under oil and gas.[2] Thus Interior anticipated that the same legal and administrative problems that had led the agency to impose a moratorium obviously would still exist once the moratorium was lifted unless a combined hydrocarbon lease was created to solve the problem. Because the 70 percent of tar sands resource encumbered by oil and gas leases would be necessary to develop the rest, it had to be included in the combined lease area.

The act, debated in both 1980 and 1981, resolved this problem by putting a combined hydrocarbon lease under section 17 of the Mineral Leasing Act. Key sections of the legislation (Public Law 97-78) are summarized below.

*Section 4:* This section required that the new lease be applied to special tar sands areas designated as such by the secretary of Interior. The tar sands triangle was so designated on November 20, 1980.

*Section 6(a):* This section provided for competitive bidding for new combined hydrocarbon leases.

*Section 6(c):* Competitive leases would be for a primary term of ten years.

*Section 8:* Owners of oil and gas leases issued prior to the enactment of this act (November 16, 1983), as well as owners of valid claims to hydrocarbon leases based on mineral locations prior to 1926, were entitled to convert the lease or claim to a combined hydrocarbon lease for a primary term of ten years. Leaseholders had to apply for such a conversion within two years of the act's enactment. The conversion application had to include an acceptable plan of operations that assured *reasonable protection of the environment and diligent development of the resource.* The secretary of the Interior was required to issue regulations implementing the act within six months. Upon submission of a plan of operations in substantial compliance with these regulations, the secretary had to *suspend* the running of the lease proposed for conversion until the plan was approved. The secretary had fifteen months to act on proposed plans.

*Section 11:* This section is the most important for this study. It stated:

"The secretary shall apply the provisions of this Act to the Glen Canyon National Recreation Area, and to any other units of the national park system where mineral leasing is permitted, in accordance with any applicable minerals management plan if the Secretary finds that there will be *no resulting significant adverse impacts* on the administration of such area, or on other *contiguous* units of the national park system" (emphasis mine).[3]

During hearings on the legislation, some observers thought the tar sands resource would eventually be produced by surface mining rather than the in-situ process.[4] This was likely because of the relative newness and uncertainty of the in-situ method of recovery.

Santa Fe Energy Company did not want the lease conversion decision to be subject to the National Environmental Policy Act (NEPA).[5] Santa Fe would later become one of the companies that would apply for a hydrocarbon lease, and its interest in avoiding the NEPA process is understandable. The lease conversion process was, however, subjected to NEPA.

Preservationists were active in the legislative process as well. The Wilderness Society argued that the legislation protected only the recreational resources of the recreation area and thus requested that the Park Service minerals management plan be required to consider impacts on other resources, including air quality and nearby parks. The society also recommended that the word "contiguous" be changed to "adjacent," thus bringing at least one other national park, Arches, into the scope of section 11.[6] Congress did not adopt these changes, but later events would allay some of the preservationists' fears.

There was an aura of boosterism present during the 1981 hearings. Utah Senator Jake Garn predicted that present technology would allow for a "100,000 barrel-per-day oil production facility for almost 100 years," while noting that environmental factors were "much less imposing" than other synthetic fuels development and more easily adapted to existing technology than other synthetic fuels production.[7] Garn's statement appeared to view tar sands development in an optimistic and imminent light.

Most important, the similarity between the language of section 11 of the CHLA and the proposed Park Protection Act discussed in chapter 2 is striking. Section 11 gave the secretary of the Interior authority to lease the tar sands resource if there were "no significant adverse impacts" on Glen Canyon or contiguous park units. The Park Protection Act also spoke to the secretary's leasing authority but split that consideration into two parts. Leasing within park units could be done only if it was not likely to have a "significant adverse effect." Determination of such had to be done with a hearing on the record, in coordination with other planning and decision-making processes and with the determination published as a separate document. For "adjacent" leasing under the jurisdiction of the Department of the Interior, the secretary was required to weigh the public interest in allowing the activity versus the public interest in preventing the same "significant adverse effect." Thus the language of the Combined Hydrocarbon Leasing Act provides a test case of what might occur should legislation worded like the Park Protection Act pass.

During the floor debate by the House on the CHLA, a very important exchange happened between John Seiberling of Ohio and James Santini of Nevada:

> Mr. SEIBERLING: And section 11 thus precludes tar sands leases which would involve significant adverse impacts on the administration of a national park system unit, even though that unit is not withdrawn from operation of the mineral leasing laws?
> Mr. SANTINI: Yes.
> Mr. SEIBERLING: And would the gentleman agree with me that in that context the word "administration" involves more than such matters as the provision of visitor services and the like—and would include such aspects of administration as control of air or water pollution or other matters impacting on the lands within the unit?
> Mr. SANTINI: Yes, all that is involved in "administration" of a national park system unit.
> Mr. SEIBERLING: And further, is it not correct that section 11 clearly precludes activities which would have an adverse impact on any national park system unit not open to mineral leasing, if that unit were contiguous to a unit open to leasing?
> Mr. SANTINI: Yes, that is right.
> Mr. SEIBERLING: So, for example, any leasing under this bill of lands within the Glen Canyon National Recreation Area, which is open to leasing under the Mineral Leasing Act, could only be done if that leasing would not adversely impact the values of the Canyonlands National Park, which is contiguous to Glen Canyon and which is withdrawn from mineral leasing?
> Mr. SANTINI: Yes, that is right.
> Mr. SEIBERLING: And the values of Canyonlands that are protected by section 11 of the bill include such matters as air quality, water quality, and the like?
> Mr. SANTINI: The gentleman has all the good lines. Yes, that is correct.
> Mr. SEIBERLING: Well, I think the "yes" line is the best one of all.[8]

This exchange should be remembered in light of the events that followed enactment of the bill. The next stage in the tar sands issue would involve the promulgation of regulations required by the 1981 act.

The activities described above took place in 1981. During that year, oil reached its highest per barrel price ever. In 1972, when the Glen Canyon National Recreation Area was created, it was $3.39 per barrel. By 1981, it had reached $33.71 per barrel, a tenfold increase.[9] One engineer ventured his opinion that 1981 oil prices "might" have made tar sands development economically feasible for a short time.[10] Also during this period, a great deal of attention was being paid to the possibility of synthetic fuels development, of which tar sands is an example. The new Reagan administration was struggling with a policy dilemma regarding synthetic fuels. As Regina Axelrod asked, "How could the government subsidize synthetic fuels if the market provided insufficient incentives?"[11] If oil prices fell, the question would become an acute one for an administration committed to a free-market philosophy.

## THE TAR SANDS REGULATIONS

The Combined Hydrocarbon Leasing Act resulted in the promulgation of a set of regulations on leasing of the tar sands resource. These regulations focused primarily on two aspects: new competitive leases and conversion of existing oil and gas leases. I will focus on just one of these—conversion. The competitive leasing program has been under indefinite suspension by the BLM since July 18, 1984.[12]

The conversion regulations have several key sections that are important to understand because they structure decision making for the tar sands triangle. First, any application for a conversion of an oil and gas lease to a combined hydrocarbon lease requires submission of a "plan of operations" explaining how the applicant proposes to develop the tar sands resource. The plan could contain an exploration phase but had to contain a development phase that showed "reasonable protection of the environment" and diligent development of the resource.[13] Second, the regulations provide for the "unitization" of leases either before or after conversion.[14] Unitization allows leaseholders to combine leases into one large development unit to jointly develop the resource.

Third and most important, the regulations clarify the role of the Park Service in conversion decisions on leases within units of the park system. Any approval of a plan of operations within a unit of the system required the consent of the regional director of the Park Service, in this case the director of the Rocky Mountain Region headquartered in Denver. More specifically, this consent required that the regional director "shall find that there will be no resulting significant adverse impacts on the resources and administration of such areas or other contiguous units of the National Park System."[15] From a reading of the tar sands regulations, it is clear that the definition of "significant adverse impacts" was the key to any Park Service decision on the conversion of leases on agency-administered lands.

It soon became apparent that decisions on the conversion of oil and gas leases would be subject to NEPA. Because of the scope of the tar sands resource and possible development, NEPA's "tiering" process was involved. Tiering "refers to the process of addressing a broad, general program, policy or proposal in an initial environmental impact statement [EIS] and analyzing a narrower site-specific proposal related to the initial program, plan or policy in a subsequent EIS."[16] In this case, it meant that the BLM would prepare a regional EIS addressing the impacts and implications of proposed conversions and new leases for all of Utah. But no decisions regarding any implementation of specific parts of the tar sands program was to stem from this regional analysis. Thus "conversion decisions will be made following preparation of the subsequent site-specific analysis (EIS's and Environmental Assessments) prepared for individual projects."[17] The "trigger" for an EIS would be the submission of a plan of operations.

On December 16, 1982, a group of energy companies—Santa Fe Energy, Altex Oil Corporation, and thirteen other holders of oil and gas leases—submitted a conversion application for leases in the tar sands triangle. The application involved a proposal to combine (unitize) all of the converted leases into one 66,040-acre operating unit that would develop the resource using the in-situ processing method (see Maps 4.1 and 4.2). The development proposal involved four phases of production. Attention should be paid to the fourth stage of development, because it had the most potential to cause environmental degradation to various park units.

Phases I and II, involving the drilling and testing of 2 and 15 coreholes respectively, are primarily exploratory activities designed to further define the characteristics and extent of the tar sands deposit within the proposed federal lease unit. Phase II could require up to 12 miles of new temporary access trails to the individual drill sites and a 200 x 200 foot cleared and leveled area for each drill pad. Drilling would be accomplished with trailer-mounted air drilling rigs.

Phase III would be a pilot-scale project for testing in-situ extraction processes and identifying optimal procedures for producing hydrocarbons from the deposit. This phase would require drilling of two adjacent five-spot wells and eight production wells. The applicants are currently proposing a steam-drive process. The pilot plant

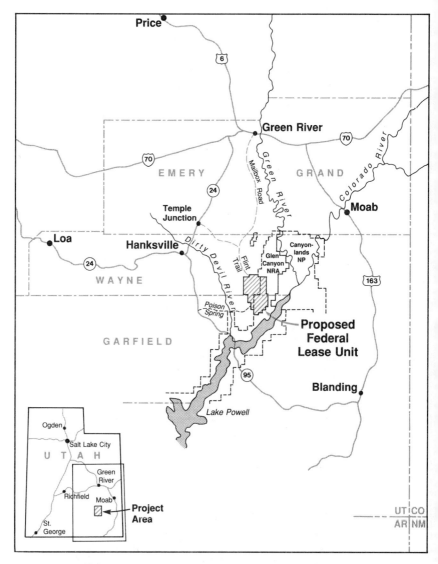

Map 4.1. The Location of the Tar Sands Triangle (from DEIS)

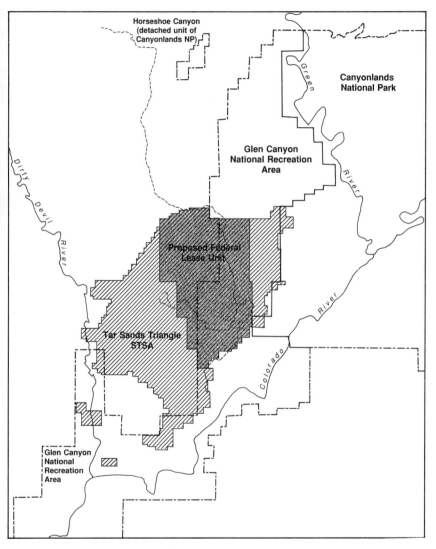

Map 4.2. The Tar Sands Triangle Leasing Proposal Area (from DEIS)

would include a portable 10 to 15 million Btu/hr boiler for steam generation, a 125 KW diesel powered electrical generator, two water wells, and associated piping and pumping facilities. Leveling and clearing of approximately 15 acres would be required for the extraction zone and associated ancillary facilities. In addition, phase III could require widening, paving, or other improvements to the Flint Trail. The pilot phase would also include testing of upgrading methods on the extracted bitumen at an offsite laboratory.

Phase IV would be full commercial development, including eventual development of the entire leased acreage for extraction and ancillary facilities. At any given time during phase IV, activities would be concentrated in a single extraction zone (prospective area). Each extraction zone would be developed to produce bitumen at a rate of 30,000 barrels per day (bpd), with an active wellfield of approximately 1,000 production wells and 940 steam injection wells. To the extent possible given terrain constraints, each well field would be developed in 25-well modules, each drilled from a central wellpad served by a blacktopped road. A pump station on the Dirty Devil River and a 12 to 15 mile pipeline would be built to supply water needs, estimated at 1,679 acre/feet a year. The steam required for bitumen extraction and electrical power generation (up to 2.27 million pounds/hour) would be generated onsite in five fluidized bed combustion units. An onsite steam turbine (32 MW capacity) would generate electricity for future facility needs. The bitumen would be processed in an onsite upgrading facility. This refinery-type facility would produce about 20,700 bpd of syncrude which would be transported to market via an as yet undetermined method (pipeline or truck), and the remaining 9,300 bpd of production would be used as fuel for steam generation and other onsite needs. Numerous other onsite facilities would also be required including solid waste handling and disposal facilities for boiler waste (800 yd$^3$/day) and silt (170 yd$^3$/day), coking facilities, sulfur recovery plant, syncrude tankage, water storage reservoir (approximately 130 million gallons), water treatment plant, and reinjection wells for wastewater disposal. Access to these phase IV activities would be via the Flint Trail which would require major upgrading, including crowning, ditching, paving, and possibly bridging of major canyons.

As the tar sand resource is depleted within each active extraction zone, new prospective areas would be developed (up to 18 such areas are proposed), and the depleted areas would be reclaimed sequentially until the entire lease unit is depleted and restored. Because of uncertainties regarding the production process an accurate schedule for the project cannot be established. However, it is esti-

Gordon Flats—this terrain is typical of areas where in-situ development would occur (by the author).

mated that the progressive development of extraction zones could continue for up to 160 years. This "rolling" of the extraction zones would necessitate moving and resiting (from 3 to 5 times) of ancillary facilities such as the fluidized bed steam generators.[18]

The production potential here had been significantly down-scaled from Senator Garn's initial forecast of one hundred thousand barrels a day to around thirty thousand.

It soon became clear that a proposal of the scope envisioned by this plan of operations would lead to the preparation of an EIS. Before the tar sands triangle EIS was prepared, there had been some debate within the Park Service as to whether an EIS was even needed. For a time, agency officials debated whether or not the information contained in the submitted plan of operations was sufficient to make an adverse effect determination without an EIS. A decision was made to go ahead with preparation after what was described as rather animated discussion.[19]

## THE ADVERSE-IMPACTS DIRECTIVE

During preparation of the draft EIS (DEIS) for the tar sands triangle, the Washington office of the Park Service issued a directive to the regional director of the Rocky Mountain Region to guide any possible finding of "no significant adverse impacts" regarding the proposed oil and gas lease conversion in Glen Canyon National Recreation Area. The regional director's decision was to be a management determination based on a review of a technical analysis, of a submitted plan of operations, performed by specialists within the agency.

The directive noted that there was little guidance (presumably from Congress) on the definition of "significant adverse impacts," and thus the agency defined the key terms based on its own interpretation of relevant law, regulations, and Park Service policies. These terms were as follows:

> "Resulting"—any impact that is directly or indirectly attributable to, a consequence of, or a logical outcome of tar sands development activities that could occur as a result of converting the leases in the consortium's proposal and/or ensuing exploration, operations or other activities. Resulting also includes impacts on NPS resources that occur from regional population growth and industrial, energy and other development necessitated by or associated with the project.
>
> "Significant Adverse"—an impact shall be deemed to be a significant adverse impact when that impact or combination of impacts is of such magnitude, scope, location, timing, extent, frequency, or duration that the impact or combination of impacts conflicts with the preservation of the resources, values, or attributes of a park unit, or portion thereof, for present or future visitors.
>
> "Impact"—any quantitative or qualitative change in environmental, ecological, historic, cultural, aesthetic or visitor experience factors or indicators.[20]

The regional director, Lorraine Mintzmeyer, was then given three ranked criteria on which to base her decision. The first considered impacts that violated mandatory statutory responsibilities; the second considered violations of values for which GCNRA was established (such as scenic panoramas); and the third was similar to the second but considered cumulative impacts on lands, resources, and visitor experiences. The regional director *had* to make a finding of significant adverse impact if the first criterion was met; the other two required "reasoned judgment" based on available information.[21] Any Park Service decision regarding an adverse impact required written notification of the Bureau of Land Management.

It did not take long for the BLM to respond to the Park Service directive. In a memo that passed through both assistant secretaries with respective authority over the two agencies, the BLM stated its concerns. The agency focused on three issues: legislative and administrative intentions regarding GCNRA; prior Park Service–BLM agreements regarding tar sands; and the Park Service directive's relation to NEPA. The BLM first argued that the Park Service had made mineral development "virtually impossible" in GCNRA by broadly defining the values (purposes) for which the area was established.[22] Put another way, the BLM's position was that the recreation area was established for recreation and that the Park Service was trying to manage the area like a national park. The BLM also pointed out that Glen Canyon had a minerals management plan which directed that certain areas of the recreation area be open to minerals development; the Park Service, however, appeared to be moving away from this prior managerial commitment.

The BLM also objected to what it thought was Park Service inattention to existing agreements between the two agencies.[23] The BLM believed that the Park Service was ignoring both the joint EIS that the two agencies were preparing and the tiered and phased review that BLM thought the two agencies had agreed to. Put simply, the BLM thought the Park Service was "rushing" a no-development decision that could be made at a later point in the process.

Finally, the BLM argued that the Park Service was ignoring established NEPA law and procedure as it set forth its significant adverse impact criteria. This was because NEPA, NEPA regulations, and resultant court interpretations of NEPA had already defined the terms the Park Service was attempting to explain in its directive. It should be made clear, though, that the BLM argument was that the Park Service should adopt language used already, not that it had to. As the BLM stated, "There is no reason to 'reinvent the wheel' here and confuse what is already an established procedure."[24]

A clear understanding of the overall position of the BLM on the Park Service directive can be seen in the following comment: The "Park Service has a Minerals Management Plan for GCNRA opening and closing areas in the GCNRA to minerals development—GCNRA is not necessarily a park but a recreation area—this appears to be a strategy to frustrate any mineral activity in or near GCNRA. Entire notice reflects a predetermined intent to reject all tar sand activities without giving fair and objective consideration to CHLA."[25] The BLM seemed afraid that the adverse impacts directive would preclude tar sands development. Since both agencies had jurisdiction over different parts of the tar sands resource, a joint EIS was obviously necessary. One might predict, however, that the climate around EIS preparation was somewhat clouded. Some of that clouding could easily be attributed to the multiple-use mandate of the BLM opposing the preservation mandate of the NPS. Yet this does not necessarily mean that the BLM would allow leasing to occur. What is probably equally important is the BLM's desire to fully *consider* leasing, without NPS hints that it was not likely to occur due to the adverse-impacts directive.

THE TAR SANDS DEIS

In late 1983, the BLM and NPS issued their joint DEIS. It proposed five development alternatives that can be summarized as follows.

*Alternative 1:* Conversion of all leases except those in areas of the GCNRA that were closed by the Minerals Management Plan. A production rate of 30,000 bpd was assumed. The total size of the lease proposal was 54,546 acres.

*Alternative 2A:* Conversion of all leases with additional restrictions to protect critical resources. A production rate of 5,000 bpd was assumed. The total size of the lease proposal was 23,541 acres.

*Alternative 2B:* Conversion on BLM wilderness study areas was denied. Protective restrictions were placed on the rest of acreage. The total size of the lease proposal was 14,090 acres. (Areas managed by the BLM that have the potential for inclusion in the U.S. wilderness system are to be inventoried and reviewed as wilderness study areas. They will remain in this status until Congress either designates them as wilderness or releases them back to multiple-use management.)[26]

*Alternative 2C:* Conversion of all leases in the recreation area was denied. The total size of the lease proposal was 14,745 acres.

*Alternative 3:* Conversion of all leases was denied.

Extensive environmental analyses were performed for each of the development alternatives, based on the four-phase production scenario described earlier, to help the Park Service and BLM come to an agreement on which alternative to recommend.[27] This recommendation would not be offered until the issuance of a final EIS, but, as will be seen, the agreement and final EIS were never written.

There were many new environmental laws passed in the 1970s that would affect the EIS decision. The most important of these are the Clean Air Act Amendments (1977), the Clean Water Act Amendments (1977), the Endangered Species Act (1978), and the Archaeological and Historical Data Preservation Act (1974). These acts, much like the constantly changing energy picture, provide another context in which to view the tar sands issue. Their very existence allows one to surmise how events might have proceeded ten years earlier had tar sands been feasible to develop.

Analysis contained in the draft EIS revealed that there were serious environmental consequences possible for all the development alternatives. Perhaps the most serious, because of statutory requirements, were the air-quality violations projected under what is called the "new source permitting process," or prevention of significant deterioration (PSD). Air-quality analysis in this process involves the use of complicated computer models that estimate both pollutant concentrations and visibility impairment.[28] If certain "increments" of air pollution standards for sulfur dioxide ($SO_2$) and fine particulates are exceeded, it will be harder to get a construction permit approved. The models predicted a series of air pollution problems. The most serious were caused by the projected emissions from the phase IV development under alternative 1, though all the development alternatives forecast some visibility problems and PSD increment violations.[29]

The Glen Canyon National Recreation Area, a federal class II PSD area (see chapter 5), was predicted to have $SO_2$ and fine particulate PSD increment violations, as well as national ambient air quality standards (NAAQS) violations under alternative 1. The other development alternatives did not violate the NAAQS, but they did violate certain PSD increments. Under the 1977 Clean Air Act Amendments, an air-quality permit cannot be issued if these violations are not mitigated. Other violations were predicted for Canyonlands and Arches national parks, including visibility degradation. Even under the reduced development alternatives of 2A, 2B, and 2C, short-term PSD $SO_2$ increment violations, as well as reduced visibility, were predicted in Canyonlands.[30] Both of these areas are class I, where air-quality degradation is most strictly regulated. Interestingly, had these class I violations been the only air-quality violations, the necessary air-quality permits for tar sands development could have been granted if the federal land manager (the Park Service, in this case) had been able to certify that no adverse impact would have resulted from the violations. But, since the class II violations preclude, by law, a permit for construction *without* exception, there was no opportunity for certification at this point, and thus the proposed development could not be allowed under alternatives 1 and 2A, 2B, and 2C unless the extraction plant was redesigned.

The EIS analysis looked at many other potential impacts on other resources should the tar sands development take place. These resources included water quality and quantity, soils, vegetation, wildlife, noise, scenic and recreational values, cultural resources, and socioeconomic impacts. None of these resources is protected under statutory guidance such as that provided by the Clean Air Act, with the exception of certain wildlife that might fall under the scope of the Endangered Species Act. What is important to note is if any of the analysis of potential impacts contained in the DEIS was used by the Park Service in its adverse-impacts decision making on this issue (to be discussed later).

## PUBLIC RESPONSE TO THE DEIS

Public response to the draft environmental impact statement came in two forms, written and oral. The oral comments were given at three public hearings held August 21, 1984, at Hanksville, Utah; August 23, 1984, at Salt Lake City; and August 28, 1984, at Lakewood, Colorado. The Hanksville hearing took place in a small, rather isolated town that was the closest settlement to the tar sands triangle. Three people spoke at this meeting, all in favor of the proposed development. Two of the three—Ferrel Chappel and Meeks Morell—were Wayne County commissioners. Their testimony was brief and to the point: They all favored development because of their perception that the development would be of economic benefit to the Wayne County area.[31]

The next hearing, at Salt Lake City, was not much better attended than the Hanksville meeting, but several comments are worth noting. Jim Peacock, representing the Rocky Mountain Oil and Gas Association, argued that lease conversion itself did not involve any environmental impact and thus questioned the need for any EIS,[32] although he supported the development interpretation of the CHLA.[33] Terri Martin, representing the National Parks and Conservation Association, supported the "no conversion" alternative and took the opposite position on the intent of key mandating legislation.[34] She also made the point that the plan of operation had not been adequately analyzed for meeting the diligent development requirements. Diligent development was not defined in the regulations but appeared to mean that development had to occur in a timely and focused manner. Martin also noted that the DEIS had reconfirmed a point in the regulations asserting that a right to conversion was based on an ability to produce tar sands.[35] At least one person in the Park Service confessed that the agency had also questioned some of the same aspects of the plan of operations and whether it could be disapproved before the EIS process even began because diligence and the ability to produce were not shown.[36]

The final meeting was held in Colorado. Only one person spoke, but he represented a key actor in the tar sands issue. He was Robert Montgomery of Kirkwood Oil and Gas, one of the major leaseholders in the tar sands triangle.[37] Montgomery echoed an earlier argument that the DEIS was not needed at that point.[38] Montgomery said the EIS should be done once the development phase of the proposal was perfected, which could happen during the exploration phase: "The only acceptable alternative is the conversion of all oil and gas leases with stipulations and mitigating measures that pertain only to the exploration through pilot phases of the plan of operations. . . . [A]n extensive environmental analysis should be required upon acceptance of a perfected plan of development."[39]

Written comments obviously fell into two categories, those that suggested conversion of the leases and those that opposed conversion. Preservation organizations predictably opposed lease conversion and recommended the adoption of alternative 3. Both the National Parks and Conservation Association and the Environmental Defense Fund (EDF) submitted lengthy comments on the conversion issue. The NPCA document was wide-ranging in scope, citing impacts on park resources such as air quality and archaeological sites.[40] The group also reasserted the familiar preservationist interpretation that the Orange Cliffs were intended as a buffer for Canyonlands.[41] Finally, the NPCA expressed some reservation about the Park Service draft adverse-impacts directive, noting that any Park Service change of decision criteria should be open for public comment.[42]

The Environmental Defense Fund chose to focus on air quality and visibility impairment, arguing for more comprehensive visibility models and study of the regional haze problem.[43] The radical group Earth First! provided a passionate counterpoint to the comments of the older, more traditional preservation organizations in a handwritten note that urged the Park Service to "show some guts" and not become a "patsy for industry."[44]

The preservationists found allies in two places: the Environmental Protection Agency (EPA) and the state of Utah. The EPA, citing both air and groundwater degradation, supported the "no action" alternative unless a level of development could be found that was not environmentally harmful.[45] The agency also questioned the air-quality model chosen for the DEIS, suggesting that possible impacts might have been understated.[46]

The state of Utah also supported the "no action" alternative. The argument for its position was familiar: The data suggested that too much degradation would occur for the development to be permitted. But the state had two other concerns as well. First, it questioned the timing of the development plan. Noting that the state was supportive of development generally, Governor Matheson pointed out: "I am still concerned with the timing for the submission of the development plans prior to obtaining adequate knowledge of the resource and the high level of uncertainty surrounding potential impacts arising from undefined diligence requirements and inadequate knowledge of the extractable resource or appropriate extraction technologies."[47]

A similar view was often expressed during my interviews with various officials involved in the tar sands issue. The problem, it seems, was with various decisions made by Congress. Some Park Service officials thought the origin of the problem was the act that created the recreation area; it ended up as a compromise between a park and almost no additional protection. Congress should have been clearer on the primary purpose of the recreation area. But, some Park Service supporters said, it was only proper that the Park Service try and protect the recreation area with appropriate statutory and discretionary authority, allowing mining if it was compatible.

However, most officials, in both the Park Service and the BLM, saw the CHLA as the real culprit. Through it, Congress had prematurely drawn attention to the development of a resource that was still faced with extraction technology problems. The Utah congressional delegation was seen as promoting the CHLA as the means to bring economic development to the state, but without really examining the reality of tar sands development in the early 1980s.[48] Senator Garn's statement in 1981 certainly adds credence to this viewpoint.

Utah also suggested a solution to the problem: competitive leasing. Under this approach, a more reasonable time frame would allow for "appropriate exploration and research and development upon which technologies for extraction may be developed."[49] This opinion resulted in part because the state believed that the CHLA's restrictions made conversion not economically viable at that time.[50] Interestingly, the state paid attention to the buffer zone concept in its written comments. It suggested that a new alternative be developed that denied conversion on GCNRA and BLM wilderness study lands and other sensitive areas. This would "have the effect of providing a 'buffer zone' between the industrial development to the west of Glen Canyon and the sensitive Canyonlands National Park to the east."[51]

Another set of actors wrote in favor of some level of tar sands development. One group we have seen before—the local and regional governments of southern Utah. Their positions in favor of the development were again to the point: It would be of great economic benefit to the region.[52] The local representatives argued optimistically that technology would improve during the exploration and test phases of the projected development.[53]

The two companies that held a major portion of convertible oil and gas leases—Kirkwood and Santa Fe—contributed extensive comments on the DEIS. Santa Fe's comments centered on the role of the commercial development phase of the proposed project (phase IV). The company contended that the phase IV project proposal had been forced on it by the BLM's interpretation of congressional intent regarding the plan of operations contemplated by the CHLA.[54] The company's position was that a phase IV project would only be proposed if the results of the first three phases were positive enough to warrant it.[55] Thus, argued Santa Fe, the environmental analysis of the DEIS should be limited to only the first three phases of production.

The regulations on conversion appear to speak to this question quite clearly in section 3140.2-3(f), when they require that the plan of operations "*shall* include a development phase" (emphasis mine).[56] The plan could still be approved even if work under the exploration plan was needed to perfect the development phase.[57] The preamble to the conversion regulations also clarified the question of a development phase by supporting the contention of several commentators that "the intent of the authors of the legislation was that the applicants not be allowed to convert before they are fully committed or prepared to pursue diligent development of the tar sand resource and that the mechanism for ensuring this commitment was a complete plan of operations."[58]

Santa Fe also protested the "no action" alternative as it had been developed in the EIS. The company contended that under the "no action" alternative, it could still try to develop the tar sands under existing oil and gas leases. Thus the "no action" alternative should provide for that possibility.[59]

In one of the technical analysis sections of the company's lengthy comment on the EIS, Santa Fe made note of a new study of the resource potential of the tar sands triangle. This study had estimated the potential recoverable oil from the region at 6.3 billion barrels, down significantly from the 12–15 billion of previous estimates.[60] The key question, of course, was how much of the tar sands was actually recoverable. The plan of operations predicted a 30,000 barrel per day production rate for 160 years for a total of 1.75 billion barrels, for that particular project. That total represents about six months of U.S. consumption of oil (1988).[61]

Finally, Santa Fe included its response to the Park Service draft adverse-impacts directive of May. Although this response was first sent to the Park Service before the EIS comments, the Park Service was to make its determination on the complete development proposal, including phase IV, which was being analyzed in the EIS. Thus the wording of the adverse-impacts directive was crucial and of great concern to Santa Fe. Santa Fe's contentions revolved around the purpose of the recreation area and the company's perception that it was the duty of the Park Service to prescribe mitigation measures to "allow" development to go forward. Santa Fe thought the directive "appeared to ignore the special status of GCNRA and to treat it as a national park" and later stated that it was "incumbent" on the Park Service to propose mitigating measures rather than oppose conversion.[62]

Kirkwood focused on many of the same concerns as Santa Fe. In addition, the company emphasized the section of the conversion regulations that allowed conversion even if more work was needed on the development phase. The exact wording of the regulations, however, was that the plan "can be approved," not that it had to be.[63] Kirkwood also argued that since the regulations provided for the possible amendment of a plan of operation, a phased approval was the proper way to proceed, because, in Kirkwood's view, the development phase of the plan was really only conceptual at that point.

## POST-DEIS NEGOTIATION AND CONFLICT

All of the comments made upon issuance of the DEIS were designed as input to the final EIS, the next step in the decision-making process. As mentioned, the two Interior agencies had postponed a recommendation on which alternative they preferred until the final EIS was issued. On December 5, 1984, the Park Service notified the BLM that it preferred alternative 3 (no conversion).[64] This notification mentioned the Park Service's understanding that the BLM alternative would be 2A—with restrictions on development as outlined in the DEIS. The course of action at that time appeared to suggest the possibility of the Park Service's supporting the adoption of alternative 2C (no development within the recreation area), absent, the memo said, "escalation within the department."[65] On December 27, 1984, the Park Service Energy, Minerals, and Mining Division revised the adverse-impacts directive, subject to Washington clearance, with "no substantive changes."[66] Three months later, the final directive was issued, again with no significant changes.[67] All of the DEIS activity had no apparent influence on the final version of the adverse-impacts directive.

Events in January and February 1985 saw the BLM and Park Service attempt to come to an agreement on the tar sands issue. In January, the BLM tried to get a discussion going between the two agencies based on a "working" assumption that alternative 2A (conversion with additional restrictions) had been adopted without the production limits specified in the original 2A alternative.[68] The Park Service, as could be expected, strongly objected to this and presented an option that would focus on alternative 2C (no development on GCNRA land) with additional NPS stipulations.[69] The BLM position, coupled with an NPS view that the BLM did not take Park Service management concerns into account, led the agency to propose its own possible solution to the impasse.[70]

The Park Service strategy was intriguing. The agency offered two ways to proceed on the issue: Both alternatives 2A and 2C with additional stipulations were suggested as possible courses of action.[71] Alternative 2A as approved by the Park Service would allow for only phases I and II to proceed. Phases III and IV were disapproved on Park Service lands but could be continued on BLM lands. Results of these activities would be used to assess the environmental effects of the phase I and II operations. Before any activity was allowed on BLM lands, all permits would have to be obtained. Thus, for example, all air-quality problems, such as increment violations, would have to be addressed and solved before a permit for construction could be granted. The Park Service reserved its right to make an adverse-impacts evaluation on any additional resource development (phases III and IV) on Park Service lands.

The 2C stipulations clearly illustrated Park Service preference for this alternative. These stipulations would allow conversion only on BLM lands. The Park Service would permit drilling to delineate the resource during the time of unexpired oil and gas leases. Thus to the Park Service, "alternative 2C would allow exploration and resource delineation on Park Service lands, allow development of extraction technology on BLM lands, and leave the NRA lands available for leasing under the competitive system. An advantage of the competitive system is that it contemplates and provides for phased resource development."[72]

While the BLM was preparing its response to the Park Service proposal, a curious thing happened. The Park Service received a memo from the assistant secretarial level of the Interior Department that conflicted starkly with prior Park Service positions on the tar sands issue.[73] The memo stated that the Park Service did not find a significant adverse effect on the 2A conversion decision. Certain conditions were attached: The pilot plant would be located outside the GCNRA, and production would be limited to between one thousand and thirty-five hundred barrels per day. Second, the memo stated that the Park Service and BLM were "equal" partners in any decisions affecting GCNRA lands, including the provision of additional stipulations, rather than the usual position of the Park Service's having jurisdiction over the recreation area.

The Park Service reacted strongly. The agency asserted that it had not made any adverse-impacts decision—nor would it, until after a final EIS was issued—and that any agreement to conversion was "definitely not the case."[74] The agency also pointed to language in both the leasing regulations and the CHLA that required Park Service consent on any conversion decisions on its lands, plus the right to develop stipulations on any leases converted.[75] Evidently, the memo from the secretarial level was intended as a policy "feeler," because no further evidence exists that Interior officials pursued it after the Park Service objected to it.

In late February, the Park Service and BLM had a series of exchanges over each other's position on the tar sands question. A memo from the

Park Service to the BLM reveals the areas of disagreement between the two agencies. The Park Service commented on the BLM's response to the Park Service's additional proposed stipulations on the 2A alternative.

The first disagreement between the two agencies was over the scope of the approval of the submitted plan of operations. The Park Service's position was that under its compromise proposal, the plan of operations was only approved in part (phases I and II) under either alternatives 2A or 2C. Reflecting concern about phase IV of the project, the BLM's reaction to the Park Service position was that a plan of operations had to be approved in its entirety, with the provision that "certain aspects of the operation may not be allowed until the plan is amended."[76] The Park Service claimed that the BLM had always adhered to a policy of phased plan approval and was now reversing that policy and going along with the Park Service policy of making an adverse-impacts determination based on a complete plan of operation. Of course, the BLM position was approval of the entire plan of operation, with stipulations. But, according to the Park Service, the agency was attempting to compromise on a level of tar sands development that it could "live with."[77] Thus the Park Service "must either deny its consent to the entire proposal or deny its consent to that portion of the proposal with which the resulting significant adverse impacts are associated" (phases III and IV).[78]

On the question of the siting of the phase III pilot project, the Park Service's position was to locate the plant on BLM land. The BLM opposed this location because it might interfere with its own wilderness study areas.[79] The Park Service used this argument to its advantage by applauding the BLM's desire to protect its areas, and "in the same vein the Park Service seeks to protect GCNRA, an area which Congress has already declared to be of national significance for natural resource values unrelated to tar sands."[80] What the BLM wanted to protect as possible wilderness, the Park Service wanted to protect as the already established recreation area.

As part of its argument, the BLM proposed that any decision regarding modification of the plan of operation's phase III pilot project would be made in consultation with the Park Service. The Park Service answered that it had consent authority over plan revision within the GCNRA, not merely consultation privileges, and referred to consultation as "wholly inadequate and unacceptable."[81]

There were several other Park Service–BLM disagreements over various aspects of the Park Service 2A stipulations. The basis of disagreement was obvious. The Park Service was opposed to more than phase I and II development on its lands but left the door open for phase III development on BLM lands under strict environmental stipulations. Phase IV development was opposed by the Park Service and favored by the

BLM. The Park Service once again used its potential-adverse-impacts authority to make its policy recommendation. The BLM favored phase IV development even though it had admitted that the phase IV project was conceptual and not complete enough to be used to approve commercial development.[82]

The thrust of the discussion is clear. The information in the DEIS led the Park Service to make an adverse-impacts determination but to try a compromise as well. The BLM, supporting conversion and development, apparently felt constrained by the Park Service compromise and continued to try to get approval of the whole project, even though the BLM itself had doubts about the last phase of the development proposal.

In March, Interior and agency officials and industry representatives continued to meet to try to resolve the dispute over which alternative to recommend. Apparently, an idea surfaced to exchange leases to solve part of the problem.[83] Interior's solicitor's office questioned whether there was any legal authority to make such an exchange. More important, there was some indication that Secretary Donald Hodel was leaning toward a "no conversion" decision in the GCNRA and possibly in the BLM's wilderness study areas, though no decision had yet been reached on a preferred alternative.[84] In April, the two agencies still had not come to an agreement. When the BLM issued a briefing statement for Secretary Hodel's use on his visit to the tar sands triangle and nearby areas, the Park Service reacted to what it perceived as inaccuracies. The BLM briefing listed several "points to consider" that the Park Service contradicted.

First, the BLM and Park Service continued in their long-standing disagreement over the purpose of the GCNRA. Second, the BLM had identified 2C as the preferred alternative of the Park Service; the Park Service stated that its preferred alternative was 3 (no conversion) and had been since December.[85] Third, the BLM, according to the Park Service, had minimized the still unacceptable impacts of the 2A, 2B, and 2C alternatives. Fourth, there was disagreement between the two agencies over where the bulk of the resource was located, though recent data indicated that it was close to evenly divided.[86] Fifth, the two agencies disagreed over the intent of the CHLA: The BLM believed that it emphasized development (conversion) with diligent development and environmental protections; the Park Service believed that conversion should proceed only if there were no projected adverse impacts.[87]

This exchange had several other interesting aspects. The Park Service claimed that phase IV was "submitted at the request of the Bureau of Land Management to satisfy a regulation. The applicants have consistently stated that they need to carry out exploration before it would be known where in the unit commercial tar deposits (if any) are distributed."[88] The BLM's briefing statement also mentioned the attempt to exchange leases, noting again that the exchange would be difficult.[89] Finally, the BLM rejected the "compromise" 2C alternative put forth by the Park Service in March.[90]

By late April, it appeared that the attempt to reach consensus was over. The regional director of the Park Service notified the director that the agency, at that level, was sticking with alternative 3 and that some agreement had to be reached on a preferred alternative. Discussion with the BLM was to be concluded and a decision made at higher levels within the Interior Department.[91]

In June, the associate director for natural resources, Richard Briceland, sent the regional director a memo that summarized the agency's latest position. The Park Service rejected alternatives 1, 2A, and 2B as not protective enough to allow a "no adverse impacts" determination. Alternative 2C (no conversion within the recreation area) was seen as only marginally better and still not protective enough.[92] Briceland concluded:

> This matter has been before the Secretary for months. We understand that both the Secretary and the Under Secretary favor the Park Service no development position; however, no final decision has been announced. We understand further that the Secretary has asked the Solicitor to see if there is some land exchange or other concession that might be offered to the consortium to induce them to withdraw their lease conversion application and tar sand development proposal. To the best of our knowledge, no satisfactory solution has been identified to date, nor is one likely.[93]

The Park Service urged that the secretary endorse the publication of the final EIS with alternative 3 as the preferred choice.

In February 1986, events remained unchanged. During an interview with me, a high-level Park Service official stated that a final decision on the tar sands question had been placed on indefinite hold. This official reported a conversation that supposedly occurred between Secretary Hodel and Park Service Director Mott. Hodel had told Mott that no tar sands development would happen within the recreation area but that the Interior Department would not declare this as official policy.[94]

On January 31, 1986, the BLM released its statewide wilderness DEIS for Utah. Part of the tar sands triangle contains a BLM wilderness study area called French Spring–Happy Canyon. The BLM wilderness proposal suggested that none of this area's twenty-five thousand acres be managed as wilderness. The BLM proposal thereby rendered the DEIS 2B alternative moot for the time being.[95]

That ended the tar sands saga for now. By 1986, oil prices had declined to $13–14 a barrel.[96] Tar sands development had once again become too expensive. Also in 1986, the Western Research Institute performed a laboratory combustion test on tar sands material that was not successful, once again suggesting that technology still had a ways to go before tar sands would be recoverable.[97] Secretary Hodel, apparently torn between two constituencies represented by the BLM and the NPS, chose not to make a decision on a final EIS recommendation, and so the document was never written. The tar sands were not developed, the recreation area and surrounding parks remained protected, and the leases were suspended from running out.

## CONCLUSION

The tar sands issue involved a "layering on" of different actors, interests, and statutes from the first expression of interest in making the area a national park to the events of early 1986. We saw preservationist and Park Service interest in having much of the region that encompasses the tar sands triangle put under Park Service management, first as Escalante National Monument and later as Canyonlands National Park. Once Glen Canyon National Recreation Area was created, preservation groups urged that most of that area be managed as "naturally" as possible.

Natural-area management also turned out to be the policy that the Park Service felt most comfortable with in its management of Glen Canyon. Although the recreation area was not in the strictest sense a national park, the Park Service still believed that the area's parklike qualities had a much higher priority than minerals development. Congress had, after all, mandated recreation as the primary purpose of the recreation area. From there, it is not much of a leap to managing the area like a national park.

Opposing the preservationists and the Park Service was an informal coalition of interests composed of the BLM, local officials and citizens, and parts of the mineral extraction industry. The state of Utah also supported minerals development but apparently was concerned that adequate technology be available to develop the tar sands resource, something not clear from the lease conversion application.

What does the tar sands case tell us about the external threats issue? It presented an interesting opportunity to analyze how a park protection law similar to John Seiberling's might fare in practice. One lesson learned from the tar sands case is that a law that might seem to be clear in its intent may not be applied, or implemented, with that intent in mind. There was not much question that the tar sands development project was likely to cause harmful impacts on both Glen Canyon and nearby Canyonlands. Yet no policy decision ever emerged from the secretary's office denying the lease conversion application because of projected harm to the park units. There has been no development, but the running of the leases remains suspended so that the leases are in force indefinitely. Although dormant, the issue is likely to become active again should energy concerns and prices rise once more on the national policy agenda.

Secretary Hodel could have either opposed development or deferred it, because lower energy costs rendered development too expensive. Instead, he chose to do nothing at all. And so the battle will have to be refought at a later time. One can only speculate on why Hodel picked this path; nothing exists in the public documents that would help explain his decision. Yet it is not hard to reach the conclusion that the natural resource policy ideology of the Reagan administration was probably the salient factor at work. Much has been written about Reagan's resource policy, most of it negative.[98] Thus, although it may have been difficult for the Reagan administration to approve the lease conversion, it was not as difficult to simply defer the matter. A final decision made either way would likely have angered a lot of people, especially potential supporters of the president's policies on the environment. At the same time, it was difficult to justify lease conversion because of evidence that the proposed lease development would indeed prove harmful to the resources and values of Glen Canyon and Canyonlands. Therefore, the decision became no decision, with no clear losers or winners.

All of this is disquieting. The evidence suggests that a park protection statute may not have the results intended. Rather than forcing a decision to be made about the value of park protection versus the value of resource development, decisions can be postponed. Postponement may be politically wise but not fundamentally helpful in creating a consensus on the need for and scope of park protection. Problems that are supposed to be dealt with through a park protection mechanism could end up never being resolved.

During several interviews with BLM officials in Utah, I broached the subject of buffer zones in the tar sands case. The question was hypothetical but designed to see what BLM officials involved in tar sands decision making thought about a buffer around Canyonlands and Glen Canyon (which some people thought was already a type of buffer). The officials I spoke with were not in favor of a buffer zone for BLM lands next to parks, preferring expanded boundaries over constrained decision making on BLM lands. Their argument fell along the lines of asserting that sensitive land should probably belong in a park (if that could be proved) but that the BLM should not be expected to make decisions based on the welfare of nearby parks. This would be a constraint upon the BLM multiple-use mission and the expertise of BLM officials.[99]

A few points need to be made about the role of the National Park Service in the tar sands case. The Combined Hydrocarbon Leasing Act provided the Park Service with a framework—the adverse-impacts directive—to address the effects of tar sands development on Glen Canyon and Canyonlands. This directive, coupled with information gleaned from the DEIS, enabled the Park Service to take an assertive stand on tar sands development.

The adverse-impacts directive might serve as a useful model should a sympathetic secretary of the Interior decide to act on the question of park protection. There would be nothing to stop that secretary from ordering the Park Service to prepare a generic adverse-impacts directive to evaluate Interior activities. Such a directive would provide a structure, supplementing NEPA, by which some external threat activities could be better evaluated. It would not by itself solve the problem, but it would certainly help inform the choices that would still have to be made.

But it was the role of the Park Service resource professionals that allowed the tar sands directive to work the way it did and which may be the most important thing to emerge from the tar sands case for the Park Service. The Park Service is currently in the throes of organizational change. During the early 1970s, the agency reorganized in response to the Yosemite riots. Those riots, in which the Park Service was faced with a "classic counterculture confrontation with the establishment," led to increasing concern for law enforcement.[100] Today, the growing concern is resource management, and the Park Service has begun to increase its expertise in this area.

Resource management can take two forms. The Park Service has specialist divisions that focus on air quality, water quality, and energy and minerals management. It also has scientists outside the divisions at the park, regional, and national levels. Finally, the agency has a growing cadre of resource management specialists—some in the "025 park ranger" series, others in the "401 park biologist" series. Agency specialists such as these were instrumental in providing crucial information to higher-level decision makers, information that was used to make the adverse-impacts determination in the tar sands case.

It seems probable that future threats problems are likely to need this type of clear and specific information if the Park Service is to make progress on other external threat issues, provided, of course, that the agency has the authority to act. We must remember that the tar sands resource was partially included within Glen Canyon, a unit of the park system and thus a primary reason why the agency was given the authority, through the secretary of the Interior, to make the adverse-impacts decision. If a developable resource lies outside a park, that, of course, is a different situation.

The Reagan administration consistently maintained that new legislation dealing with the threats issue was unnecessary, because existing statutes were adequate to address the problem. It would seem that the tar sands case belies that assertion to some extent. The two examples of threats legislation discussed in chapter 2, though different, nevertheless centered on some accounting mechanisms by which an activity's impacts on nearby parks could be judged. The Combined Hydrocarbon Leasing Act appeared to provide a similiar accounting mechanism, which Secretary Hodel chose to ignore. Thus it seems that the Reagan administration's insistence about the adequacy of existing legislation remained untested. The law may have been adequate in the tar sands case, but it had to be used.

The preservationist community displayed interesting behavior during the tar sands controversy. Their support for inclusion of the tar sands resource within a national park and later opposition to the development of the resource are hardly surprising and need no further discussion. They have been, and continue to be, very concerned about external threats to parks.

Yet one of the most important aspects of the external threats problem is that it is one that affects both park resources and visitor enjoyment of those resources. In other words, the external threats problem has the potential to unite the two parts of the national park constituency, the preservationists and the park-using public. However, something happened during the saga of the tar sands issue that suggests that the unification of these two groups may be hard to achieve.

During the 1971 hearings to enlarge Canyonlands National Park, the Sierra Club made the following statement about a region near the tar sands triangle called North, or Panorama, Point:

> Both of these areas are as spectacular, perhaps more so, from an overlook where one can take in the whole panorama than they are from the intimacy of the canyon bottoms. For this reason we are proposing that the area . . . be made instead a part of Canyonlands National Park. This would make the Maze and the Land of Standing Rocks available to everyone from North Point and Panorama Point. For many Park visitors, this would be the major Park Experience on the west side of the Colorado River.[101]

In 1971, preservationists were involved in the politics of land designation. They were in favor of expanding the boundaries of Canyonlands National Park. One way to build support for the enlargement was to talk

in terms of overlooks where visitors could get a sense of the vast undeveloped lands that lie below in the less accessible parts of Canyonlands.
Today, the Park Service manages the Maze area of Canyonlands for a
very primitive wilderness experience.

In 1977, the argument was different. Land designation politics had
given way to internal land-management decisions facing the Park Service. North Point and Panorama Point were now within Glen Canyon
National Recreation Area and very close to the tar sands triangle. This
time, the preservationists—in this case, the Sierra Club—said about
North Point that

> the vastness of the landscape, the emptiness of it, and the variety of
> form and color are completely overwhelming. This is truly one of
> the most beautiful places that God has created.
>
> The Park Service proposes to keep open the Road to Panorama
> Point. This would be total folly, and we most strongly protest such
> ill-advised plans. The road to Deadhorse Point [a nearby state park]
> has effectively destroyed the sanctity of that overlook by encumber-
> ing it with fences, walls, asphalt, and signs.[102]

Apparently, once an area is under Park Service administration, concern
for overlooks and park visitation can drop off the preservationists'
agenda.

This is too bad. The preservation and environmental movements
have done many important and necessary things, including fighting for
parks and later wilderness. But there is a growing chorus of criticism that
these groups have become anti-people, an especially disturbing charge
when applied to the national parks. It is hard to see, however, how preservationists and environmentalists can expect to win the external threats
battle without including visitor experience as one of the most important
threatened park values. Inclusion of the park experience might build a
formidable constituency. One need only recall the famous ads condemn-
ing plans to construct dams in the Grand Canyon to see how important
constituency building can become. Without showing some sympathy if
not respect for the ordinary park visitor, it is hard to see how progress
will ever be made on the problem of external threats to parks. One cannot talk about the threat of mining next to Canyonlands while continuing to narrow the scope of those who might be familiar with the park.

In the end, it seems that land use in the northern Colorado Plateau is
constantly subject to redefinition based on new resource discoveries, societal needs, and outside events. Much of the region might have become
a national park, but World War II intervened. After the war, preservationists were able to stop the damming of Dinosaur National Monument,

but growing water demands and the preservationists' own ignorance of the area led to the creation of Lake Powell. Canyonlands National Park was established, but so was Glen Canyon, a recreation area open to minerals development. The tar sands resource seemed destined for nondevelopment, however, until the energy crisis of the 1970s drew attention to the resource. Now the region appears to be in a preservation-development truce until the need for tar sands emerges once again and technology improves enough to be able to economically extract the resource with less environmental damage. Thus the region's resource politics appears destined for continued conflict; the Colorado Plateau is rich in mineral resources but also in parklands. The tar sands case, unfortunately, did not help us sort out how we wish to value and prioritize this wealth.

# CHAPTER FIVE

# Protecting National Parks from Existing Visibility Impairment

It is both fitting and understandable that the problem of visibility impairment in national parks was first noticed on the Colorado Plateau. The region contains many units of the national park system known for their sweeping vistas and grand viewpoints. The sight of the Grand Canyon from any point on the South Rim, of Bryce Canyon and Navajo Mountain from Yovimpa Point in Bryce Canyon National Park, and of the La Sal Mountains from the Needles in Canyonlands National Park are three examples familiar to visitors from all over the world. It is hard to imagine these parks without the views. Thus protecting these panoramas that have astounded visitors for decades would seem an important task.

In 1977, Congress mandated the protection of certain areas, including many of our older and larger national parks, from visibility impairment, both existing and future. In this chapter, I will focus on the protection of national parks from existing visibility impairment, from the time of the 1977 Clean Air Act Amendments until August 1989. It is a long and sometimes technically complex story. For friends of the national parks, it is a frustrating story as well. For students of natural resource policy, it is an excellent example of how well-intended legislation can be slow to reach its goals.

## AN OVERVIEW OF VISIBILITY

Visibility has traditionally been defined as "the greatest distance at which an observer can just see a black object viewed against the horizon sky."[1] From this definition, it is easy to see why the question of visibility impairment has become such an important one for certain units of the national park system. Many of the parks of the Colorado Plateau were created in part because of the long-ranging, colorful views one has from points within them. The need to protect vistas like these led to the inclusion of section 169A in the 1977 Clean Air Act Amendments. As the Park Service said: "Visibility is . . . closely associated with conditions which allow appreciation of the inherent beauty of landscape features. It is important to be able to see and appreciate the form, contrast detail, and color of near and distant features."[2]

Visibility impairment is caused by "light scattering and absorption by atmosphere particles and gases which are nearly the same size as the wavelength of the light."[3] "Scattering" refers to light being redirected from its original path, and "absorption" to light being "taken up" by another material. Assessing visibility impacts is concerned primarily with the origin and transport of fine particulates (particles smaller than 2.5 micrometers in diameter), because they scatter light very efficiently and are believed to generally cause most visibility problems. Particles in the 0.1 to 1.0 micron range are the most efficient scatterers.

Scattering also occurs naturally. The sky is blue because blue photons, which are bundles of light energy, are closer to the size of the molecules that make up our atmosphere than photons of other colors. This closeness allows the molecules to scatter blue photons more efficiently and thus the sky appears blue to us.[4] However, anthropogenic fine-particle scattering, from particles originating as a result of human activities, is often of much greater magnitude than molecular scattering.

The man-made pollutants that are the worst contributors to visibility degradation in most areas are either the fine particulates formed in the atmosphere from nitrogen-dioxide ($NO_2$) and sulfur-dioxide ($SO_2$) gases or these gases themselves. Some more-common sources of these pollutants and their visible signs are

$SO_2$: a gas. Source: fossil fuel–fired power plants, copper smelting and refining, industrial boilers, chemical production, oil shale/tar sands extraction and processing. Sign: converts in the atmosphere to a sulfate, which is "visible" as a uniform, or regional, haze.

$NO_2$: a gas; one of several nitrogen oxides ($NO_x$). Source: coal-fired power plants, diesel- and gasoline-powered motor vehicles. Sign: brown cloud or plume, because it absorbs blue light as a gas; also contributes to photochemical smog.

*Fine particulates:* created in atmosphere primarily as sulfates and nitrates from the two gases above; can travel a long distance and contribute to regional haze by reducing visual range.[5] Sign: uniform, or regional, haze.

Uniform haze impairs visibility in all directions, whereas layered haze appears as a band across the view area with a boundary between it and the background. If the haze layer is seen originating from a source, it is called a plume.

The problem of visibility is still more complicated. Because visibility concerns human perception, a series of linkages must be made to establish the effect that visibility impairment has on park visitors. These linkages can be diagrammed this way:

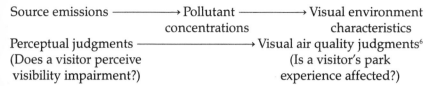

Source emissions ─────────→ Pollutant ─────────→ Visual environment
concentrations                characteristics
Perceptual judgments ────────────────→ Visual air quality judgments[6]
(Does a visitor perceive                    (Is a visitor's park
visibility impairment?)                    experience affected?)

The last linkage is very important because, as we will see, a pollution source can apply for exemption from pollution controls if it can prove that it does not contribute to "significant impairment" of visibility (that is, does not interfere with the visitor's visual experience of an area). Research is ongoing to establish all of the linkages above. Research on the effects of air pollution on park resources is, of course, not limited to visibility; nor is it the only focus of the Clean Air Act.

## THE CLEAN AIR ACT AMENDMENTS OF 1977

Concern over visibility gained focus during 1977 as Congress entered the third year of a struggle to revise the Clean Air Act. Here, for the first time, Congress addressed the question of visibility as it related to, among other areas, national parks. During the lengthy process to revise the Clean Air Act, it was the House that initially included a section on visibility impairment in its version of the amendments to the act, HR 6161, in 1977. The Senate later adopted this section with some revisions.

One of the most important catalysts for the concern over visibility in national park units came from several preservation groups, among them the National Parks and Conservation Association and Friends of the Earth. In early 1977, several groups and individuals testified to both the House and the Senate about visibility impairment.[7] Michael Williams of the John Muir Institute reported that both the Navajo (near Page, Arizona) and Four Corners (near Farmington, New Mexico) power plants were impairing air quality. Park rangers at Mesa Verde National Park had reported that Shiprock, a prominent geological feature on the Navajo Indian Reservation, was "often hidden in smoke and haze."[8] The plume from the Navajo plant was at times seen "travelling over the northern end of the Grand Canyon."[9] Park officials at Glen Canyon National Recreation Area and Wupatki and Sunset Craters national monuments had reported their concerns about Navajo to their regional director, Williams said. The NPCA agreed with Williams, telling Congress that Navajo and Four Corners were the likely sources of visibility problems in places like the Grand Canyon.[10] The House decided to write visibility protection into its version of the 1977 Clean Air Act Amendments.

The House committee report explained the intent of the visibility protection section of HR 6161 (then numbered section 116). It noted the

The Navajo Generating Station, Page, Arizona (by the author)

importance of scenic vistas in the creation of many of the western parks.[11] Visibility problems were caused primarily by emissions of "sulfur dioxide, oxides of nitrogen, and particulate matter."[12] Relatively pristine areas like parks were especially vulnerable because a small increase in particle concentration greatly reduced visibility.[13] The report cited possible examples of visibility impairment caused by existing pollution sources and provided testimony by the NPCA that had helped alert Congress to the visibility problem.[14]

At the time of the 1977 amendments, Congress had come to realize, through various court decisions, that certain areas of the United States had air that was "cleaner" than other areas and even cleaner than air judged acceptable by national ambient air quality standards (NAAQS).[15] To prevent the deterioration of this cleaner air, Congress classified it: class I, II, and III. The cleanest areas were given the class I designation and comprised international parks and national wilderness areas over five thousand acres that were established before August 7, 1977, and national parks over six thousand acres, also established before August 7, 1977. This included a total of 158 areas, 48 of which are Park Service units. Any national park, monument, preserve, recreation area, lakeshore or seashore over ten thousand acres established after the August date was given class II status, with the possibility of redesignation to class I by the state in which the unit was located.[16] Thus section 116 was added by the House to establish a "national goal of remedying existing impairments of visibility in these areas [class I] and of preventing future visibility problems from occurring in such areas."[17]

A note is in order regarding visibility impairment that might be caused by new, as opposed to existing, sources of air pollution. The federal land manager (FLM) was given an "affirmative responsibility" to protect the air quality–related values (including visibility) of such lands within a class I area.[18] (The term "federal land manager" refers to the federal agency that administers a federal class I area. This responsibility is delegated by the secretaries of Agriculture and the Interior to the Park Service, Forest Service, or Fish and Wildlife Service. The exception is the Roosevelt Campobello International Park in Maine, which is administered by a commission.) This section, 42 U.S.C. 7475, gives the FLM the authority to participate in permit reviews for major new or modified sources of possible pollution.

The House report summed up the structure of section 116 regarding existing visibility impairment:

This provision . . . requires State plans for States with such areas (class I) and States whose emissions cause or contribute to visibility problems in such areas, to be revised to include two types of measures. First, the State plan must provide for the Best Available Retrofit Technology (BART) for existing sources which are causing or contributing to visibility impairment in such areas. In determining best available retrofit, consideration is to be given to costs, nonair quality environment impacts, energy requirements, the remaining useful life of the source and the anticipated benefits to visibility which would result from the use of such technology. The Administrator [of the EPA] would not be authorized to require retrofit on any source older than 15 years and could not require use of a scrubber on any powerplant of less than 700 megawatt capacity. Second, the State plan must incorporate a long-term (10–15 year) strategy for making maximum feasible progress toward attaining the national goal. Prior to holding hearings on plan revision, the State must consult in person with the Federal land manager concerning the revision and publish the land manager's conclusions.

The Administrator, with the concurrence of the Federal land manager, may exempt by rule from the retrofit requirement, a source that he determines will not cause or contribute to significant visibility impairment in Federal mandatory class I areas. The exemption provision does not apply to fossil-fuel-fired powerplants with total generating capacity of 750 megawatts or more.

This section prohibits citizen suits from being brought to compel attainment of the national goal by any specific date. Moreover, the Administrator is prohibited from requiring the use of any mandatory or uniform buffer zone for the purposes of this section.[19]

The "State plans" are state-prepared documents that implement federal clean air requirements and are usually referred to as state implementation plans (SIPs). The federal government, in this case the Environmental Protection Agency, must approve all SIPs to make sure they are in compliance with the Clean Air Act. Once they are approved, the day-to-day implementation of the Clean Air Act is done through the process and procedures developed in each SIP.

The House, in a section-by-section debate on HR 6161, passed the legislation without much discussion about the visibility section. Henry Waxman of California noted that visibility was "the most precious air quality value in places such as Grand Canyon."[20] During the floor debate, section 116 was amended to give existing power plants of over 750 megawatts the right of exemption from BART requirements if the plants could prove to be far enough away from a class I area to, by themselves or with other sources, not significantly impair visibility.[21] Concurrence of the federal land manager was required for any exemption.

Since the Senate had no comparable section in the bill it passed addressing visibility (S 252), and since there were many other differences between the two bills, a congressional conference committee was necessary to try to put together a bill agreeable to both houses of Congress and thus possible to be signed by President Carter. The conference committee chose to accept visibility protection as part of the compromise legislation and made several minor changes in the House visibility section.

First, the secretary of the Interior, in consultation with the federal land manager, was required to identify all federal class I areas where visibility was an important value and pass that list on to the EPA. The list was to be published by the EPA and could be updated. The first list was due August 8, 1978 (it was published in the *Federal Register* on November 30, 1979).[22] Second, clarification was made that the state (or the EPA if no SIP revision was done by the state) identified the source of visibility impairment and the type of BART required. For fossil fuel–fired power plants greater than 750 megawatts, emission guidelines and specifications for BART had to be based on EPA guidelines.[23] Which agency is to have the power to identify and regulate sources of pollution is obviously an important consideration and has remained controversial, as we will see. Third, the twenty-six major stationary sources that might be required to retrofit were listed by type. Two of the most important sources are fossil fuel–fired electric plants and copper smelters. Fourth, in perhaps the most significant revision, "maximum" progress was changed to "reasonable" progress in meeting the goals of visibility protection.[24]

There was a significant exclusion of sources that might be required to retrofit. The law did not include major stationary sources in existence before 1962. This exempted nine copper smelters in southern Arizona and southern New Mexico.[25] Research indicates that these smelters contribute a majority of the sulfur oxides emitted in the Four Corners region and thus are possibly major causes of visibility impairment in the parks of the Four Corners states.[26] Because of concern about the economic difficulties facing the American copper industry, these plants were also exempted from $SO_2$ ambient standards until 1988.[27] This exemption precluded any regulation under the visibility requirements as well.[28] Yet economic hardships facing the copper industry may also mean that some of the smelters may not be in operation much longer.[29]

During the floor debate on the conference version of the bill, Congressman Waxman made the following observation about the intent of the visibility section regarding existing visibility impairment: "For the first time, the Congress will write into law explicit protection for visibility. This will mean that the Four Corners and Navajo powerplants can expect to retrofit with additional pollution controls to limit the vast deterioration in visibility which their plumes have caused."[30] Thus it seems clear that the visibility section was directed in large part at certain existing sources of air pollution that were thought to be causing impairment of visibility in parks of the Colorado Plateau. It appears that in 1977 source identification, and the expectation of source retrofit, were almost foregone conclusions on the part of some members of the House—for example, Congressman Waxman. It also appears that in 1977 visibility impairment was believed to exist.

The Senate seemed to agree. James McClure of Idaho remarked that "the visibility section was aimed at retrofitting those facilities constructed in the recent past which have already impaired the quality of the air over many of our national parks and wilderness areas."[31] Once again, Senator McClure's statement appears to indicate that source retrofit was expected by some members of the Senate active in passing the Clean Air Act Amendments.

In conclusion, the 1977 amendments provide the Park Service a significant role as the federal land manager. The agency had to identify areas where visibility was an important value. Second, the SIP revision process involved Park Service consultation with the states and state consideration of Park Service recommendations regarding the certification and identification of existing visibility impairment. Third, any proposed exemption from BART required Park Service concurrence. Fourth, the Park Service, as the FLM, was given an "affirmative responsibility" to protect air quality–related values (including visibility) during the new source review process for PSD and nonattainment areas. Finally, Congress took the rare step of naming a specific park resource to be protected from harmful activities external to the boundaries of the affected park.

Even though protection of visibility was mandated by Congress, it was also given a structure that involved multiple agencies and levels of government. Thus if the Park Service wanted to take an aggressive role in protecting visibility in national parks, it would have to persuade other actors in the visibility regulatory arena to take the same role. The Clean Air Act Amendments of 1977 required the promulgation of regulations to implement the visibility section, regulations that would speak among other things to the role of the Park Service as the federal land manager.

## THE VISIBILITY REGULATIONS

The EPA did not promulgate visibility regulations by the statutory deadline of August 1979. The agency was sued for noncompliance by the Friends of the Earth. EPA administrator Douglas Costle told the court that the EPA would propose rules by May 1980 and finalize them by November 1980. Both dates were accepted by the court.[32] On May 22, 1980, the EPA proposed its visibility rules by issuing draft visibility regulations. Three hundred eighty-three comments were received from private citizens, environmental groups, businesses, and other governmental organizations.[33] Public response was so great that the EPA had to publish a two-hundred-page document summarizing the comments that had been received.[34] On December 2, 1980, the EPA issued the final visibility regulations that still govern the visibility protection process today.

Although it might appear that the protection of visibility in national parks is a rather simple and clearly defined goal, it is not. Congress actually spoke in very general terms about how that protection should come about or, in the terminology of political science and public administration, be "implemented" by the actors charged with protecting visibility. Once the Clean Air Act Amendments were law, Congress left it up to the EPA to study how to best identify, characterize, and protect against visibility impairment. Visibility impairment, for example, has to do with the perceptions of a park visitor and his/her park experience. That is, some attempt has to be made to determine whether there is impairment of visibility, whether it is noticed by the visitor, and whether he/she is unhappy about it. For reasons such as these, the EPA regulations take center stage.

The initial problem that faced the EPA was how to define visibility impairment. This problem is interesting in itself, because it shows that

Congress had no real idea what visibility impairment was when it passed the 1977 act except to assume that it already existed. Congress expected the EPA to answer that research question after the law was passed. Visibility impairment was defined as "any humanly perceptible change in visibility (visual range, contrast, coloration) from that which would have existed under natural conditions."[35] Visibility impairment had to be categorized. That is, some problems are caused by single or several sources, resulting in plumes or layered haze, and can be more easily traced to those sources. Other problems are caused by large numbers of sources (as in Los Angeles) and result in regional haze. Quite obviously, the regulation of several unique sources with visible plumes is different from the regulation of a large urban area with multiple sources. Thus the EPA chose to take a "phased" approach to visibility impairment, developing a regulatory program that sought to address impairment that could be "reasonably attributable" to a source or small group of sources.[36]

Only the first type of visibility problem was addressed by the EPA regulations, because of the complexity of monitoring, modeling, measuring, and regulating regional haze.[37] Consequently, the pollutants of primary concern for the first phase of the visibility program were $NO_2$ and particulates that cause a visible plume or layered haze, with $SO_2$ emissions relegated to the second stage of the program.[38] Both types of visibility pollution were categorized as

> caused by factories, plants and other sources that emit particles and gases into the air. These substances either absorb or scatter the light a person can receive from a viewed object. The practical effect is that impaired visibility degrades the aesthetic value of the surrounding landscape by (1) discoloring the atmosphere to produce a visible plume, (2) whitening the horizon and causing objects to appear flattened so that landscape colors and textures become less discernible, or (3) in the case of a discernible plume, obscuring some portion of the landscape.[39]

Existing visibility impairment was dealt with in the following way by the regulations. (This process is the core of the regulatory structure for existing visibility impairment.) First, the FLM could certify to the state at any time that visibility impairment existed on class I lands. This step in the regulatory process gives the Park Service a responsibility to research visibility to make such a certification.

For any visibility impairment so certified by the FLM at least six months prior to SIP revision, the *state* was to identify the existing stationary facility that caused the visibility impairment. The Park Service could suggest, through research, which source might be the cause, but the actual source identification was the responsibility of the state with the class I area. It is therefore possible that a state could disagree with NPS conclusions regarding source identification. The state had to perform a BART analysis on any source it identified. The state was given certain flexibility regarding evaluation of various means of control, costs, energy and environmental impacts, the length of time the facility would operate, and the extent to which BART would improve visibility. A BART analysis would, if this point was reached, specify emission limitations. Re-analysis of pollutants not covered by a prior BART review was required if technological improvements made it possible. Emission limitations, BART schedules, and other procedures were all to be part of the SIP revision.[40] The preamble to the regulations made note that existing techniques for controlling $NO_2$ emissions might not perceptibly improve visibility.[41]

Finally, sources could apply and receive exemption from BART if the source did not cause or contribute to "significant impairment" of visibility and if the federal land manager concurred in the exemption. Significant impairment was defined as impairment that "interferes with the management, protection and enjoyment of the visitor's visual experience" of the class I area.[42] States were also required to develop a monitoring strategy and use any available monitoring data as part of their visibility protection planning.[43]

The preambles to the regulations, which are often more informative to the reader than the regulations are themselves, made interesting statements about existing sources and BART requirements. Reviewing a preliminary modeling analysis done to identify potential existing sources that might have to retrofit, the EPA stated that

> we found that this screening overstated the potential impact of these regulations. Most of the sources which were initially identified as potential BART candidates are not now anticipated to be affected because the visibility impairment cannot be reasonably attributed to these facilities. Other sources identified in this analysis are not now believed to be affected by these regulations because either existing problems are currently being dealt with by other air quality programs or because currently available control techniques will not perceptibly improve visibility.[44]

Apparently, this was a "first stab" by the EPA at categorizing visibility in class I areas.[45] As EPA official Julie Horne noted: "Subsequent investigations may alter these results somewhat as land managers' knowledge about visibility increases."[46] Horne went on to note that technical limitations might make the regulation of all forms of visibility impairment except obvious plume blight impossible at that time.[47] Even plume blight regulation was questionable, because $NO_x$ control technology did not reduce the plume below a level where it became invisible.[48] These 1980 visibility assessments by the EPA seemed to render problematic the earlier assertion of Congressman Waxman that certain sources in the Colorado Plateau would be expected to retrofit. According to the EPA, there was not enough evidence to identify a visibility-impairing source of pollution—that is, no visible plume could be conclusively traced back to an offending source. This finding seemed to contradict the expectations of those who had written the 1977 act.

## Enter the Integral Vista

A new concept not mentioned in the 1977 legislation, the "integral vista," appeared in the visibility regulations. An integral vista is a view from within a class I area "of a specific landmark or panorama located outside" the class I boundary.[49] Each federal land manager was given the option of identifying integral vistas by December 31, 1985, with certain requirements placed on the states to consider impacts on the vistas should the vistas be named six months prior to initial SIP revision or six months prior to the submission of a permit for new source construction. The regulations treated integral vistas as part of the visibility considerations for federal class I areas.[50] However, the states once again were permitted to consider costs, time of compliance, remaining life of the source, and degree of visibility improvement before regulating source impacts on integral vistas.[51] The integral vista concept was extremely controversial since the term did not appear in the original legislation passed by Congress. The Interior and Agriculture departments chose not to exercise their option to identify integral vistas (more will be said about that decision).

The EPA, in its summary of comments on the proposed regulations, noted that the integral vista concept received the most response.[52] In its initial May rule-making, the EPA developed the integral vista concept, using as justification the legislative history of the Clean Air Act Amendments, the legislative history of the establishment of many class I areas, and the belief that visibility was a perceptual value occurring "in" the class I area. Thus to the EPA, the integral vista was a permissible extension of something occurring "in" the class I area as well as a vital part of the reason the area was established.[53]

Integral vistas were directly related to the existing visibility impairment review process. Properly identified vistas were to be included in the BART process. Thus it was possible that an existing source could be required to apply BART because it was impairing an integral vista and not the class I area. The final regulations gave the state more flexibility on integral vistas than the draft regulations, because the state ended up having the final say on source identification and BART. But this wasn't enough to satisfy the utility companies.

Utility companies remained opposed to the integral vista concept even with the various regulatory changes and checks and balances.[54] The utilities thought that the concept was an improper discretionary act by the EPA. The Utility Air Regulatory Group (UARG) filed petitions with the EPA for reconsideration of the visibility regulations, but the EPA did not respond.[55] An attempt by the Mountain States Legal Foundation and other parties to obtain judicial review of the regulations was terminated by the courts, subject to reopening.[56]

The integral vista concept is a wonderful example of the power of federal agencies to interpret the intent of Congress. The question is whether or not the EPA had any justification to invent the integral vista. If the agency did have justification, and a case can be made that it did, should the agency be able to make such an interpretation?

A second area of the draft regulations that resulted in a great deal of public reaction concerned the role of the federal land manager. The EPA originally proposed that the state document the reason it did not accept the FLM's claim that visibility was reasonably attributable to a source.[57] The final regulations required instead that the state identify the source suspected of causing visibility impairment based on certification of the impairment from the FLM. Second, the EPA noted that many industry and state commentators had opposed giving authority to the FLM to certify impairment in class I areas.[58] The EPA kept the requirement because, the agency argued, Congress gave the FLMs responsibility to manage the class I lands, and thus they were familiar with the air resources of those lands.

In 1978, the Park Service created an air quality office to deal with air pollution problems. Known today as the Air Quality Division (AQD), it is headquartered in Washington with technical support staff located in Denver and Fort Collins, Colorado. Much of the credit for the institutionalization of the division and subsequent funding belongs to its first chief, Barbara Brown, who played an active role as a Park Service "policy entrepreneur" in arguing the merits of the division.[59] She was able to secure an effective budget for the AQD and establish it as an operating division of the National Park Service at a time when established divisions were strongly competing for funds.

The AQD is split into three branches: a research branch, a policy and implementation branch, and a permit review branch.[60] The AQD is the part of the Park Service that evaluates and documents potential visibility impairment from existing sources, among other resource management responsibilities. Any final decisions regarding the Park Service and Fish and Wildlife roles under the EPA visibility regulations and their implementation are to be made by the assistant secretary of the Interior for Fish and Wildlife and Parks.[61]

In conclusion, the visibility section of the 1977 law, as well as the regulations, mandated active participation by the NPS as the federal land manager for its class I lands. The requirements to categorize and identify visibility impairment seemed to demand that the Park Service develop the expertise and staff to do so. At the same time, both dependence on and cooperation with the states were necessary in order to adequately protect Park Service class I areas from visibility impairment.

Finally, one must pay attention to the role of the EPA from 1977 to 1980, during the presidency of Jimmy Carter. The EPA took a very active role during this period. The best example is the development of the integral vista, beyond the scope of any direct congressional guidance. What the Carter EPA had created, the Reagan EPA might take away. If the Reagan administration tried to alter EPA policies, would the Park Service be able to protect parks from visibility impairment?

THE POLITICS OF VISIBILITY
SINCE THE 1980 REGULATIONS

One cannot follow the politics of visibility protection in the 1980s without understanding the context of the election of Ronald Reagan and his administration's policies toward the EPA and, to a lesser extent, the Park Service. It became clear, early in the Reagan term, that a fundamental policy shift was to be undertaken at the EPA. Reagan appointed Ann Gorsuch (later Burford) to head the EPA. Burford announced five objectives: regulatory reform, budget reduction, fewer program delays, a strengthened federal-state-local partnership, and a better scientific basis for major agency decisions.[62] Yet the strong anti-regulation, anti-environment ideology of Burford quickly destroyed whatever might have been positive about some of these goals. As Richard Harris and Sidney Milkis concluded: "There is little doubt that the policies pursued by Ann Burford had immediate and significant impacts on the agency: fewer rules were written, enforcement actions declined, workforce decreased dramatically, morale and initiative among staff plummeted, institutional memory was destroyed, and implementation of newer, more complex statutes [such as the 1977 amendments] was delayed."[63] This was the policy context for visibility protection as the 1980s began.

The context for the Park Service had changed as well. The Park Service, according to Paul Culhane, had three priorities: staffing needs, problems to address with park concessionaires, and external threats.[64] James Watt, Interior's new secretary, had other priorities. Watt told the concessionaires that he would remove any Park Service people causing them problems, decided to improve park infrastructures like sewers and roads, and said nothing about external threats.[65] As discussed in chapter 2, it also became questionable how much control Park Service officials would have over park policy.

Since the publication of the visibility regulations, then, progress on remedying visibility impairment from existing sources has been slow and often taken a path not foreseen by Congress in 1977. On December 20, 1982, three environmental groups, led by the Environmental Defense Fund (EDF), filed a suit that sought to compel the EPA to promulgate regulations for states that had failed to revise their SIPs required by the 1977 law. At the time of the suit's filing, Alaska was the only state out of thirty-six required to revise SIPs to have done so.[66] The parties involved (the EDF and EPA) signed a complex settlement agreement in April 1984 that established specific guidelines and schedules for SIP revision.[67] The EPA thus began writing SIP revisions for the states that had not done so. The states would continue to have the opportunity to revise their own SIPs, but the EPA revisions would be in place should the new deadlines set by the settlement agreement not be met.

The settlement agreement divided the visibility regulations into two parts for sequential promulgation and implementation. The first part dealt with SIP revisions regarding a visibility monitoring strategy under section 51.305 of the 1980 regulations and new source visibility assessments under section 307.[68] The rest of the regulations were to be promulgated and implemented during the second stage. These second-phase revisions were general plan provisions, emission control strategies for existing sources, integral vista protection, and long-term strategies.

The settlement agreement established a timetable for EPA implementation. The EPA was required to propose first-stage rules by October 1984 and finalize them by July 1985. States were given until April 1985 to amend their own SIPs with EPA approval of any state SIP amendments required by December 1985. The second-stage plan revisions for the long-term strategy and the general plan requirements were due August 31, 1988. (Integral vistas and emission control strategies, part of the phase two agreement, will be discussed later.)

The 1984 draft EPA regulations made some important assertions regarding visibility monitoring. Two significant points from earlier regulatory policy were restated: the responsibility of the FLM to identify visibility impairment, and the lack of standard methods for measuring visibility impairment.[69] More important, the regulations gave credit to the National Park Service: "The [Park Service] has been active in developing visibility monitoring in many of the national parks and has experience with many of the techniques for visibility monitoring."[70] Yet the draft regulations ended up restating the 1980 EPA view that few existing sources "are expected to be required to install control technologies because of their age or because control techniques are not available to significantly reduce the contributing pollutants."[71] The draft regulations proposed establishing two monitoring programs. Some monitoring would be done to establish background data for the new source permitting program. The federal land managers were recruited to monitor visibility within their own class I areas if the EPA provided equipment. The EPA also stated that a monitoring program would be established to document existing impairment attributable to one or a small group of sources.[72]

On July 12, 1985, the final EPA regulations were published. They contained several important concerns about existing visibility impairment and all were in the visibility monitoring strategy proposed by the EPA. The EPA assumed the role of collecting monitoring data in class I areas located in states lacking approved visibility SIPs,[73] with the cooperation and assistance of the FLM, by setting up a national monitoring network that would include selected Park Service class I monitoring sites.[74] Also, the agency required a new source permittee to collect visibility data if the source planned to locate near a class I area that was not adequately represented by the national network. Monitoring sites would be established based on two criteria: lack of available data and potential for growth near the class I area. Utah, one of the Four Corners states of original concern by Congress, has an approved SIP revision for visibility monitoring. Its SIP revisions were: continued monitoring by the FLM (there are five class I areas in Utah managed by the Park Service, two of the areas closely monitored); and the future implementation of a state monitoring network.[75] I will discuss the Utah SIP in more detail later.

Second, the EPA asserted that a single method for visibility monitoring remained undeveloped. The agency noted that although the original regulations defined "visibility impairment" in a workable way, the EPA was going to begin a program in 1986 to develop a single visibility monitoring reference method.[76] Thus, said the agency, a state that submitted an SIP revision for visibility did not have to use monitoring equipment such as that used by the EPA or the Park Service.[77]

Finally, the regulations called once again on all the FLMs to identify visibility impairment in each of their class I areas. Should a problem be identified, "priorities for implementation [of BART] will be based on availability of existing data, the severity of the suspected impairment, and the probability of an effective control strategy."[78] Thus for states with nonapproved SIPs, the FLM would be submitting the pertinent data to another federal agency—the EPA.

### Integral Vistas: Part of the Park or Part of the Problem?

Perhaps the most controversial concept to appear in the 1980 visibility regulations was that of the "integral vista." Again, the term was defined in the final regulations as "a view perceived from within the mandatory Class I area of a specific landmark or panorama located outside the boundary."[79] The EPA's justification for its development of the integral vista concept was drawn from several sources. First, the agency noted that many national parks were set aside "because of their extensive vistas, expansive scenic views, unique natural formations or primitive value."[80] Second, the EPA pointed out that many parks' enabling statutes had included words such as "grand," "distant," and "vistas."[81] Third, the agency boldly stated that "nowhere is there the suggestion that grand vistas integral to public enjoyment of a mandatory Class I federal area were not entitled to protection if the place viewed lay outside the area."[82] This last contention was disputable; as Jerome Ostrov noted, "One may take pause at the notion that the absence of prohibitory language is by itself sufficient authority to support affirmative agency action."[83] The FLM was given until December 31, 1985, to identify such vistas, but the key language stated that the FLM "may" identify any integral vista.[84] The base criterion by which an FLM was to identify an integral vista was whether the vista was important to the visitor's visual experience of the class I area.[85]

The regulations intended the integral vista concept to apply to existing and new sources. BART review had to be done for any sources identified by the FLM at least six months before SIP revision as impairing a vista.[86] Sources identified later as affecting vistas could still be subject to BART review.[87] States had to list vistas appropriately identified by FLMs in their SIPs but had the opportunity to disagree with vistas the states thought were not properly identified under FLM criteria, with resolution of any disagreement made by the governor of the affected state.

On January 15, 1981, the Park Service published in the *Federal Register* its preliminary list of integral vistas, as well as draft guidelines for the determination of vistas. The Park Service used two general criteria for the selection of its preliminary list based on criteria established earlier by the EPA: (1) the importance of the vista to the objectives for which the area was established, and (2) vistas that "significantly" contribute to visitor enjoyment of the area.[88] Some of the factors the Park Service developed to aid consideration of possible vistas included the existence of observation points and prominent media attention given to the vista.[89] Not surprisingly, the parklands of the Colorado Plateau were well represented in this list. One of the vistas was the view from Yovimpa Point in Bryce Canyon toward Navajo Mountain (photographs of that view had been shown to Congress in 1977).

There was no further Park Service or Interior activity on the integral vista issue until late 1985, close to the deadline set by Congress. Several congressional attempts had been made to delay or overturn the visibility regulations, but they were unsuccessful.[90] On September 9, 1985, Park Service director Mott sent a memo to his political superiors (the assistant and under secretaries) regarding the promulgation of a final list of integral vistas.[91] Mott viewed the designation of the vistas as a minimal responsibility given to the Park Service and Interior by the Clean Air Act, which required state cooperation and agreement for implementation.[92] The Park Service director expressed concerns about litigation, then went on to say that "we would be derelict in our responsibilities if we chose to ignore the opportunity provided by the Clean Air Act to identify integral vistas. . . . Such inaction would certainly result in severe criticism of the Department and the Administration both by environmental groups and by a public that will perceive that highly important park attributes are being sacrificed."[93]

In October, Assistant Secretary Horn sent Mott a memo regarding Interior's position on the vistas that included several points that "led" Interior to its decision not to publish a final list of vistas. First, the memo asserted that the states had the authority under the Clean Air Act to protect integral vistas if they so chose through the SIP.[94] Second, the memo relied on a Park Service regulatory impact assessment on the impact of proposed new sources (through 1998) on integral vistas that had concluded that the impacts would be minimal.[95]

The Reagan administration's position on identifying integral vistas was aptly illustrated in a speech given by Secretary Hodel to the National Recreation and Park Association's 1985 congress in Dallas. In a stunningly convoluted set of arguments, Hodel spelled out the reasons for not listing the vistas:

First, the guidelines could have the effect of providing a false sense of security to land managers. "The guidelines are serving to protect . . . so I don't have to be as alert." That is not good.

Second, identification of specific sites and areas could give the impression that we do not view as important those areas not listed. That is not good.

I simply am not prepared to send the message to park superintendents and employees at nearly 300 other park units that their vistas are not important.

Third, it could falsely suggest that there is some kind of hierarchy in threats, with vistas having higher priority than pollution, crowding, development and the like, and that is not the case. Nor is it good.[96]

Hodel also noted that litigation would result from listing the vistas rather than from failing to do so.[97] The argument was poor but the point clear. The Reagan administration would not support protection of integral vistas.

What can be made of the strange end to the saga of integral vistas? On the one hand, it is obvious that the EPA decision to develop the concept was controversial. Good arguments can be made on both sides concerning the EPA's decision.[98] The question is now moot because the deadline for Interior to develop a final list has passed, though states can always identify integral vistas. Still, the integral vista concept is an excellent example of policy discretion on the part of an administrative agency and shows us how an agency must often fill in the gaps that Congress chooses or forgets to include in its legislation.

There is some uncertainty, however, about the rationale advanced by Interior in its decision not to list the vistas. For Secretary Hodel to argue that the states had adequate authority to protect vistas seems to miss the point: The history of state action on visibility protection hardly suggests that many states would voluntarily list vistas. Indeed, as of 1988, only two states—Alaska and Washington—had included the integral vista in their SIPs. Of course, neither of these states is anywhere near the source of "inspiration" for section 169A, the canyon country of the American Southwest. Second, Hodel's claim that the FLMs would ignore areas not listed, as well as be "miffed" that they didn't get their own vistas, is absurd and contrary to common understanding about how the Park Service views the resources under its care.[99] One can hardly imagine one park superintendent in a sulk because his/her park was not awarded an integral vista.

Third, to suggest that a list creates some sort of "hierarchy" of external threats is perplexing. One could argue as well that the Clean Air Act is one of the few pieces of legislation that speaks to a specific external threat problem and to not act where possible would in itself be a policy decision about air pollution and the national parks. Fourth, Hodel pointed out that existing laws were adequate to protect park air quality. To test this assertion, one must examine how successful the Park Service (with Interior support or lack thereof) has been in dealing with existing visibility impairment (which I will address shortly).

Finally, Hodel was accurate on one point: Industry appeared ready to challenge a list of integral vistas.[100] But for this to occur, Interior would have to publish the list and thereby send a signal that it favored the vista concept. We must remember that publishing the list was a discretionary task of Interior and thus really dependent on the fundamental environmental policy outlook of the administration in power. In this sense, the integral vista concept was really a bellwether for the environmental policy outlooks of the Carter and Reagan administrations: It was the Carter administration—especially the official in charge of air programs for the EPA, David Hawkins—that developed and pushed the vista concept from 1977 to 1980. From 1980 to 1985, the Reagan administration chose to do nothing about integral vistas, and they died a regulatory death at the federal level. Even the preservationists, while outraged, could do nothing about changing the decision until the Clean Air Act was changed.[101] In the end, a somewhat chagrined Mott had to report back to NPS underlings Hodel's conclusion that a listing of integral vistas would weaken NPS ability to protect vistas not on the list.

## RESEARCH AND VISIBILITY:
## THE 1985 HOUSE HEARINGS AND BEYOND

In May 1985, the House Interior Subcommittee on National Parks and Recreation held oversight hearings on the impact of air pollution on national parks. These hearings are especially useful because they provide a look at the status of visibility in the national parks five years after the regulations were promulgated. It should be noted, however, that visibility was not the only focus of these hearings; air pollution impacts on aquatic, cultural, and biological park resources were also discussed in depth.[102]

Because of the different technical questions that surround regulatory solution of visibility impairment, perhaps the most important information to come out of the May hearings was the status of visibility research. It seems evident that the original 1980 visibility regulations intended for the EPA to be the coordinator and the leader of the visibility research effort. The Park Service, as an FLM, was to both categorize visibility in its class I areas and document to the relevant state officials possible visibility impairment.[103] However, in conversations and interviews that I held with NPS Air Quality Division officials, they suggested that the EPA had not actively pursued its research role.[104]

There seem to be two reasons for this inaction on the part of the EPA. First, Park Service officials, as well as some environmentalists, suggested that EPA officials appointed by the Reagan administration had chosen to ignore visibility concerns, going so far as to eliminate visibility research money from the EPA budget.[105] Thus visibility research "defaulted" to the Park Service, and the Park Service in turn made an active commitment to increase its own air pollution research efforts. The results, for example, can be seen in the 1985 fiscal year budget for the AQD of $3.5 million and the staffing of eighteen full-time positions.[106]

Second, Park Service officials indicated that visibility was simply not a priority concern for the EPA, even if the research budget had not been cut. This was an allocative policy decision: health-related policy and regulatory tasks simply were seen by key EPA officials as more important than visibility.[107] Therefore, said the Interior people, EPA officials who were concerned about visibility faced a "selling job" with upper-level EPA decision makers to convince them that visibility protection was important.[108] Yet the recent court order forcing the EPA to take over implementation of visibility protection from states whose SIPs had not been approved had rung alarm bells at the EPA. In fact, in November 1985, the Park Service provided information requested by the EPA on existing visibility impairment of Park Service and Fish and Wildlife Service class I areas, as the regulatory process required.[109] Thus it appears the EPA had begun taking a more active role in the visibility program because now the agency simply had no choice in the matter.[110]

The Park Service Air Quality Division was obviously well represented in the May hearings. The 1980 visibility regulations, in their phase I program, had focused on existing impairment resulting from visibility plumes likely caused by nitrogen dioxide gas and particulate emissions. The May hearings revealed that these plumes were not the major source of visibility impairment. Rather, the attributed cause was primarily sulfates resulting originally from sulfur dioxide gas. As the Park Service summarized:

> Visibility data, when combined with particulate composition and concentration, allow for developing an understanding of which of the many atmospheric constituents are responsible for visibility reduction ("light extinction budgets"). Because different size particles reduce visibility with varying degrees of efficiency, it does not automatically follow that an aerosol species making up a certain fraction of total mass will be responsible for that same fraction of visibility reduction. Sulfates are especially important contributors to visibility impairment because their size usually makes them very effective scatterers of light. Therefore, the relative contribution of sulfates to visibility reduction can be significantly greater than their percentage contribution to the total airborne mass. Statistical analysis of currently available visibility and particulate data show the following:

Sulfates are the single most important contributor to the visibility impairment in Park Service units except in the northwestern United States, where fine carbon plays a more prominent role.

*In the Colorado Plateau, an area containing Grand Canyon, Bryce Canyon, and Canyonlands National Parks as well as a number of other park units, sulfates are responsible for 40 to 60% of visibility impairment* [emphasis mine].

On the average, soil-related material is responsible for 10–30% of the visibility impairment.

Typically, 20% of the visibility reduction is associated with other fine mass, which is comprised of organic carbon, elemental carbon, and nitrates.[111]

The result of Park Service research was confirmed by other researchers and suggested, as the Congressional Research Service pointed out, that "there seemed to be agreement among many witnesses that the primary concern with regard to visibility impairment in the national parks was the result of regional haze and not specific smokestack plumes."[112] Reduced visibility due to regional haze was, in the original regulations, considered much harder to regulate because of the difficulty in tracing the haze to specific sources. William Malm, chief Park Service researcher on air pollution and visibility, summarized the current understanding of regional haze at the Grand Canyon:

From the standpoint of Grand Canyon, what appears to be the single largest contributor to pollution at Grand Canyon comes from air masses that come out of the San Joaquin Valley, down in front of the Sierras, through the L.A. area, Los Angeles contributing, and then flowing into Grand Canyon. We refer to that as the southern California plume. The southern California plume flows up in this direction. It impacts Grand Canyon, Bryce, Canyonlands. We have tracked it back. Even to the Rocky Mountain National Park we see the impact of the L.A. plume as it moves out across the Western United States.

That is the single biggest contributor to pollution at the Grand Canyon.

The second biggest contributor to pollution at the Grand Canyon comes out of southern Arizona. That is, of course, the copper industry that has an effect on that. You see pollution coming from southern Arizona moving up into Grand Canyon, mostly in a circular fashion like this.

[At?] other areas at Grand Canyon, as I said, we have done a substantial amount of work. We have identified impact from the

Navajo powerplant, from the Four Corners powerplant, from the smelter up in Salt Lake City, possibly from the Hayden and Craig powerplants up in Colorado. So we have identified some pollutant impact from all these sources.

That is the only area that we have done that sort of intensive analysis on, to the point where we can identify these various sources that actually impact the area.[113]

Malm went on to say that

source attribution, that is, determining the relative impact of the various sources on a receptor site such as Grand Canyon, is something that is intensively being investigated right now. . . . The technology really doesn't exist at this point with a high degree of accuracy to say what percentage of the time this source is impacting a receptor site or that source. . . . To tie it down to highly precise numbers, that is something that is under investigation at this point.[114]

Here is clear evidence that the original focus of the 1977 Clean Air Act Amendments, visible plumes, was not the problem. The general research conclusion of the Park Service was that "in excess of 90% of the time scenic vistas are affected by man-made pollution at all Park Service monitoring locations within the lower 48 United States."[115]

As of May 1986, the Park Service had thirty-five long-term monitoring sites throughout the parks, with fourteen of these sites in operation in the Southwest since 1978. The three basic methods used by the Park Service to monitor visibility are cameras, which take series of photos that can be compared; fine particulate monitors; and teleradiometers, which measure the brightness of a specific point in the sky or a vista.[116] There were two types of responses to these research conclusions. The first was to challenge the research, the second to recommend policy changes.

As can be expected, industry—represented by a group of western electric utilities (Western Energy Supply and Transmission Associates)—challenged the Park Service research by claiming that both the teleradiometer and the camera system used by the Park Service were faulty. The teleradiometer was faulted for being too open to subjective interpretation of data results by its user. The cameras were challenged for a focal length of 135 mm and not well representative of the human eye.[117] Under questioning from Congressman Hansen of Utah, Malm defended the Park Service monitoring system as accurate.[118] That Hansen did not pursue further questioning of Park Service monitoring equipment was significant, because he was not known for his pro-environment positions on many issues, as can be seen from his comments during the Park Protection Act debate. Hansen could have taken the opportunity to raise some of the concerns expressed by industry but apparently chose not to.

Industry was also on record as urging more research on visibility impairment before any new regulatory approaches, such as regional regulation, were tried.[119] In fact, J. Robert White of the Western Regional Council Clean Air Committee cited EPA figures showing a decline in both ambient air-quality levels for sulfur dioxide and particulates, suggesting that a projected continuing decline would solve most air-quality problems in the parks.[120] His testimony on visibility, however, did not mention any projected improvement and instead focused on industry opposition to the integral vista concept.[121]

Recommendations on what to do about visibility appeared to stress the need for more research and monitoring, as well as to urge a more regional approach to the problem.[122] A majority of the testimony reflected the growing awareness that most visibility impairment was caused by regional haze and not identifiable smokestack plumes. Thus, for example, James Lents of Colorado's Air Pollution Control Division testified that long-range transport required a regional approach on visibility, with regional visibility standards and multistate cooperation.[123]

In summary, the May 1985 hearings provided a look at current understanding of the visibility issue as related to national parks. It is significant that eight years after the passage of the Clean Air Act Amendments, no mention was made of any BART review done for any existing source-caused visibility degradation. The complexity of the visibility problem appeared to have rendered the original intentions of Congress in 1977 problematic at best.

In November 1985, the Department of the Interior, through the assistant secretary for Fish, Wildlife, and Parks, sent the EPA a letter on visibility in the Park Service and Fish and Wildlife class I areas.[124] The EPA had asked for all federal land managers of class I areas to update their listing of integral vistas and to report on any existing visibility impairment suspected by the land managers.

The reason for the EPA request stemmed from the settlement agreement discussed previously. The EPA was faced with writing regulations for those states that had not yet revised their SIPs to deal with visibility protection. It was the FLMs' duty to notify the relevant states about suspected visibility impairment in any class I areas in those states. Then it was the states' duty to analyze for BART any existing facility that might be reasonably anticipated to be contributing to visibility impairment of the class I areas.

Furthermore, by 1983, there had been a change at the EPA. William

Ruckelshaus, the EPA's first administrator, had returned to head the agency. Ruckelshaus and his successor, Lee Thomas, tried to resurrect some of the legitimate goals of cost-effective regulation without ideological polarization. They wished to improve the scientific basis for regulatory decision making, as well as consider the costs of regulatory policies.[125] They were committed to environmental protection but with a full accounting of the benefits and the costs involved. Yet at the same time, the EPA was not given a green light to proceed with environmental protection. Even though the EPA might move forward, other Reagan administration officials would not. Thus, as Harris and Milkis noted, "the Department of Justice and OMB . . . sought to limit the enforcement activities of the EPA. In a sense Meese [Department of Justice] and Miller [OMB] were fighting an administrative rearguard action on behalf of regulatory relief, while the Congress, public lobby groups, and in some cases the EPA once again were forging ahead with an aggressive environmental policy agenda."[126]

The Park Service letter to the EPA reported two major findings. The first was that scenic views at all of the agency's monitoring stations in class I and class II areas in the lower forty-eight states were affected by anthropogenic pollution, or uniform haze, over 90 percent of the time.[127] Uniform haze is, of course, regional haze, and the primary pollutants contributing to this haze were sulfates.

The Park Service also provided a list of suspected impairments where impairment may have been traceable to specific sources. The agency's data were based either on surveys of field staff at the class I park unit or on evidence presented in a videotape of impairment at Bryce and Grand Canyon national parks.

In March 1987, the EPA responded to the Park Service report through a proposed rule designed to address the phase-II SIP revisions. The regional haze problem was once again dismissed for the time being, because of the lack of an appropriate regulatory program. For five class I areas—Bryce, Carlsbad Caverns, Isle Royal, Pinnacles, and Mesa Verde—the EPA stated that "the documentation is not sufficient to determine if the impairment is within the park boundaries."[128] This left five park units.

The first, Voyageurs National Park in Minnesota, was reported to have ground-based and elevated layered haze, as well as uniform haze. Two major sources were close to the park, one of them in Canada. The EPA concluded that "neither [the] EPA nor [the] NPS have sufficient documentation which would support an attribution decision at this time. The EPA, in cooperation with the NPS, has installed photographic monitoring equipment in Voyageurs National Park in order to develop the type of information necessary to make this decision."[129] The EPA also decided to defer until August 1988 any decision on BART for the suspected sources, hoping by then to have enough data to attribute impairment to one or both of the sources.

The remaining park units with possible visibility impairment were in or near the Colorado Plateau. At two of the units, Grand Canyon and Canyonlands, the Park Service had submitted documentation of visibility impairment. The EPA concluded that the impairment was not within the parks. Furthermore, the EPA held off on source attribution until August 1988 when the Park Service finally completed a study it was undertaking on sources of the suspected impairment.[130]

The last two park units were Saguaro and Petrified Forest. Saguaro National Monument is near Tucson; it reported both uniform and layered haze. Petrified Forest National Park reported a yellowish-brown layered haze. The EPA noted the existence of two power plants within thirty miles of Petrified Forest and a number of power plants within sixty-five miles of Saguaro, plus the cities of Tucson and Phoenix. Once again, the EPA deferred BART decisions until more information could be gathered from monitoring studies.[131]

THE 1986 VISIBILITY CONFERENCE

The suspected impairments listed by the Park Service are but one aspect of the large research effort being undertaken on visibility. In September 1986, the Air Pollution Control Association held a conference at Grand Teton National Park on the research and policy aspects of visibility protection. The conference was to serve as a forum for the presentation of research on various aspects of visibility protection, including such topics as human perception of visibility, progress in the development of modeling techniques, source attribution, and the results of various field studies. Some of the difficulties in regulating visibility protection were also discussed, but no attempt was made to prescribe policy options for the future. In short, the 1986 meeting was primarily a scientific conference, filled with technically complex reports.

In 1977, when the Clean Air Act Amendments became law, the driving force behind the visibility section was concern over visible plumes in the parks of the Colorado Plateau. Mesa Verde National Park was one of those parks. The Park Service submitted evidence to the EPA indicating that it could document visibility impairment in the nearby "integral vistas" of that park through photography and that it suspected impairment within the park's boundary. The source of the impairment was identified as the Four Corners power plant in Farmington, New Mexico.[132] As it turned out, however, the evidence was inconclusive. First, the visible plumes photographed outside the park boundaries could not be shown to have entered the park. Second, the research equipment in use by the Park Service could not show that particulate matter measured in the park actually came from the suspected power plants.[133]

One of the most important of the visibility impairment linkages concerns the park visitor. The visibility regulations defined "visibility impairment" as any humanly perceptible change in visibility, whereas "significant impairment" (in terms of BART exemption) meant impairment that interfered with aspects of the visitor's visual park experience. Thus research was necessary to establish whether park visitors noticed visibility impairments and whether those impairments interfered with their park experience. Unless those two linkages could be established, existing sources of visibility impairment might not have to retrofit, even if, for example, atmospheric scientists could identify impairment through instrumentation.

According to research reported at the visibility conference, clean air was a highly valued part of most park visitors' experience. Yet clean air also appeared to belong to a more general grouping of attributes dubbed a "cleanliness cluster" by researchers.[134] That is, a park's overall cleanliness, which included unpolluted air and water, was what mattered most to park visitors. By inference, then, polluted air could have the potential to adversely affect a visitor's park experience. Of course, the visitor would also have to recognize polluted air when he/she saw it and express some measurable disapproval to park officials. Thus this link in the visibility impairment chain has been strengthened but not completed by research.

The visibility conference also reported on various ongoing research projects regarding visibility impairment. The most studied area, the Grand Canyon region of northern Arizona, is part of three research efforts. The Electric Power Research Institute, the Department of Defense, the Salt River Project, Southern California Edison, the EPA, and the Park Service are all involved in SCENES, a five-year research project (begun in 1984) studying visibility impairment in the American Southwest.[135]

The federal government also recently entered into a cooperative monitoring effort—IMPROVE—stemming from the EPA "take-over" of visibility protection from states that did not revise their SIPs. IMPROVE, which involves the Park Service, EPA, Fish and Wildlife Service, Forest Service, and BLM, evaluates all one hundred fifty-six mandatory class I areas and prioritizes sites based on the likelihood of monitoring.[136] Park sites included Grand Canyon, Bryce, Canyonlands, and Mesa Verde in the Colorado Plateau.

Monitoring of suspected existing visibility impairment was expected to be constrained by budgetary considerations and thus limited to those highest priority sites where visibility impairment was already suspected. The EPA had initially committed $480,000 per year to IMPROVE, while the Park Service committed about $700,000 to the program. Only about 10 percent of the EPA money, however, was to go to the existing-source monitoring program. Thus two units likely to receive additional monitoring under IMPROVE are Grand Canyon and Canyonlands national parks. The Park Service, as will be seen, recently completed a special monitoring of the Canyonlands–Grand Canyon area, with equipment from both IMPROVE and SCENES, on the winter regional haze problem.

IMPROVE is also designed to assist in the development of better technology to measure visibility impairment through the construction of a particle monitoring device and a "transmissometer" (a device capable of measuring atmospheric extinction due to light scattering and absorption). The transmissometer uses a man-made light source to measure extinction. The IMPROVE program will also be used to supplement the existing NPS monitoring program, the Visibility Trend Monitoring Network (see Maps 5.1 and 5.2).

This research conference confirmed that there was more to the visibility issue than originally thought. In 1985, during testimony to the House Interior committee, NPS researchers pointed out that regional haze appeared to be the most significant problem at Grand Canyon and perhaps other parks of the Colorado Plateau. Regional haze was not addressed by the phase-I EPA visibility regulations, but it has become the most controversial part of visibility regulation.

THE REGIONAL HAZE PROBLEM

In mid-1985, the multi-agency regional haze task force released its report on findings and recommendations for developing long-range strategies to deal with regional haze. The report stated concerns about EPA progress on visibility that had been previously expressed to the author by Park Service officials:

> Progress has been made, but significant opportunities were lost by subsequent reductions in EPA's visibility research program. . . . Although the Task Force recognizes that visibility is not the highest EPA research priority, it is nevertheless important to restore at least a moderate program that takes maximum advantage of coordination with other visibility and related research programs.[137]

Perhaps the most important conclusion drawn by the task force was that visibility was best understood as a regional problem; regional haze–related visibility problems in the East were much more severe than those

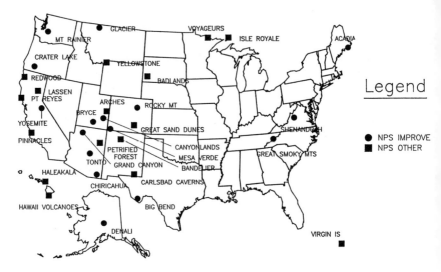

Map 5.1. The National Park Service Visibility Trend Monitoring Network (courtesy of National Park Service)

in the West.[138] Moreover, the eastern United States had another air-quality problem closely related to visibility and again more severe than in the West: acid precipitation, or, more popularly, "acid rain." Thus the EPA task force was prepared to suggest that more attention be paid by policymakers to $SO_2$ reductions in the East and the relation between these reductions and acid precipitation as well as visibility.[139] The task force said an integrative solution was also favored by most public commentators on the regional haze issue.[140] These commentators were split, however, on how quickly action should be taken on the eastern problem. Preservationists favored new legislative initiative on haze, whereas industry urged more research on visibility and on whether $SO_2$ controls would result in improvements in visibility.[141] An effective policy to deal with the relation between acid rain and visibility might well have to consider new legislation.[142]

Western visibility problems were different. The task force stated that

> protection of western visibility may be effected well enough without new legislation. Assuming implementation of current regulatory programs, the western analyses suggests [sic] that delaying development of new regional haze programs for several years while awaiting improved source-receptor information would probably not result in unacceptable or irreversible degradation. As new research results improve our ability to predict regional impacts of emission

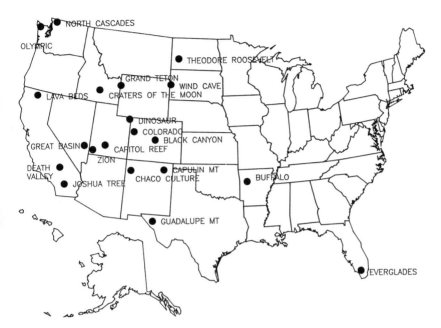

Map 5.2. The National Park Service Visibility Trend Monitoring Network: Camera-Only Sites (courtesy of National Park Service)

source limitations, "phase II" regulations can be developed under the existing section 169A. Protecting visibility in class I areas while implementing existing NAAQS, PSD, and mobile source controls will provide substantial protection against impairment from haze throughout the west.[143]

For western class I areas, the key was the "vigorous enforcement of current regulations, particularly those designed to attain the current NAAQS."[144] More specifically, the task force pointed to the smelters in southern Arizona, expected to begin cleanup in 1988, as examples of future improved visibility in the West.

The task force also stressed the need for continued work on documentation of current visibility impairment caused by regional haze, something we know is being actively pursued by the Park Service.[145] Finally, the task force noted that some air policies were potentially contradictory: Residential growth in the deserts of Los Angeles designed to reduce ozone in the L.A. area could increase ozone amounts near desert class I areas. Thus the task force recommendations on western class I areas appeared to urge continued research on existing regional haze impairment as well as active enforcement of all existing regulations. Any comprehensive phase-II regional haze programs could be deferred in the West for a few years because the problem was not yet severe.

For the East, the key to progress on visibility seemed to rely more on the linkage of regional haze to acid rain problems and the reduction of SO$_2$. Perhaps most important, active adoption of these task force recommendations would require support from upper-level EPA management. Conversations with EPA and Park Service officials involved in visibility regulation revealed that EPA management received the task force recommendations without indicating whether it was for or against them.[146]

One of the recommendations of the task force was to consider further the possibility that a revision of NAAQS secondary standards developed under Clean Air Act procedures might be an effective strategy to address the regional haze problem in the East. Secondary standards are public welfare– rather than public health–related and not as strict as the health-related primary standards. In an effort to solicit public comment, the EPA, in July 1987, issued advance notice of a proposed rule for secondary NAAQS standards for fine particulate matter. The secondary standards would be developed primarily for class I areas in the eastern United States, as was urged by the task force on regional haze. In addition, the development of secondary standards for fine particulates would also be linked to the acid rain problem in the eastern part of the country.[147]

Interior's response to the EPA's request for comments was made from the secretarial level and did not include any direct statements from the Park Service, indicating that key park policy was being made by political appointees. The department's comments were reminiscent of those of Secretary Hodel's on integral vistas. Interior argued, for example, that focusing on secondary standards might "cause" states to not explore other methods of visibility improvement.[148] Interior also urged that the EPA consider not just secondary standards for the East but also additional regional standards, while at the same time it apparently argued against national standards, something not under active consideration by the EPA. This was the first mention of multiple regional standards in the eleven-year saga of visibility protection. Since it took the EPA eight years to arrive at the point where it wanted to consider a western versus eastern approach to regional haze, one must view Interior's proposal as a stall.

Interior once again displayed its ability to reason in the convoluted manner it had during the integral vista decision. The department objected to what it said was overreliance on "user values" in conducting cost-benefit analysis on various approaches to visibility regulation and argued that preservation of visibility for future use of visitors ought to be included in the analysis. The problem with including such future values is obvious. The visibility regulations as currently written are based on determining adverse effects on today's visitor enjoyment of class I areas in order to require BART for identified existing sources of pollution. The visibility regulations focus on current visitor use and experiences. Thus future value calculations would miss the point of the regulations.[149]

In summary, Interior's approach to secondary standards for fine particulates favored the status quo and opposed the setting of standards. One could view both the integral vista concept and the secondary fine particulate standards as ways to address the problem of visibility (as well as acid rain in the East) based on new information gleaned from research. However, Interior's support of section 169A without change appears to favor a status quo approach to visibility protection. Progress thus seems to rely on the individual agencies with class I areas or on aggressive states. States in the Northeast may be showing some aggressiveness. In early 1988, Vermont and some of its neighbors took the EPA to court because of the lack of progress on the phase-II visibility regulations. This issue began with Vermont's proposed SIP revisions.

## VERMONT AND REGIONAL HAZE: FORCING THE ISSUE

There is no question that Vermont's SIP revision for visibility protection is the most far-reaching, as well as the most controversial, plan yet adopted by a state, because it identified regional haze as the source of visibility impairment in Vermont. Vermont has one class I area, the Lye Brook wilderness area in the Green Mountain National Forest, managed by the Forest Service. It has no class I Park Service area, but the state's arguments about regional haze and the phase-II visibility regulations have the obvious potential to affect Park Service units.

Vermont, in its proposed SIP revision, provided a legal justification for the scope of its visibility plan. Citing the lack of national legislation to deal with either acid rain or long-range transport of sulfates, the state claimed it had used section 123 (smokestack heights) and section 126 (interstate pollution abatement) of the Clean Air Act to address the problems.[150] But, said the state,

Section 123 has proved ineffectual, as the general nature of the wording leaves Congressional intent unclear and permits a wide range of interpretations. Section 126 contains more specific language, but has also proven ineffectual to date, largely because the specific language is not well suited to addressing multiple source, regional scale problems resulting from non-criteria pollutants like sulfate.[151]

Certain Park Service officials indicated that Vermont was angry at EPA inaction on the "regionalism" of acid rain and sulfate transport and so it chose its SIP revision as a way to highlight its concerns.[152]

Vermont, in an executive summary of its visibility SIP revision, stated the conclusions on which it based its plan:

> 1. There are, in addition to Lye Brook, many other "sensitive areas" [areas above 2,500 feet as declared in the SIP revision] in Vermont for which visibility protection is important to the welfare of Vermont's citizens. [Vermont has contracted with its state university to do an economic evaluation of the value of good visibility in Vermont.][153]
> 2. There is *no* existing impairment in Lye Brook or other "sensitive areas" which results from "Plume Blight." If Vermont were to merely comply with EPA's (phase I) regulations, it would result in no progress whatsoever toward the national goal set forth by Congress in 169A. Vermont's implementation plan must therefore either extend beyond EPA's regulations or be in violation of the Federal Law. [Vermont has stated that the "phased" EPA approach has now begun to frustrate congressional intent.][154]
> 3. There is considerable impairment of visibility throughout Vermont which occurs on a regional scale and is particularly severe during the summer—the season when Lye Brook receives the vast majority of its annual visitors.[155]
> 4. This summertime regional impairment is predominantly caused by sulfate particulate of anthropogenic origin.

These findings led Vermont to set a statewide secondary twenty-four-hour ambient sulfate concentration standard to protect its designated "sensitive areas."[156] Using sulfate transport models, Vermont concluded that $SO_2$ concentrations from eight midwestern states (Ohio, Pennsylvania, West Virginia, Indiana, Illinois, Michigan, Kentucky, and Tennessee) "are major contributors to Vermont's summer sulfate concentrations, especially on episodic days of high sulfate and poor visibility."[157] Vermont employed the "reasonably attributable" clause of section 169A to point to these eight states as the source of its visibility problems.

Vermont established a program to monitor compliance with the sulfate standard, stating that attainment of that standard by 1995 would reduce sulfate levels by 50 percent and constitute "reasonable progress" toward visibility improvement.[158] Vermont noted that it would have liked to include a more complex monitoring method (such as those used by the Park Service) in its plan, but costs made such a network prohibitive.[159] The key to the reduction of sulfur dioxide lay outside Vermont. The state essentially prescribed an emissions reduction schedule for the lower forty-eight states.[160] Vermont also requested that the EPA disapprove the SIPs of these eight midwestern states and require them to revise their SIPs to protect visibility in Vermont's Lye Brook wilderness.[161]

In the summer of 1987, the EPA acted on Vermont's SIP revision. The EPA found itself straddling a typical environmental policy debate. Allied with Vermont were Maine, Connecticut, Massachusetts, New Jersey, New York, the Conservation Foundation, the Environmental Defense Fund, the Natural Resources Defense Council, the Sierra Club, and the eastern regional office of the Forest Service. Opposing this coalition were the Utility Air Regulatory Group, the Mining and Reclamation Council of America, and Ohio.

The EPA chose to take no action on the four most controversial parts of Vermont's SIP revision—ambient sulfate standards, forty-eight-state emission reductions, requested SIP disapprovals, and designation of sensitive areas. The reason for this decision was the EPA's lack of a regulatory regional haze program because of the inadequacy of scientific certainty about the regulation of regional haze.[162]

The EPA's decision to take no action on these aspects of Vermont's plan led the state into the legal arena. Vermont, with allies in both the Northeast and the environmental community, tried two approaches. First, it challenged the EPA's refusal to act on parts of the SIP revision regarding regional haze. The U.S. Second Circuit, in *Vermont v. Thomas*, 87-4119 (June 23, 1988), supported the EPA position, arguing that the regional haze SIP revisions were outside the scope of the original 1980 visibility regulations and thus the EPA's action to "not act" was reasonable.[163]

Vermont and its supporters then tried a different legal approach. Section 7604 of the Clean Air Act states that the district court is the appropriate court for bringing a suit based on the EPA's failure to perform a nondiscretionary duty.[164] So the plaintiffs brought their suit to the U.S. District Court for the District of Maine (Maine was a party to the suit). The suit revolved around whether, eleven years after the passage of section 169A, the EPA had a discretionary duty to promulgate regional haze regulations or whether the EPA *must* now develop such regulations. As one environmental source argued, "The question of EPA's discretionary duty is moot. It's a purely legal issue—the law required them to promul-

gate section 169A regulations and they haven't; therefore they're break-
ing the law."[165]

Maine, Vermont, and their supporters in court argued that the EPA
had the duty to implement visibility regulations that would address the
regional haze problem and thus meet the congressional goal of visibility
protection.[166] The EPA's nonattention to regional haze is the substantive
issue in this case. The plaintiffs argued that the EPA's duty to develop regional haze regulations was a "non-discretionary" task and thus the EPA
should be compelled by the courts to address regional haze in the agency's visibility regulations.[167]

The EPA position (supported by industry) asserted that Congress left
the implementation of visibility protection to the EPA because of the lack
of scientific information on the problem. Recognizing this information
shortage, the EPA promulgated its two-phased approach to visibility protection. In so doing, the EPA carried out its duty to promulgate visibility
regulations and therefore was not liable under section 7604.[168] The EPA
went on to argue that the only thing the plaintiffs could do at this stage
of the visibility policy was to petition the EPA to promulgate newer regulations that would address regional haze.

The district court, in its decision, agreed with the EPA on the question of jurisdiction, thereby refusing jurisdiction in the case. The plaintiffs were told to seek action in the U.S. Court of Appeals for the District
of Columbia under section 7607(b) of the Clean Air Act.[169] The district
court argued that the visibility regulations were "final actions" under
section 7607 and thus only reviewable by the appellate court:

> These decisions [prior court decisions] indicate that once the EPA
> has publicly announced a formal decision not to act or to defer
> action [as it did with the phased regulations] and the basis for that
> decision is set forth in an administrative record,[as it apparently was
> in the *Federal Register*] such inaction or deferral of action becomes a
> final action for purposes of review under 7607.[170]

Because the district court did not assert jurisdiction, it did not reach
the substantive issues in the case. However, the district court did add
some thoughts on whether the appellate court was likely to be sympathetic to the substantive appeal of the plaintiffs. Noting that the Second
Circuit Court had upheld the EPA decision to take no action on Vermont's visibility regulations in *Vermont v. Thomas*, the Maine court stated
that the plaintiffs had "difficulties on the substantive issues in this
case."[171] Because the court did not act on the substance of the appeal of
Maine et al. because of jurisdictional grounds, the plaintiffs appealed to
the First Circuit Court of Appeals for judgment.

On May 18, 1989, the First Circuit Court issued its decision. The appellate court sustained the decision of the district court for Maine, arguing that the 1980 visibility regulations were indeed final and so not subject to the jurisdiction of the district court. Thus even though the EPA deferred the regional haze regulations, this was a final action under the provisions of the Clean Air Act.[172]

There was, however, still a course of action available for the plaintiffs. The appellate court noted that "Congress intended citizens to have an ability to confront EPA with new information arguably sufficient to merit revision of extant regulations."[173] If the plaintiffs thought that sufficient progress had been made in scientific understanding of regional haze, they could petition the EPA for new regulations that took the new knowledge into account. At this writing, such a petition has yet to occur. One can safely assert, however, that lengthy wrangling about whether enough new knowledge is or is not sufficient for new regulations is likely. The saga of the phase-I regulations ought to make that clear.

## UTAH AND VISIBILITY PROTECTION: DEVELOPMENT VERSUS PRESERVATION

We now return to visibility protection on the Colorado Plateau. Our battleground this time is Utah, home of numerous national parks and monuments, and the state's SIP revision process. Utah's visibility SIP is important if for no other reason than the state contains five class I areas, all administered by the Park Service and all well known: Bryce, Zion, Canyonlands, Arches, and Capitol Reef national parks. Utah's SIP, like the EPA regulations, set up its own phased approach to visibility protection. The first phase dealt with the implementation of a visibility monitoring strategy and new source review. The strategy involves implementation of a three-part monitoring network: FLM visibility monitoring, new source monitoring if the proposed source was going to locate near a class I area, and implementation of a state monitoring network.[174]

The Utah SIP has this to say about the state's own monitoring program: "It is the desire of the Committee to establish a state operated visibility monitoring network to complement the monitoring required by the SIP and to provide additional baseline data. Contingent upon obtaining necessary funding, the Bureau of Air Quality will begin installation of a continuous visibility monitoring network by September, 1987."[175] One must question the level of commitment suggested by this quotation. Seventy-five percent of the state's air pollution funding came from the federal government in 1983.[176]

If we assume that Utah increasingly had to confront replacing federal funding with its own, Charles Davis and James Lester have suggested key factors that would influence such a replacement decision: "A willingness to intervene in the sphere of private sector activities for the public good while also demonstrating the political will to assume the administration of federal environmental policies [is] more likely to produce the necessary revenue to maintain these [environmental] programs."[177] Utah's "contingent" clause appears to provide a justifiable reason why its monitoring plan might not be implemented and thus suggests that Davis and Lester's "political will" might be lacking.

Utah's phase II deals with existing visible plumes and regional haze. The regulation of existing visibility impact seems to defer completely to FLM research, noting that no plume impairment has yet been identified by the FLMs.[178] Regional haze regulation was to be addressed by an "anticipated" SIP revision by December 20, 1986, with that visibility problem characterized as "little known" by current research.[179] Also, Utah's plan noted that current research indicated that the source of regional haze impacts may be outside the state and thus not subject to Utah regulatory authority.[180] Utah never did revise its SIP to address visible plumes, so that regulatory function was taken over by the EPA. In summary, the Utah SIP revision appeared to be a minimum regulatory scheme that addressed federal monitoring and nothing else. The state visibility monitoring network did not seem to have the commitment of the Utah Air Conservation Committee, which formulated and adopted the plan, because of the funding contingency "escape" clause.

Yet, in the spring of 1986, some startling news came out of Utah. The state's governor, Norman Bangerter, appointed the Citizen's Advisory Committee on Visibility to study state designation of integral vistas. The advisory committee took a protective stance toward what it called Utah's scenic vistas, recommending that the integral vistas first identified in 1981 by the Park Service within Utah be incorporated and protected by the state. The committee then recommended that large coal-fired electric power plants, smelters and steel mills, major lumber and aluminum plants, and coke ovens be prohibited in identified integral vistas.[181] These prohibitions applied only to new sources of visibility impairment. Finally, the advisory committee urged the development of interstate compacts to mitigate the impacts of regional haze on Utah's national parks and vistas.

Utah's Air Conservation Committee, the state's official air-quality policymaking body, chose not to adopt the scenic vistas of the advisory committee. Environmentalists were very disappointed, charging that the Air Conservation Committee had "turned its back" on the "visionary recommendation" of the advisory group.[182] Park Service officials were more optimistic, finding the Air Conservation Committee still making a "strong policy statement" on visibility protection in the scenic vistas of southern Utah, even though these vistas were not specifically identified.[183] The Park Service also hoped that Utah governor Bangerter would follow the committee recommendation to urge the Western Governors Association to establish a task force on regional haze.

The politics of integral vistas within Utah was not dissimilar to that at the federal level. In an address to the 1986 visibility conference at Grand Teton, former Utah governor Scott Matheson had quite a lot to say about integral vistas. Matheson began by acknowledging that visibility protection which stopped at the border of national parks such as Bryce was essentially meaningless.[184] Yet he also believed that the current Clean Air Act did not support the integral vista concept. Matheson pointed with some alarm to the consequences of what he thought was improper discretionary policymaking by the EPA. He referred to a 1982 study by the Office of Technology Assessment (OTA) indicating that over 20 percent of the total land area of Utah would be affected by the designation of integral vistas originally identified by the Park Service.

Matheson proposed to return the question to Congress. He argued for a scheme by which a revised Clean Air Act would allow the federal land manager to nominate integral vistas but leave approval of them to the state. Matheson believed that the federal land manager would be an excellent advocate for the more "national" goal of visibility protection. At the same time, however, he thought that only an elected official familiar with the need to balance visibility protection with economic development—that is, the state governor—should make the final decision. His argument was based on the premise that the governor is more accountable to the public for a decision than either the EPA or the NPS. Presumably, if the public did not like the governor's decision, they would vote accordingly at the next election.

Gordon Anderson, the former Park Service ranger who took some of the first photographs of the Colorado Plateau in 1977 that helped lead to section 169A, was also displeased at the status of integral vistas. He wanted to see them returned, presumably through amending the Clean Air Act.[185] Yet final authority should not rest with the governor of a state with an integral vista but with the federal land manager who had jurisdiction over the viewshed. Anderson's policy prescription is the opposite of Matheson's. To Anderson, a strong advocate of visibility protection, the federal land manager would be much more likely to protect an integral vista than a governor. In the case of the Park Service, he is undoubtedly correct. The Park Service is held accountable, and indirectly at that, only for resource protection and visitor enjoyment, both of which are adversely affected by visibility impairment. Economic development is not a primary concern of the agency. Anderson, in fact, goes so far as to suggest that the final say on BART be removed from the governor as well.

## BREAKTHROUGH AT THE GRAND CANYON: ARE EMISSIONS FROM THE NAVAJO GENERATING STATION *"REASONABLY ATTRIBUTABLE"*?

In April 1989, results of the multi-agency research effort on winter visibility at Grand Canyon and Canyonlands were released. It was this study that the EPA had been waiting on before making BART determinations for the suspected impairments at these parks. The study was called the Winter Haze Intensive Tracer Experiment, or WHITEX. As discussed, the Park Service has had a visibility monitoring program at the Grand Canyon since 1978. That research identified sulfates as the dominant man-made visibility pollutant at the park, with most of the summer impairment caused by long-range transport of pollutants from southern California, southern Arizona, New Mexico, and Mexico. Yet as the Park Service noted:

> When these same tools were used to predict sulfate contributions on an annual basis, there was a poor correlation between the concentrations measured at the Park during the winter months and those that would be expected to occur if long-range transport were the dominant cause. This discrepancy led researchers to believe that wintertime haze in the Grand Canyon might be primarily caused by more local air pollution sources.[186]

The Park Service had already, in 1985, identified the Navajo Generating Station (NGS) as a suspected local source of wintertime visibility impairment at Grand Canyon, Canyonlands, and Bryce Canyon national parks. Thus WHITEX was an attempt to gain more information about NGS and its contribution to regional haze. The study was also designed to test whether certain techniques could attribute emissions to a single source, as the phase-I visibility regulations had required.

The WHITEX study took place during six weeks in January and February 1987. The Park Service used a number of attribution methods, including placing a "tracer" (deuterated methane) in NGS to distinguish its emissions from other sources. Various monitoring techniques were employed, with intensive monitoring done at Hopi Point in Grand Canyon, Canyonlands, and Page.[187] In addition, the Park Service used complex statistical and deterministic models to help with its analysis.

Four conclusions were drawn by the agency in a draft report:

1. Visibility at the Grand Canyon between November and March of each year is perceptibly degraded by manmade pollution at least 15 percent of the time (21 days) and perhaps as much as 30 percent of the time (42 days). On the average, sulfates are responsible for 55 percent of the non-rayleigh extinction [scattering by natural gases]; on the highest extinction days, sulfates cause over 70 percent of observed visibility impairment.

2. The Navajo Generating Station is the single largest contributor to visibility impairment at the Grand Canyon on 90 percent of the episode days during the winter.

3. The Navajo Generating Station, on the average, causes 40–50 percent of the visibility impairment during winter.

4. On days with the worst visibility during the winter, the Navajo Generating Station is highly likely to cause 70 percent of the observed visibility degradation.[188]

The WHITEX study mentioned all the owners of the power station: the Salt River Project (21.7 percent), the Bureau of Reclamation (24.3 percent), Los Angeles Water and Power (21.2 percent), Arizona Public Service (14 percent), Nevada Power Company (11.3 percent), and Tucson Gas and Electric (7.5 percent).[189] Some of these owners were quick to criticize the Park Service study. Larry Crittenden, spokesman for the Salt River Project, noted that "the Park Service used selective data, and they used unproven methods," as well as chastised the agency for not using peer review.[190] The battle lines were drawn, and the terrain seemed familiar. How much evidence was needed, and how conclusive should it be, for the EPA to require NGS to install BART?

On July 6, 1989, the settlement agreement between the EPA and EDF was revised again. The EPA would rule on whether any facility could be identified as contributing to visibility impairment at Grand Canyon by August 31, 1990, as well as rule on possible impairment in the Moosehorn Wilderness in Maine and Canyonlands National Park. On September 5, 1989, the EPA responded to the WHITEX report and to the two other open questions of possible visibility impairment. In a *Federal Register* notice, the EPA decided that BART was not necessary for suspected impairment in the Moosehorn Wilderness or in Canyonlands National Park. In Maine, plant modifications rendered BART requirements unnecessary, and in Canyonlands no source could be identified as contributing to visibility impairment.

The conclusion was different for Grand Canyon. The EPA proposed to tentatively accept the Park Service data identifying the Navajo Generating Station as a suspected source of visibility impairment and proposed a BART analysis for Navajo subject to the final Park Service report.

Visibility impairment at the Grand Canyon caused by pollution from the Navajo Generating Station, Page, Arizona. These photographs were taken at 3 P.M. over several days. Note that the canyon rim is almost completely obscured in the last photograph in the series. (courtesy of National Park Service)

The EPA opened a sixty-day comment period on its proposal and promised a BART decision by February 1, 1990. Since Navajo is in Arizona, the EPA was proposing the February date as the date for deciding whether to revise the Arizona Federal Implementation Plan to include BART, or other possible control strategies, for Navajo.[191]

There was immediate opposition to the EPA proposal. The Salt River Project, as well as the Alabama Power Company (a consortium of electric utility firms), brought up four legal and regulatory issues. The first argued that the impairment was "regional," and the second that all contributing sources needed to be identified.[192] The EPA dismissed both of these claims, arguing that the NPS had identified a specific source and that BART analysis was therefore proper. The other two objections were legal points over whether the EPA had the authority to act as it was; the EPA asserted that it did have that authority.

The Department of the Interior also entered the fray. Secretary Manuel Lujan called for a new study by the National Academy of Sciences (NAS) to recheck the Park Service study.[193] Lujan did not challenge the study or the EPA's preliminary finding.[194] Lujan had good reason for requesting the NAS study. Another Interior bureau, the Bureau of Reclamation, owns 24 percent of Navajo. Thus if Navajo is forced to install BART, at a cost estimated between $330 million and $1 billion, Interior would have to pay for part of the cleanup.[195]

The final Park Service report was issued on December 4, 1989, and was essentially the same as the draft report. On January 9, 1990, the U.S. District Court for the Northern District of California granted a motion by the Salt River Project and Alabama Power Company et al. to extend the rule-making deadlines. The EPA was given until February 1, 1991, to propose BART, and until October 2, 1991, for final action on it. This extension, however, did not preclude the EPA from acting earlier than the deadlines.

On February 8, 1990, the EPA submitted a notice of proposed rule-making to the Office of Management and Budget (OMB). That notice confirmed the EPA's preliminary finding that visibility impairment in Grand Canyon was reasonably attributable to Navajo. Based on the results of a BART analysis done on Navajo, the EPA proposed reducing $SO_2$ by 90 percent, as well as stabilizing $NO_2$ and particulate emissions at current levels.[196]

The EPA also found, in two supporting documents given to OMB (BART and regulatory impact analyses), that the cost of requiring BART would range between $103.5 million and $145.2 million per year.[197] The increase for residential customers of Navajo power was estimated to be less than 5 percent, or about $2.55 a month.[198] Since Navajo power was also used to pump water for the Central Arizona Project (CAP), cost estimates were made in this area too. Costs were estimated to rise about 3–4 percent for twenty-three hundred farmers, or about $22,000.[199] CAP, however, plans to phase down its obligations to these farmers. If this phase-down happens, cost increases would drop to 1–2 percent a year, said the EPA.[200]

In addition, the EPA noted that visibility would "perceptibly" improve at Grand Canyon one hundred days during the winter season, "noticeably" improve fifty-eight days, and "very apparently" improve twenty-one days.[201] The 90 percent $SO_2$ reduction would improve visibility an additional forty-four days over the 70 percent reduction.[202] The EPA tied a benefit analysis onto this visibility improvement estimate, though not required, and performed a cost-benefit analysis to check the "reasonableness" of its BART results. The EPA found that "estimated net benefits are positive for all examined control levels, and are maximized at the 90 percent level," confirming its BART analysis.[203]

The Salt River Project also began its own winter visibility study at Grand Canyon. The EPA promised to look at the results of that study, plus the NAS report, if they were issued by August 31, 1990, and if they appeared to affect the conclusion of the proposed rule-making.[204] As of early May 1990, the OMB had still not acted on the proposed rule.


VISIBILITY PROTECTION: SOME CONCLUSIONS


What is perhaps most striking about the saga to protect our national parks from existing visibility impairment is the technical complexity of the task. Concerned environmentalists first brought the problem to the attention of Congress in 1977. In a sense, this early action was an emotional, gut-level "I know visibility impairment when I see it" response. Many people who examined the slides of Gordon Anderson and others could see, or thought they could see, impairment of viewsheds in parks of the Colorado Plateau.

Today, eleven years after revisions of the Clean Air Act passed Congress, not one polluter has yet had to apply retrofit technology to the source of pollution. It has become apparent that visibility protection was a much more complicated problem than many people thought it would be. The National Park Service has finally been able to document visibility impairment at the Grand Canyon, as well as to identify a source suspected of causing that impairment. But here the process may once again come to a halt. Any source so identified can apply for an exemption from BART. Getting an exemption requires the source to prove that its emissions are not affecting visitor enjoyment. It is not clear that research on visitor perception and enjoyment is anywhere near being able to firmly establish that visitors either notice or are affected by visibility impairment. Yet the burden of proof seems to lie with the pollution source.

Also, the time of visibility impairment must correlate with actual visitation. There is evidence that some of the most serious visibility impairments may occur in the winter, at least in parks of the Colorado Plateau. Visitation at these parks is traditionally less during the winter. Thus the park visitor may be essential to preventing visibility impairment. Yet, paradoxically, a charge can be leveled at many environmental groups that they have become increasingly hostile to the average park visitor.[205] Whether environmentalists are able to rise above their at times condescending attitudes and link up once again with the majority of park visitors for the protection of visibility may be a key to the protection of this invaluable resource.

Another important aspect of visibility protection is the role of the EPA. There is abundant evidence that the EPA simply has not placed visibility protection on a par with its health-related protection programs. Yet, at the same time, EPA behavior has varied quite a bit over the last eleven years. The Carter EPA was quite sympathetic to visibility protection if one considers that it was the Carter EPA that developed the integral vista concept. It is also clear that the early years of Reagan's administration saw a major change of direction regarding environmental protection.[206] Today, forced to respond by the settlement agreement reached with environmentalists, the EPA has begun to alter its behavior of the early Reagan years. This change remains slow, however. In 1988, the EPA cut back on some of the research monies it had allocated for visibility monitoring.[207] In the words of Nevada senator Harry Reid, such cutbacks "come at a time when our previous investment in these monitoring networks is beginning to produce results."[208] Such cutbacks also seem to render progress on the phase-II regional haze regulations slower than it needs to be. The crux of the EPA's position has been that more research must be done on regional haze and its contribution to visibility impairment. It is hard to see how progress can be made when funds for monitoring are reduced, yet that is what the EPA did. In 1989, funding was restored to previous levels.

Another related question appears to be the EPA's attitude toward regional haze. The EPA has so far argued successfully that it does not yet have enough information on regional haze to proceed with active regulation in this area. The agency has begun to address the "regionalness" of the haze issue by soliciting comments on a secondary standard for fine particulates. One of the reasons for EPA action was increasing recognition of the linkage between visibility protection and acid rain in the East. At the same time, the EPA has been taken to, and ultimately supported in, court for its progress on the regional haze aspects of visibility protection. The unanswered question remains, How much research is "necessary" before some sort of phase-II regulations are written? For critics of EPA progress, perhaps the election of a new administration may offer the best prospect for speedier action. One test of President Bush's promise to be the "environmental president" would be the EPA's response to the Navajo Generating Station visibility issue.

Another interesting aspect of visibility protection has been the effect it has wrought on the National Park Service. Today, the Air Quality Division of the Park Service is one of several centers of research on visibility. The Park Service does not have much actual policy control over visibility, in that the agency can only identify suspected sources of visibility impairment to the EPA. Yet it is clear that the first identification is going to come from the Park Service.

The Park Service has filled a void left by the EPA regarding visibility research. Most people, when they think of the National Park Service, usually do not conjure up visions of atmospheric scientists and air-quality specialists. Yet it is the air-quality professionals who have allowed the Park Service to develop the expertise it now has in visibility. For an agency increasingly concerned with all aspects of research on natural resources, the air-quality specialists might serve as a useful model of how to promote research within the agency.

Of course, the Park Service has other important aspects to its mission—perhaps still the most important is providing for visitor management and protection. Indeed, this aspect of the agency's mission may always remain the most important. Yet it is the research on visitor valuation of various park resources, stemming from visibility studies, that may provide the Park Service with a better handle on what park visitors value most about a national park. Such research might serve as an effective way to guide the rather difficult process of making policy for the national parks.

All of this leads to the issue of revising Clean Air Act provisions on visibility protection. Some environmentalists have urged that the integral vista be added to the legislation,[209] because there is a good possibility that some of the source attribution programs would be able to document visibility impairment, as well as identify the offending source, in an integral vista. Integral vistas enlarge the area for study and increase the likelihood that visibility impairment can be identified. This is the reason, of course, that industry first objected to the integral vista concept, fearing regulation that extended far beyond the boundaries of class I national park units.

The obvious political question related to integral vistas centers on which decision maker would have the power to recommend protection of them. As we have seen, people such as former Utah governor Matheson prefer one actor, and environmentalists another. In fact, Gordon Anderson goes so far as to suggest that the recommendation on BART be given to the federal land manager, rather than the governor of the affected state.[210]

Another possible revision to the Clean Air Act lies in the area of regional haze. Eastern states, notably Vermont, have been unhappy with EPA progress on regional haze, especially as it relates to acid rain. Some attention to this linkage has been paid in congressional debates, but as yet no change has occurred.[211] President Bush, in 1989, attempted to introduce new legislation on acid rain. Environmentalists were pleased with Bush's initiative but were also worried about some aspects of his plan. They suggested four necessary additions to the president's plan: capping emissions from utilities at 1985 levels; keeping offset reductions in the West if the source was also in the West; not allowing the reduced emissions from closed copper smelters to count as offsets, because the plants were in violation of air pollution laws when they closed; and maintaining current PSD provisions.[212]

Perhaps the most important lesson to be learned from our study of visibility is how a well-intentioned law became difficult to implement in practice. Because Congress is not a body of technical experts, it left the writing of the "rules" on visibility protection to the experts in the EPA. A presidential election brought new direction to the EPA and slowed progress on visibility protection. The Park Service picked up the slack in research but never had the regulatory power to enforce any BART decision it might have made if it had had the power. Governor Matheson would applaud this example of our federal separation-of-powers system in action. Environmentalists have not applauded.

If visibility protection is to be speeded up, it will be either in the hands of a new administration or in the hands of Congress. Perhaps Congress is where the final decision should be made. The visibility of our national parks is no doubt an important value worthy of protection. If Congress speeds up that protection, it will be only because the necessary political coalition has been formed to accomplish protection. That coalition may reflect the success of American environmentalists in bringing the urgency of visibility protection to a majority of Americans. This in turn requires environmentalists to do something they have seemingly been reluctant to do recently—that is, talk favorably about the average park visitor and that visitor's national parks.

# CHAPTER SIX

# Conclusion: Resolving External Threats to National Parks

At first glance, the two case studies may not suggest a promising resolution to the external threats problem. Both studies involved laws that supposedly gave structure and direction to the resolution of each of the activities considered. Congress mandated the protection of class I areas and thus many of the older crown jewel national parks from visibility degradation and existing sources of air pollution. Congress also mandated that tar sands development could take place only if it did not cause "adverse impacts" on certain units of the park system. Yet despite these congressional directives, not one source of visibility impairment has had to apply retrofit technology, and the tar sands development was never formally approved or disapproved.

Perhaps the most important factor in determining such outcomes is institutional. As the popular saying goes, "Congress proposes and the President disposes." Once Congress passes a law, that law must be put into action or implemented. Implementation usually involves the agencies of government with jurisdiction over the policy area in question. Thus in the tar sands case, it was up to the Park Service to make the "no adverse impacts" determination that Congress required. Increasingly, however, other political actors besides agency officials are involved in implementation decisions.

Political scientists and public administration scholars have called this involvement by other officials the "administrative presidency."[1] The term refers to the use of the appointment power by a president and his advisers to place people of similar philosophy and ideology in decision-making positions, usually at the level of secretary, assistant secretary and so forth. A critical component of the administrative presidency is having these officials make substantive policy decisions for the agencies they supervise. Opponents of whatever administration is in power are likely to respond by charging that administration with "politicizing" public policy.

The administrative presidency was a hallmark of both the Carter and the Reagan years, at least in terms of the Park Service. The Reagan presidency's effect on the outcomes of the two case studies is obvious. The Reagan administration's philosophy toward the environment was well defined, usually favoring development over preservation by requiring

131

balance of proof decisions to lie more heavily on the environmental side than on the developmental one.[2] As the Reagan presidency showed, use of the administrative presidency can greatly influence how external threat problems are resolved.

In the tar sands case, the natural resource policies of the Reagan administration influenced the outcome of the leasing decision. Section 11 of the Combined Hydrocarbon Leasing Act was specific regarding the leasing of tar sands. Leasing could not proceed unless there were "no significant adverse impacts" on Glen Canyon National Recreation Area or Canyonlands National Park. Congressman Seiberling restated what this section meant in his exchange with James Santini of Nevada, noting again that leasing could not go forward if it affected these two parks.

The draft environmental impact statement appeared to indicate that adverse impacts were probable, and the Park Service used this information to oppose leasing. Such a scenario must have been what congressional sponsors had in mind when they wrote the proposed 1983 Park Protection Act. That act required the secretary of the Interior to make a determination of no significant adverse effect before allowing leasing on land under his/her control that was adjacent to a unit of the national park system. With the DEIS done, the Park Service's adverse-impacts determination made, and the BLM in disagreement, the decision was up to Interior secretary Hodel. His office never issued one.

This solution, or nonsolution, is not what the sponsors of the Park Protection Act had in mind. Yet it illustrates how the resource policy of the Reagan administration was able to confound what appeared to be a clear-cut set of decision guidelines. In the tar sands case, the Reagan administration could not have authorized the lease conversion and development because the data were clear on the effects and impacts it would have. But because the administration saw development and preservation the way it did, it apparently could not overtly oppose the lease conversion either. So it did nothing.

Perhaps the only way to address such a problem is for Congress to mandate that park values be given the highest priority, or for that body to resolve conflicts such as the tar sands issue itself. But Congress is not likely to do the former because of political conflict over giving protection of parks higher priority than development. That is the main reason no park protection bill has yet passed any Congress. If Congress were to pass such legislation, it would signal an end to the external threats issue, because it would suggest that the necessary coalition had been assembled in affirmation of park protection over adjacent development.

Congress has usually been hesitant to resolve questions such as that presented by the tar sands case. Congress usually prefers to delegate responsibility to the various agencies that have jurisdiction over a substantive policy, only intervening when there has been an obvious policy disaster or public outcry over agency policies. When Congress delegates authority out of necessity and allows discretion on how a law is to be interpreted and implemented, Congress leaves the door open for interpretations its members may not have intended. Add to this a president elected on a perceived public mandate and with a prodevelopment ideology about how the nation's public lands should be managed and the tar sands solution is understandable.

The role of the Reagan administration was just as obvious during the battle over visibility protection. The integral vista concept was not in the 1977 Clean Air Act Amendments but was added by the Carter EPA through what it saw as a logical extension of congressional intent. Since many of the western national parks were created in part because of views in and from them, those views needed protection. So when Congress mandated visibility protection, it inferentially intended to protect integral vistas. There was strong opposition to the integral vista concept by industry and other developmental interests, but environmentalists favored it. The Reagan administration chose not to list integral vistas. Now development interests applauded while environmentalists complained.

The integral vista saga illustrates the policymaking power held by administrators in our political system. It also illustrates the significance of a change in the White House, especially when that change reflects different natural resources policy priorities. When Congress provides for policy discretion, it should not be surprised when there are policy shifts such as the one over integral vistas. The integral vista saga also suggests that external threats prevention based simply on discretion and legislative interpretation and cooperation will likely be captive to the ideology of the current administration.

## THE ADMINISTRATIVE PRESIDENCY
## OF REAGAN: POLICY RESPONSES

The natural resources policies of the Reagan presidency led to a reaction from the environmental community and sympathetic members of Congress. In 1988, the NPCA issued a multi-volumed document entitled the *The National Park System Plan*, a comprehensive look at various issues and policies surrounding national parks. The NPCA proposed that the Park Service be removed from the Department of the Interior and made an independent agency and that the director of the agency be subject to approval by the Senate. The association also called for the establishment of a board of regents to oversee the Park Service and reflect "business acumen, scientific expertise, and citizen preservation advocacy."[3]

The Park Service director at the time, William Penn Mott, requested comments on the plan from key agency officials. Almost all respondents, including Director Mott, disagreed with the suggestion that the Park Service be removed from the Department of the Interior. Comments ranged from supporting the "buffering" provided the Park Service as one of several Interior agencies, to Director Mott's insightful statement to NPCA president Paul Pritchard that "I suspect that NPCA would prefer more political guidance from an Administration that shares your views on how parks should be managed."[4]

Many Park Service comments also took the NPCA to task for neglecting the park visitor in its plan and not recognizing the "enjoyment" aspect of the Park Service organizational mission: "There is little concern in dealing with the issue of providing recreational opportunities. A blueprint for the future of the park system would need to provide a balanced approach between recreation and conservation for the mission of the Service."[5] The responses frequently mentioned surveys showing that over 90 percent of park visitors were satisfied with their experiences,[6] leading one commentator to assert that "you would never know, reading the subject sections, that parks are for people also."[7]

Mott's comment to Pritchard illustrates the real purpose of the administrative presidency. The question may not be so much where the Park Service is located as who has control over agency policy. Because the Reagan administration made policy decisions with which the NPCA disagreed, the group wanted to minimize the administration's power over the agency by pulling it out of the Interior Department. Thus the NPCA was really reacting to the presidency and policies of Ronald Reagan. During the Carter years, the administrative presidency favored environmentalist positions, so groups such as the NPCA probably had no objections to that administration's control over park policy.

George Hartzog, a former Park Service director, has charged that politicization through the administrative presidency also occurred during the Carter administration. In this case, however, it was environmentalists appointed by Carter who were politicizing the Park Service. During Hartzog's tenure, the Park Service developed a "three-tiered" management policy, dividing parks into natural, historic, and recreational categories. The Carter appointees altered the policy in favor of a single category of units. Hartzog complained: "Suddenly everything [each unit] had become the same and, thus, nothing was any longer special—not even Yellowstone. Instead of America's great national parks as crown jewels, all areas in the system were now jewels in the crown."[8] Hartzog was unhappy because park professionals like himself were being overruled by higher officials in the Department of the Interior. Thus the real question of the administrative presidency is whose administration is in charge. Mott's point has proved to be a good one, because environmentalists just might favor an administration and its park policies over policies made by the Park Service.

Also in 1988, the House of Representatives, led by congressional park policy specialists such as Bruce Vento, passed legislation that would have mandated that the director of the NPS be appointed by the president and confirmed by the Senate for a term of five years. In addition, many key functions of the secretary of the Interior were to be transferred to the director's office; budget and cabinet-level policymaking were the exceptions. Third, a review board was to be created to oversee the Park Service. Duties of the board would have included wide-ranging authority to review programs and activities of both the agency and individual parks.[9] This legislation was an attempt to address the policy consequences of the Reagan years. All of the Republican House members opposed the bill, and the Senate took no action on it.[10]

## ORGANIZATIONAL CONSIDERATIONS

A second factor that will affect resolution of the external threats issue has to do with the organizational dynamics of the Park Service. The Park Service, like most large bureaucracies, is not monolithic but, rather, composed of different professions as well as points of view about the purposes of national parks. Historically, when most of the problems and policies of the parks were internal and most of the parks were natural areas in the West, the agency seemed to function well with just the "generalist" ranger, an employee who was capable of performing most of the tasks needed in a national park: visitor interpretation, law enforcement, first aid and visitor aid, and maintenance. For a public servant, park rangers approach an almost mythical stature. They are, as Peter Steinhart put it, "bearers of a character we desperately want to preserve in the urban age. No other public servant seems so capable, so dedicated, so knowing and purposeful and so able to reach out to people at the level of humanity and deed."[11] Today, the park ranger series, or 025 federal job classification, is still the most sought after track to higher management positions in the Park Service. Yet from the two case studies, it should be apparent that the traditional park ranger was not the most important actor within the Park Service on these external threat problems.

In both the tar sands and visibility cases, the natural resource professionals were vital in providing necessary information to higher-level park managers. The adverse-impacts decision, in the tar sands controversy, could only have been made from data provided in the DEIS. Most of the progress on visibility has been made within the Park Service's Air Quality Division, a "specialist" division made up in large part of people with degrees in the atmospheric sciences.

These two studies suggest that clear-cut evidence will at the least be necessary for the Park Service to successfully address an external threat. Obviously, such evidence alone would not be sufficient, but without documented information that a park value is being damaged, it is hard to see how any action can be taken on an external threat. One can almost hear the objections to something being done if no visible proof exists that a park resource is being damaged.

Thus it appears that a strong research effort will be necessary on the external threats issue. This conclusion would not be surprising were it not for the many complaints that the Park Service has traditionally lacked a strong research effort. Beefing up agency research was one of the recommendations of the recent NPCA *Park System Plan*. John Chaffee's bill also proposed the creation of a new research division within the Park Service. Finally, expansion of its resource management role was an internal agency attempt to get at the resource problems facing it.

But this would require organizational change that is usually difficult to accomplish and that might result in other implications for the organization. For example, if park science efforts are strengthened within the agency, there might be a negative outcome such as this worst-case presentation in a journal dedicated to promoting research in national parks:

> What happens . . . when park science is viewed as an end in itself rather than as a tool of park management? When significant numbers of scientific and lay people [presumably environmentalists] view certain parks primarily as scientific benchmarks, gene pools, and relict environments of inestimable value to mankind in a trembling biosphere?
>
> An extreme scenario might go like this: First, certain parks or segments thereof are designated ecological reserves. Second, scientific study, not enjoyment and use, becomes the controlling purpose in such reserves. Third, traditional park management is relieved in favor of a science management board.[12]

The professional values of many scientists suggest that such an outcome, though not likely, is not impossible.

A recent event at Yellowstone provides further evidence of the dangers of scientific management. In 1986, the Yellowstone Park Preservation Council was created to counter what it said was the "prodevelopment" orientation of the park's management.[13] The group's members, made up in large part of Park Service employees, believed they could make "an important contribution to the park's planning process because of their diverse scientific and professional backgrounds."[14] What must be remembered is that scientists, like anyone else, have their personal views on how national parks should be managed. Any attempt to strengthen park science to meet the external threats issue is bound to result in an increase in scientists' opinions about how the parks should be managed.

A second organizational factor that relates to the external threats issue can be found in the Park Service's description of the nature of the external threats problem. This description noted that external threats to park resources would have to be solved in the political process. Solving a controversial problem such as that created by external threats will involve many actors, but certainly one key player would be the Park Service. Yet the Park Service is not oriented toward being a participant in natural resource politics. Some of its superintendents and directors have been successful in achieving agency successes in the political realm, but the agency as a whole does not encourage its decision makers to participate in political decisions. The Park Service traditionally has looked at most of its problems as "within the parks" and, like all natural resource agencies, has tried to assert its expertise in solving them. J. Douglas Wellman captured a dilemma facing most of our natural resource agencies:

> More and more, as well, managers will need to be able to recognize the inevitable limitations of science, and that entails a solid grasp of the scientific method. Most important is that managers bear in mind that science can only inform decisions, it cannot make them.
>
> Interpersonal skills—particularly political skills—will come to the fore in future wildland recreation management. One aspect of management which is especially dependent on such skills is management planning, where conflicting interests must be reconciled.[15]

In other words, the solution to policy problems such as the external threats issue may require a new way of thinking and acting on the part of natural resource policy bureaucracies. Thorny, value-laden resource conflicts, according to Wellman, are not likely to be resolved by better science or more deference to agency expertise but by active agency participation in the political process. Such participation would require something that Hartzog once listed as an essential skill for future Park Service directors: "a lively understanding of politics—that medium through which the public gets its common business done."[16]

How such an appreciation of politics can be instilled in key Park Service officials is hard to answer, but in-service training, entry-level recruitment, and career promotion for successful management of political conflicts are three possible avenues. The Park Service has recently begun to move in the direction of increasing park manager appreciation of the skills necessary to protect park resources and values—for example, establishing clear objectives, anticipating potential impacts, building support for park interests, having knowledge of planning and regulatory processes, being able to compromise while being consistent with a park's purposes, and communicating effectively.[17]

Park managers who had been successful in resolving external threat problems identified twelve factors that had been helpful to them. What is noteworthy about these factors is how many of them suggest skills and behaviors that are not traditionally taught in university natural resource programs or favored by resource professionals uncomfortable with the role of politics in decision making. These points are

1. Get involved early.
2. Coordinate with other federal agencies.
3. Find support from local groups or agencies.
4. Inform people about the local benefits of the park.
5. Share information freely.
6. Have facts to support your position.
7. Suggest alternatives and be positive rather than negative.
8. Ask for what you believe is necessary.
9. Be prepared to negotiate.
10. Try to understand the interests of others.
11. Keep in touch with the players.
12. Be persistent and patient.[18]

Another way to understand the political dimension of the external threats issue is by viewing the Park Service as a type of bureaucracy. For instance, think about how much autonomy the Park Service has over its policy decisions. An example of an agency that had a seemingly high degree of autonomy was the National Aeronautics and Space Administration (NASA) during the 1960s and early 1970s. NASA was given a clearly defined, technologically based task to accomplish (landing a man on the moon), and the rest of our political system appeared to acknowledge NASA's expertise on how to accomplish that objective and thus stayed out of that aspect of the policy by not trying to "second guess" NASA.[19] Barbara Romzek and Mel Dubnick describe NASA as having a "professional accountability" bureaucratic system during this period. Under this system, "the central relationship is similar to that found between a layperson and an expert, with the agency manager taking the role of the layperson and the workers making the important decisions that require their expertise."[20]

The Park Service does not fit the model of such an agency. If the agency task or mission were to manage parks as scientific research preserves, without providing for public use, such deference to expertise might be possible. Other actors in the political system might well defer to biologists and similar professionals about how best to manage a scientific research preserve. But this is not the sole mission of the Park Service. The noted and oft-quoted American writer Wallace Stegner suggested what the mission of the Park Service is about. Parks are, he said, "absolutely American, absolutely democratic, they reflect us at our best. . . . Without them, *millions* of American lives . . . would have been poorer."[21]

What does Stegner mean in terms of public policy and the NPS mission? The Park Service is not an expert agency with a professional accountability system but, rather, a more responsive one with a "political accountability" bureaucratic system. According to Romzek and Dubnick, a political accountability system is concerned with questions of representation, access, and responsiveness to public demands. "The potential constituencies include the general public, elected officials, agency heads, agency clientele, other special interest groups, and future generations. Regardless of which definition of constituency is adopted, the administrator is expected to be responsive to their policy priorities and programmatic needs."[22] Such an agency is squarely within Stegner's definition of parks as "absolutely democratic." The conclusion is inescapable. For the Park Service to address the external threats issue requires the agency to mobilize its most politically adept employees whenever and however possible. The threats problem will be resolved, if it is ever resolved, in the political system. And the Park Service, as part of that system, should have a voice.

## PARK VISITORS AND EXTERNAL THREATS

If one accepts the argument that the external threats issue is a political one, then the park visitor becomes an integral part of the equation. In 1988, there were over 280 million visits to various units in the national park system. Of those, the fifty national parks reported over 56 million.[23] These numbers suggest that there might be a large constituency concerned about the external threats issue. But for that concern to be manifested, those constituents need to be mobilized. What might mobilize them is their perception that their park experiences are in jeopardy.

Certainly, the Park Service can provide some focus through its interpretation programs. At Bryce Canyon, for example, the agency has organized displays about park visibility. But the agency is understandably nervous about being too eager in pointing a finger at external threats for fear of assuming the role of policy advocate, perhaps better played by others. Once an actual threat has entered the political agenda, however, the Park Service can play a role as outlined by the twelve points. However, it is still likely that the Park Service would need help from its supporters to make headway resolving the threats problem.

This is where environmentalists become important and may take an active part. However, Joseph Sax has argued that the environmentalist community has not talked about the visitor experience or about the parks as public places; instead it has tried to use "ecological principles" to resolve difficult public policy questions about the parks.[24] This same approach has also led to environmentalist rhetoric that appears antivisitor. The shift in opinion about Panorama Point (chapter 3) is an example. In 1971, environmentalists supported a road to Panorama Point and argued that the area, including the road, belonged in Canyonlands National Park. In 1977, environmentalists (represented by the Sierra Club) opposed the Park Service plan to keep the road open to Panorama Point in what had become the Glen Canyon National Recreation Area. Even though Glen Canyon had been declared a recreation area rather than a national park (see appendix 3), theoretically making it less "pure" than a national park, environmentalists did not want the road they once supported kept open.

There are other examples. The Wilderness Society, in 1988, urged that all hotels and motels be removed from national parks. The Park Service response, given by then deputy director Dennis Galvin, appeared the model of moderation. The agency, he said, was not in favor of adding hotels to parks, but the "level of development in the traditional parks is appropriate and provides an opportunity for a park experience that's rapidly becoming unique, and just as valid as the backpacking experience."[25] Finally, the NPCA, also in 1988, objected to the slight enlargement of, as well as the provision of several toilets in, a relatively small campground in Canyonlands National Park.[26]

The point should be clear. The external threats issue will not be addressed, let alone resolved, unless it has strong popular support. Environmentalists have the potential to bring this about and indeed have been working on bringing the issue more attention. Yet the inability of the various preservation groups to deal with the "publicness" of the national parks renders their arguments less powerful at best and suspect at worst.

EXTERNAL THREATS:
SOME THOUGHTS ON THEIR RESOLUTION

There have been a variety of proposed legislative remedies for the external threats issue. The most significant problem associated with new legislation concerns the related questions of "who" and "what rule" decide whether an activity, either proposed or ongoing, should be allowed. The first question relates to whether the Park Service or some other actor will have authority over adjacent activities.

The question of authority has received much attention of late with various proposals to remove the Park Service from the Department of the Interior. These proposals stem directly from the policies of the Reagan years. A strong case may be made that during this time Interior did not act to protect parks from external threats. The two case studies provide examples of lack of action by the administration. Thus as William Lockhart, a legal scholar knowledgeable on external threats, argued, park protection needs an "independent institutional advocate."[27] Lockhart linked advocacy with a "grant of clear and concrete policy-making and enforcement authority."[28] He offered a combination of proposals to strengthen the hand of the Park Service. He favored an independent agency, with clear instructions to the Department of the Interior that park protection must continue to be a high priority. He also argued that the Park Service should be given independent litigation authority. Finally, acknowledging the likely political firestorm over new powers given to the Park Service, Lockhart supported legislation such as the 1983 Park Protection Act, where final authority to resolve threats would lie with the relevant congressional committees.

Lockhart's position on the resolution of the threats issue lies at one end of the policy spectrum. Creating an independent Park Service and vesting it with litigation authority is a proposal that has as yet not been entertained by many other actors on the threats issue. Yet Lockhart did not go so far as to suggest that the balance of proof regarding an external threat lies with the agency sponsoring the threat activity. He too supported a weighing of the different values involved in the external threats issue. He seemed to argue for the most effective and forceful representation of park protection values.

I discussed the question of an independent Park Service earlier. But one must be aware of other potential public policy issues that would result from such a reorganization, issues that go far beyond the problem of external threats. Until some of the proponents of an independent Park Service can show that they are not out to severely diminish the "use" side of the agency's mission, independence for the National Park Service will likely be a controversial proposal, as Director Mott has noted.

Other legislative proposals have had less to do with reorganizing the Park Service and more to do with finding an appropriate rule to structure threats decision making. A sweeping "parks come first" approach such as John Chaffee's is not likely to become law, especially when it places the balance of proof with the offending activity. John Seiberling's approach to the problem has more chance of eventually becoming law, but the likelihood still remains low. His 1983 bill did not change the decision rules; rather, it required a "weighing" of park protection versus development values. Yet many of those opposed to the bill thought it created de facto buffers around the park. More important, in 1983, the political climate surrounding the external threats issue did not favor new legislation.

But climates can change. A new administration, a turnover in Congress, or a perceived external threats crisis could all be catalysts in reviving a park protection bill. Such events often provide the crucial "window of opportunity" necessary for the adoption of new public policies.[29] As of this writing, the position of the Bush administration was not developed. Even so, the question of whether a uniform procedure to deal with all threats is justified at this point remains unanswered. There may, however, be several things that could be first approaches on the issue.

One possible approach has been discussed in some detail already. The secretary of the Interior could instruct the Park Service to develop an adverse-impacts directive to evaluate certain activities next to parks. Perhaps a useful starting point might be to demand an evaluation of any activities subject to NEPA and requiring an EIS. Such information would obviously be helpful to both decision makers and park supporters (such as the NPCA). In some cases, it might persuade the secretary to closely monitor Interior activities for their impact on parks. The key question is whether a secretary is likely to order such a directive on his/her own. If not, it would be up to Congress to require that it be done.

A second option is to prioritize the units that appear most threatened by external threats. The *State of the Parks* report made some attempt to do so, but the listing relied heavily on manager perception rather than hard data, so the ranking was suspect. Still, some rank ordering of units by number of threats, if properly arrived at, would be useful. By itself, however, such a list would be insufficient. Of the top ten parks listed in the *State of the Parks* report, three were well-known crown jewels: Yosemite, Yellowstone, and Glacier. Several others were national recreation areas close to urban centers: Cuyahoga, Santa Monica, and Chattahoochee. Yosemite, Yellowstone, and Glacier have additional distinctions. Yosemite is a world heritage site, Glacier a biosphere reserve, and Yellowstone both. A world heritage site is an area believed to have outstanding value as part of the world's natural heritage. It is nominated by an interagency panel, based on criteria developed through international agreement. A biosphere reserve is similar. As the Park Service put it: "Individual park ecosystems or park lands that are components of regional ecosystems believed to be internationally significant examples of one of the world's natural regions" are eligible.[30] The criteria were developed by the United Nations.

Such designations give these three parks special recognition. They also suggest a way to prioritize the most important parks threatened by outside activities. The "ecosystem" approach to the external threats issue could perhaps be applied selectively at Yellowstone, Glacier, and Yosemite. If these areas cannot be protected from harmful adjacent activities, what hope would there be for lesser known, less significant units? These three parks deserve more initial attention than urban recreation areas. Given budget and personnel constraints, such an approach makes sense.

When he was chief of the Water Resources Branch in the Park Service, the late Tom Lucke had a provocative idea. Noting that Congress has permitted mining in some units of the park system, he referred to the Park Service as having a "triple" mandate rather than a dual one in these units.[31] In other words, in selected areas, the Park Service manages for multiple use. Several of these areas, notably Denali and Big Thicket, were also biosphere reserves, Lucke noted. A biosphere reserve is supposed to have a core area protected from development, with development increasing as one moves away from this core. Lucke was not suggesting opening up biosphere reserve areas such as Yellowstone to development. Rather, he believed that the Park Service's multiple-use resource management skills and values could be applied to areas outside these core protected areas. This is a somewhat radical suggestion, since it turns an old argument on its head. For years, the Forest Service has argued with some success that it could manage areas for recreation and preservation as well as the Park Service while still allowing for multiple use. For critical areas like Yellowstone, the reverse may be necessary. What may be needed are multiple-use management policies that look toward the protection of the core of the ecosystem, or biosphere reserve. Could the Park Service provide those policies for these key areas?

None of these suggestions will happen, however, without an effective political coalition to support park protection. The external threats issue is a problem of competing values. The parks have so many different meanings and, consequently, values for so many different people, and we as a nation have valued our public lands for so many different things, that it is difficult to imagine the formation of a single coalition to protect the parks. Yet that is the goal. If we can come together in our love for our parks, then the external threats issue might be resolved.

# Key Legislation from the Organic Act and Its Amendments

The section of this legislation that sets administrative policy guidelines for the National Park Service reads:

> The service thus established shall promote and regulate the use of the Federal areas known as national parks, monuments and reservations hereinafter specified by such means and measures as conform to the fundamental purpose of the said parks, monuments, and reservations, which purpose is to conserve the scenery and the natural and historical objects and the wildlife therein and to provide for the enjoyment of the same in such manner and by such means as will leave them unimpaired for the enjoyment of future generations.

Further clarification of the Park Service's mission and the composition of a park unit can be found in 16 U.S.C. 1c(a) and (b):

> (a) The "national park system" shall include any area of land and water now or hereafter administered by the Secretary of the Interior through the National Park Service for park, monument, historic, parkway, recreational or other purposes.

> (b) Each area within the national park system shall be administered in accordance with the provisions of any statute made specifically applicable to that area. In addition the provisions [here follows a long list of various statutes] shall to the extent such provisions are not in conflict with any such specific provision, be applicable to all areas within the national park system and any reference in such Acts to national parks, monuments, recreation areas, historic monuments, or parkways shall hereinafter not be construed as limiting such Acts to those areas.

In 1978, in response to *Sierra Club v. Department of the Interior* (376 F. Supp. 284 [N.D. Cal., 1974]; 398 F. Supp. 284 [N.D. Cal., 1975]; 424 F. Supp. 172 [N.D. Cal., 1976]), Congress amended 16 U.S.C. 1a-1 to read in part:

Congress further reaffirms, declares, and directs that the promotion and regulation of the various areas of the National Park System, as defined in section 1(c) of this article, shall be consistent with and founded in the purpose established by section 1 of this title to the common benefit of all the people of the United States. The authorization of activities shall be construed and the protection, management, and administration of these areas shall be conducted in light of the high public value and integrity of the National Park System and shall not be exercised in derogation of the values and purposes for which these various areas are established, except as may have been or shall be directly and specifically provided by Congress.

# Units in
# the U.S. National Park System

The Park Service provides the following nomenclature for units of the park system in its 1982 *Index of the National Park System and Related Areas*:

Generally, a *national park* covers a large area. It contains a variety of resources and encompasses sufficient land or water to help provide adequate protection of the resources.

A *national monument* is intended to preserve at least one nationally significant resource. It is usually smaller than a national park and lacks its diversity of attractions.

In 1974, Big Cypress and Big Thicket were authorized as the first *national preserves*. This category is established primarily for the protection of certain resources. Activities such as hunting and fishing or the extraction of minerals and fuels may be permitted if they do not jeopardize the natural values.

Preserving shoreline areas and off-shore islands, the *national lakeshores* and *national seashores* focus on the preservation of natural values while at the same time providing water-oriented recreation. Although national lakeshores can be established on any natural freshwater lake, the existing four are all located on the Great Lakes. The national seashores are on the Atlantic, Gulf, and Pacific coasts.

*National rivers* and *wild and scenic riverways* preserve ribbons of land bordering on free-flowing streams which have not been dammed, channelized, or otherwise altered by man. Besides preserving rivers in their natural state, these areas provide opportunities for outdoor activities such as hiking, canoeing, and hunting.

In recent years, *national historic site* has been the title most commonly applied by Congress in authorizing the addition of such areas to the National Park System. A wide variety of titles—*national military park, national battlefield park, national battlefield site,* and *national battlefield*—have been used for areas associated with American military history. But other

147

areas such as *national monuments* and *national historic parks* may include features associated with military history. *National historic parks* are commonly areas of greater physical extent and complexity than national historic sites.

The title *national memorial* is most often used for areas that are primarily commemorative. But they need not be sites or structures historically associated with their subjects. For example, the home of Abraham Lincoln in Springfield, Illinois, is a national historic site, but the Lincoln Memorial in the District of Columbia is a national memorial.

Several areas administered by the National Capital Region whose titles do not include the words national memorial are nevertheless classified as memorials. The John F. Kennedy Center for the Performing Arts, Lincoln Memorial, Lyndon Baines Johnson Memorial Grove on the Potomac, Theodore Roosevelt Island, Thomas Jefferson Memorial, and the Washington Monument—all in the District of Columbia.

Originally, *national recreation areas* in the Park System were units surrounding reservoirs impounded by dams built by other federal agencies. The National Park Service manages many of these areas under cooperative agreements. The concept of recreation areas has grown to encompass other lands and waters set aside for recreational use by acts of Congress and now includes major areas in urban centers. There are also national recreation areas outside the National Park System that are administered by the Forest Service.

*National parkways* encompass ribbons of land flanking roadways and offer an opportunity for leisurely driving through areas of scenic interest. They are not designed for high speed point-to-point travel. Besides the areas set aside as parkways, other units of the National Park System include parkways within their boundaries.

Two areas of the National Park System have been set aside primarily as *sites for the performing arts*. These are Wolf Trap Farm Park for the Performing Arts, Va., America's first such national park, and the John F. Kennedy Center for the Performing Arts, D.C. Two historical areas, Ford's Theatre National Historic Site, D.C., and Chazimal National Memorial, Texas, also provide facilities for the performing arts.

Out of a total system of 79,602,170 acres, as tabulated at the end of September 1987, the following unit types are the four largest in the system:

| | |
|---|---:|
| National parks | 47,242,673 |
| National monuments | 4,717,182 |
| National preserves | 21,960,218 |
| National recreation areas | 3,686,830 |
| Total | 77,606,903 |

# Questionnaire That Formed the Basis of the *State of the Parks* Report

Park superintendents were first given the following statement from which to make their threats evaluations: "In the light of the Enabling Legislation, the Legislative History, and the Statement for Management, What Threats Are Impacting the Park Resources and to What Extent?"

The following determinations were to be made of each threat:

THREAT LEVEL (check one)
1. None that can be determined
2. Suspected, but needs research to document adequately
3. Yes, but needs research to document adequately
4. Yes, adequately documented by research and data available

SOURCE (check one)
1. Internal threat
2. External threat

PLAN (check one)
1. Addressed in Area Resources Management Plan
2. Not addressed in Area Resources Management Plan

THREATS
*Air Pollution*
Suspended Particulates (visibility)
- smoke
- dust
- chemicals
- fog (water condensate)

CO
$CO_2$
Hydrocarbons
Acid Rain
$NO_x$
Odors

Radioactivity
Other
*Water Quality Pollution (Surface and Ground) and Water Quality Changes*
Chemical
Sewage
Salt/Sediment Deposition or Erosion
Geothermal
Unnatural Flooding or Flow Decreases
Oil Spills
Radioactivity
Acid Mine Drainage
Other Toxic Chemicals (e.g., Sulfur, Acids, Biocides, etc.)
Other
*Aesthetic Degradation*
Mineral Surveys, Development, Extraction, and Production
Timbering
Grazing or Agriculture
Forest Disease/Pest Infestations
Wildland Fires
Land Development
Utility Access—Powerlines, Pipelines
Roads and Railroads
Vista (road signs, inholdings, etc.)
Urban Encroachments
Overcrowding and Vandalism
Other
*Physical Removal of Resources*
Logging
Mineral Extraction
Gas and Oil Extraction
Hunting, Poaching, or Overharvesting
Fishing, Poaching, or Overharvesting
Grazing
Berry and Fruit Picking
Specimen Collecting
Soil Erosion
Fire, Landslides, Other Catastrophies
American Indian Freedom of Religion Activities
Archaeological Collecting
Other
*Exotic Encroachment*
Animals
Plants

Unnatural Fire
Unnatural Weather (cloud seeding, etc.)
Noise
- motor vehicles
- aircraft
- industrial
- visitor

Seismic-blasting Shocks, Sonic Booms, etc.
Other
*Visitor Physical Impacts*
Campfires
Trampling
Erosion
Wildlife Harassment
Habitat Destruction
Cross-country Skiing
Offroad Vehicles
Subtle Influences (e.g., algae growth in caves)
Other
*Park Operations*
Roads and Utility Corridors
Trails
Facilities
Research (collecting, etc.)
Suppression of Natural Fires
Misuse of Biocides
Employee Ignorance
Political Pressures
Other

# NOTES

PREFACE

1. This quotation and the next are from William Newmark, "A Land-Bridge Island Perspective on Mammalian Extinctions in Western North American Parks," *Nature* 325, 29 (January 1987): 432.
2. Sue O'Connell, "Will Glacier Be Victimized by Thirst for Oil?" *San Diego Union*, January 7, 1990, p. C-6.
3. Ibid.
4. Ibid.
5. Wallace Stegner, "The Best Idea We Ever Had," *Wilderness* 46 (Spring 1983): 4.


CHAPTER ONE. STUDYING
THE EXTERNAL THREATS PROBLEM

1. *United States Code* (1982), Title 16, Section 1.
2. These two points of view can be found in Ronald Foresta, *America's National Parks and Their Keepers* (Baltimore: Johns Hopkins University Press, for Resources for the Future, 1984), p. 268, and in National Parks and Conservation Association and the Wilderness Society, "Towards a Premier National Park System" (mimeo), 1984, p. 5
3. The various types of national park units (see appendix 2), as well as variations in enabling legislation for each unit, further complicate National Park Service attempts to consistently manage these units.
4. United States, Department of the Interior, National Park Service, "State of the Parks 1981: A Report to the Congress on a Servicewide Strategy for Prevention and Mitigation of Natural and Cultural Resources Management Problems" (mimeo), 1981, p. 90.
5. Ibid., pp. vii–x.
6. William C. Everhart, *The National Park Service* (Boulder, Colo.: Westview Press, 1983), p. 182.
7. J. Douglas Wellman, *Wildland Recreation Policy* (New York: John Wiley and Sons, 1987), p. 238.
8. Foresta, *America's National Parks*, p. 233.
9. Ibid., p. 93.
10. William Malm and John Molenar, "Visibility Measurements in National Parks in the Western U.S." (unpublished manuscript), 1982, p. 14.
11. Temple, Baker, and Sloan (firm), *Mineral Ownership and Development Activity in and around the National Parks* (Lexington, Mass.: Temple, Baker, and Sloan, 1985), pp. iv–3.
12. Dave Milhalic, "Tending Alaska's Outposts," *National Parks* 59, 3–4 (March-April 1985): 19–20.

13. United States, Department of the Interior, National Park Service, "Protection Authorities" (draft), p. 30.

14. Conservation Foundation, *National Parks for a New Generation* (Washington, D.C.: Conservation Foundation, 1985), p. 51.


CHAPTER TWO. THE EMERGENCE OF EXTERNAL
THREATS AS A POLICY AND
MANAGEMENT ISSUE


1. George Catlin, *North American Indians, Being Letters and Notes on Their Manners, Customs, and Conditions, Written during Eight Years' Travel amongst the Wildest Tribes of Indians in North America*, 2 vols. (Philadelphia: N.p., 1913), 1:294–95, quoted in Roderick Nash, *Wilderness and the American Mind*, 2d edition (New Haven, Conn.: Yale University Press, 1973), p. 101.

2. Alfred Runte, *National Parks: The American Experience* (Lincoln: University of Nebraska Press, 1987), p. 47. Technically, in 1832 Congress set aside a small area in Arkansas as Hot Springs Reservation. However, it is unclear that the purpose of this reservation—to place medicinal hot springs under public control—deserves serious acknowledgment as the "first park" when compared with Yellowstone or Yosemite.

3. Aubrey Haines, *The Yellowstone Story*, 2 vols. (Boulder, Colo.: Yellowstone Library and Museum Association and Colorado Associated University Press, 1977), 1:172–73; H. Duane Hampton, *How the U.S. Cavalry Saved Our National Parks* (Bloomington: University of Indiana Press, 1971), p. 19.

4. Runte, *National Parks*, p. 27.

5. Ibid., p. 5.

6. Nash, *Wilderness and the American Mind*, especially chapters 6 and 7. See also Hans Huth, *Nature and the American: Three Centuries of Changing Attitudes* (Berkeley and Los Angeles: University of California Press, 1957).

7. Runte, *National Parks*, chapters 1 and 2.

8. *United States Statutes at Large* 17 (1872), pp. 32–33.

9. Ibid.

10. Ibid.

11. Robert Shankland, *Steve Mather of the National Parks*, 1st edition (New York: Alfred A. Knopf, 1954), p. 151.

12. *United States Statutes at Large* 34 (1906), p. 225.

13. Hampton, *How the U.S. Cavalry Saved Our National Parks*, pp. 79, 129–30, 145–46.

14. Ibid.

15. Ibid., p. 173.

16. Ibid., p. 165.

17. Donald Swain, "The Passage of the National Park Service Act of 1916," *Wisconsin Magazine of History* 50, 1 (Autumn 1966): 5.

18. For a detailed description of the Hetch Hetchy controversy see Nash, *Wilderness and the American Mind*, chapter 10.

19. Swain, "Passage of National Park Service Act," p. 7.

20. Ibid., p. 13.

21. *United States Statutes at Large* 39 (1916), p. 535.

22. *First Annual Report of the Director of the National Park Service to the Secretary of Interior for the Fiscal Year Ended June 30, 1917* (Washington, D.C.: GPO, 1917), p. 2.

23. Ibid., pp. 9–10.

24. Ibid., p. 20.

25. Ibid., p. 98.

26. Swain, "Passage of National Park Service Act," p. 13.

27. Philip O. Foss, *Recreation*, in the series *Conservation in the United States: A Documentary History* (New York: Chelsea House Publishers, 1971), p. 185; see also Horace Albright, *The Birth of the National Park Service* (Salt Lake City: Howe Bros., 1986), p. 69.

28. Foss, *Recreation*, p. 185.

29. Ibid., p. 187.

30. Ibid., p. 185.

31. For an elaboration of this facet of park promotion, see Runte, *National Parks*, chapter 5.

32. Shankland, *Steve Mather*, p. 202.

33. For a full account of this episode, see ibid., pp. 209–10.

34. Swain, "Passage of National Park Service Act," p. 16.

35. *United States Code* (1982), Title 16, Section 348.

36. United States, Department of the Interior, National Park Service, *Fauna Series 1* (Washington, D.C.: GPO, 1932), p. 317.

37. Ibid., p. 38.

38. Ibid., p. 142.

39. Ibid., p. 37.

40. Runte, *National Parks*, pp. 138–39.

41. Ibid., p. 146.

42. I thank William Supernaugh for pointing this out to me in his review of a draft of this chapter.

43. "Study of Wildlife Problems in the National Parks," *Reports of the Special Advisory Board on Wildlife Management for the Secretary of Interior* (Washington, D.C.: N.p., 1963–1968; reprinted by the Wildlife Institute, 1969), p. 3.

44. Ibid., p. 5.

45. Ibid., p. 7.

46. Ibid., p. 10.

47. National Academy of Sciences, *A Report by the Advisory Committee to the National Park Service on Research* (Washington, D.C.: GPO, 1963), p. x.

48. Ibid., p. xiv.

49. John Ise, *Our National Park Policy: A Critical History* (Baltimore: Johns Hopkins University Press, for Resources for the Future, 1960), p. 371; and the Robertson Report, quoted in *Advisory Committee on Research*, p. 85.

50. Foss, *Recreation*, p. 198.

51. Ibid., p. 199.

52. Further calls were made for increased study of park ecosystems by the Conservation Foundation in its 1972 *Parks for the Future* report and by Durward Allen and A. Starker Leopold in their review of the Park Service's science program in 1977 (see Robert Cahn, "State of the Parks," *Audubon* 22, 3 [May 1980]: 21–22).

53. Comment by William Supernaugh on a draft of this chapter.

54. Outdoor Recreation Resources Review Commission (ORRRC), *Federal Agencies and Outdoor Recreation*, ORRRC Study Report, no. 13 (Washington, D.C.:

GPO, 1962), p. 34. Further reading also illustrates the infancy of the ecology movement. Foss cites Forest Service concern that the Park Service took too much land when it acquired a park. Of course, today some conservationists argue that park boundaries do not include entire ecosystems and thus are too small.

55. Ronald Foresta, *America's National Parks and Their Keepers* (Baltimore: Johns Hopkins University Press, for Resources for the Future, 1984), p. 54.

56. F. Fraser Darling and Noel D. Eichhorn, "Man and Nature in the National Parks," in Walt Anderson, ed., *Politics and the Environment* (Pacific Palisades, Calif.: Goodyear Publishing Company, 1970), p. 207.

57. Foresta, *America's National Parks*, p. 55.

58. Ibid., p. 97. For a summary account of the growth of ecological awareness and its effect on the Park Service, see ibid., pp. 104–27.

59. National Parks and Conservation Association (NPCA), "NPCA Adjacent Lands Survey: No Park Is an Island," *National Parks and Conservation Magazine* 53, 3 (March 1979): 4–9, and *National Parks and Conservation Magazine* 53, 4 (April 1979): 4–7.

60. Ibid. (March 1979): 4.

61. Ibid. (April 1979): 5.

62. Ibid., p. 7.

63. William E. Shands, *Federal Resource Lands and Their Neighbors* (Washington, D.C.: Conservation Foundation, 1979), pp. 12–13.

64. Ibid., pp. 21 and 29.

65. Joseph Sax, in his *Mountains without Handrails* (Ann Arbor: University of Michigan Press, 1980), argues that some environmentalists have gone astray in defending the parks primarily for their ecological integrity. Rather, he says, it is the quality of the experience within a park that should be promoted and protected.

66. Shands, *Federal Resource Lands*, pp. 21 and 29.

67. Ibid., p. 43.

68. Ibid.

69. Ibid., p. 56.

70. Ibid., p. 73.

71. Ibid., p. 60.

72. Ibid., p. 66.

73. For a comprehensive discussion of NEPA, see the series of articles entitled "Enclosing the Environment: NEPA's Transformation of Conservation into Environmentalism," in *Natural Resources Journal*, 25th Anniversary Anthology (1985).

74. Michael Reagan, *Regulation* (Boston: Little, Brown, 1986), p. 183.

75. *United States Code* (1982), Title 42, Section 7401 et seq.

76. 91 Stat. 509, Section 522(e)(3).

77. United States, Department of the Interior, National Park Service, "Protection Authorities" (draft), 1986, p. 1.

78. William C. Everhart, *The National Park Service* (Boulder, Colo.: Westview Press, 1983), pp. 19–22.

79. United States, Department of the Interior, National Park Service, *Index of the National Park System and Related Areas* (Washington, D.C.: GPO, 1982).

80. United States, Department of the Interior, National Park Service, *State of the Parks, 1980: A Report to the Congress* (Washington, D.C.: GPO, 1980), pp. 37–44.

81. This quotation and next are in ibid., pp. viii and ix.

82. Ibid., p. 5.
83. Ibid., p. 56.
84. Ibid., p. 35.
85. Ibid., pp. 35-36.
86. Robert Cahn, "Forgotten Values," *Audubon* 84, 4 (July 1982): 32.
87. For a summary of the Park Service mitigation plan, see Gary Gregory, "State of the Parks, 1980: Problems and Plans," in Eugenia Connally, ed., *National Park in Crisis* (Washington, D.C.: National Parks and Conservation Association, 1982), pp. 85-87.
88. United States, Department of the Interior, National Park Service, "State of the Parks, 1981: A Report to the Congress on a Servicewide Strategy for Prevention and Mitigation of Natural and Cultural Resources Management Problems" (mimeo), 1981, pp. 1-13.
89. Ibid., p. 13.
90. Ibid., p. 44.
91. Cahn, "Forgotten Values," p. 34.
92. Ibid., p. 36.
93. This quotation and the next are in U.S. Congress, Senate, Committee on Energy and Natural Resources, "National Park Policy under James Watt," statement of the National Parks and Conservation Association, *William Clark Nomination Hearings*, November 1 and 2, 1983 (Washington, D.C.: GPO, 1983), pp. 196 and 197.
94. *Congressional Quarterly Almanac-1982* (Washington, D.C.: Congressional Quarterly Press, 1982), p. 445. For a complete text of the subcommittee hearings, see U.S. Congress, House, *Hearings before the Subcommittee on Public Lands and the National Parks of the Committee on Interior and Insular Affairs on HR 5552, 5162, and 5976*, 97th Congress, 2d session, 1982, Serial 97-8, part 3.
95. A discussion of these sections of Seiberling's bill can be found in U.S. Congress, House, *Providing for the Protection and Management of the National Park System and for Other Purposes*, 98th Congress, 1st session, 1983, H. Rept. 98-170, pp. 4-7.
96. Ibid., pp. 8-9.
97. Ibid., p. 9.
98. Ibid., p. 10.
99. For the best example of this testimony, see the comments of Russell Dickenson, then director of the National Park Service, pp. 435-52 of the 1982 House Hearings (note 94).
100. H. Rept. 98-170, pp. 12-13.
101. Paul Culhane, "Sagebrush Rebels in Office: Jim Watt's Land and Water Politics," in Michael Kraft and Norman Vig, eds., *Environmental Policy in the 1980s* (Washington, D.C.: Congressional Quarterly Press, 1984), pp. 293-318.
102. *Congressional Record*, October 4, 1983, pp. H7917-18; on the court issue, see ibid., p. H7921.
103. Ibid., p. H7919.
104. Ibid.
105. For mining industry opposition to the proposed legislation, see U.S. Congress, House, *Hearings before the Subcommittee on Public Lands and National Parks of the Committee on Interior and Insular Affairs*, 98th Congress, 1st session, 1983, Serial 98-8, part 10, pp. 431-34.
106. Ibid., p. H7920.
107. For a general discussion of the powers of Congress to regulate nonfed-

eral activities on private lands, see Joseph Sax, "Helpless Giants: The National Parks and the Regulation of Private Lands," *Michigan Law Review* 75, 4 (December 1976): 239–74, and Ronald Frank and John Eckhardt, "Power of Congress under the Property Clause to Give Extraterritorial Effect to Federal Lands Law: Will 'Respecting Property' Go the Way of 'Affecting Commerce'?" *Natural Resources Lawyer* 15, 4 (December 1983): 663–86. On the political difficulties, see Frank and Eckhardt, p. 684. The NPCA has also published a helpful book on many of the statutes that relate to aspects of the external threats issue.

108. Foresta, *America's National Parks*, pp. 248 and 284.

109. 36 *Code of Federal Regulations*, parts 25, 27, 28, 30, and 31.

110. Sax, "Helpless Giants," p. 244.

111. "An Ordinance of the Board of Supervisors of Pima County, Arizona, Amending the Natural Pima County Zoning Code," Ordinance 85-82 (draft).

112. Personal communication, William Paleck, November 12, 1988.

113. "Threatened near Tucson," *High Country News*, July 18, 1988, p. 4.

114. Luther Propst, Dwight Merriam, and Christopher Duerksen, "Local Governments and Park Natural Resources" (mimeo), Conservation Foundation, Washington, D.C., 1988.

115. U.S. Congress, Senate, *A Bill to Further Protect the Outstanding Scenic, Natural, and Scientific Values of the Grand Canyon by Enlarging the Grand Canyon National Park in the State of Arizona, and for Other Purposes*, 93d Congress, 2d session, 1973, S. 1296.

116. *Congressional Record*, August 2, 1973, S. 27539.

117. *High Country News*, February 16, 1987, p. 4; see also *Ten Most Endangered National Parks*, Wilderness Society news release, May 24, 1988.

118. U.S. Congress, Senate, *A Bill to Provide for Consistent Federal Actions Affecting Resources of the National Park System and for Other Purposes*, 99th Congress, 2d session, 1986, S. 2092.

119. Ibid., section 103.

120. Ibid.

121. Ibid., section 106.

122. Ibid.

123. United States, Department of the Interior, National Park Service, *Index of the National Park System* (Washington, D.C.: GPO, 1987).

124. S. 2092, section 110.

125. U.S. Congress, House, *Oversight Hearings before the Subcommittee on Public Lands and the Subcommittee on National Parks and Recreation, of the Committee on Interior and Insular Affairs, House of Representatives, on the Greater Yellowstone Ecosystem*, 99th Congress, 1st session, 1985, p. 2.

126. Harold Seidman and Robert Gilmour, *Politics, Position, and Power* (New York: Oxford University Press, 1986), p. 223.

127. Charles E. Little, "The Challenge of Greater Yellowstone," *Wilderness* 160 (Winter 1987): 54.

128. George B. Hartzog, Jr., *Battling for the National Parks: A Political and Personal Memoir* (Mount Kisco, N.Y.: Moyer Bell, 1988), p. 258.

129. *Hearings on Greater Yellowstone Ecosystem*, pp. 47–48.

130. Bruce Fahrling, "A Still-Wild Chunk of America Is Vulnerable to Development," *High Country News*, March 31, 1986, p. 1.

131. United States, General Accounting Office, *Limited Progress Made in Documenting and Mitigating Threats to Parks* (Washington, D.C.: GAO, 1987), p. 51.

132. For a useful starting point, see Robert Keiter, "On Protecting the Na-

tional Parks from the External Threats Dilemma," *Land and Water Law Review* 20, 2 (1985): 355–420.

133. *United States Code* (1982), Title 16, Section 1a–1.

134. Robert Keiter, "National Park Protection: Putting the Organic Act to Work," in David Simon, ed., *Our Common Lands* (Washington, D.C.: Island Press, 1988), pp. 79–80.

135. National Park and Conservation Association, *Investing in Park Futures: Executive Summary* (Washington, D.C.: NPCA, 1988).

136. Ibid., p. 23.

137. *Federal Parks and Recreation*, February 13, 1986, p. 7.

138. William Lockhart, "External Park Threats and Interior's Limits: The Need for an Independent Park Service," in Simon, ed., *Our Common Lands*, pp. 23–24.

139. General Accounting Office, *Limited Progress Made in Threats to Parks*, pp. 13–14.

140. Lockhart, "External Park Threats and Interior's Limits," pp. 23–24.

## CHAPTER THREE. THE CREATION OF GLEN CANYON NATIONAL RECREATION AREA

1. United States, Department of the Interior, *Report of the Secretary of Interior* (Washington, D.C.: GPO, 1939), p. 292. For a map of this proposal, see *Desert Magazine* 4 (April 1941): 20–22.

2. Ronald Foresta, *America's National Parks and Their Keepers* (Baltimore: Johns Hopkins University Press, for Resources for the Future, 1984), p. 49.

3. United States, Department of the Interior, National Park Service, *Parks for America* (Washington, D.C.: GPO, 1964), p. 450.

4. Phillip Fradkin, *A River No More* (New York: Knopf, 1981), pp. 186–91.

5. Ivan Goslin, "Colorado River Development," in Dean Peterson and Barry Crawford, eds., *Values and Choices in the Development of the Colorado River Basin* (Tucson: University of Arizona Press, 1978), p. 40.

6. Helen Ingram, "The Politics of Water Allocation," in Peterson and Crawford, eds., *Values and Choices*, p. 63.

7. This argument surfaces again and again throughout the hearings on the Colorado River Basin Storage Project Act in 1955. Phillip Sirotkin and Owen Stratton's *The Echo Park Controversy*, Interuniversity Case Study Series, no. 46 (Syracuse, N.Y., 1959), is a good place to start reviewing water resource policy.

8. There are several excellent accounts of the Echo Park controversy. Two are Elmo Richardson, *Dams, Parks, and Politics: Resource Development and Preservation in the Truman-Eisenhower Era* (Lexington: University Press of Kentucky, 1973), and Sirotkin and Stratton, *The Echo Park Controversy*.

9. Resources for the Future, *The Southwest under Stress* (Baltimore: Johns Hopkins University Press, 1981), pp. 14–15.

10. Ibid., p. 13.

11. United States, Department of the Interior, Bureau of Land Management (BLM), *Utah Combined Hydrocarbon Leasing Regional Final EIS*, 4 vols. (Washington, D.C.: GPO, 1984), 1:17.

12. Howard Ritzma, "Utah's Tar Sand Resource: Geology, Politics, and Economics," in J. W. Smith and M. J. Atwood, eds., *Oil Shale and Tar Sands*, vol. 72, no. 155 (New York: American Institute of Chemical Engineers, 1976), p. 48.

13. Ibid.

14. Ibid.

15. Ibid.

16. Oblad, Seader, Miller, and Burger (firm), "Recovery of Bitumen from Oil-Impregnated Sandstone Deposits of Utah," in Smith and Atwood, *Oil Shale*, p. 70.

17. Ritzma, "Utah's Tar Sand Resource," p. 47.

18. BLM, *Utah Combined Hydrocarbon Leasing*, p. 19.

19. Ibid., p. 21.

20. Ibid.

21. General discussions I have had with park personnel, as well as my own experience with the Park Service, seem to point to the public's acceptance of a generic "national park." That is, if the Park Service administers the area, it's a "park," not a monument, recreation area, or preserve. Thus certain expectations exist with interesting implications for management.

There is more confusion among the public about the specific duties and roles of federal land management agencies. Everyone they meet in a uniform appears to be a "ranger," who is expected to know and do certain things.

22. United States, Department of the Interior, National Park Service, *Index of the National Park System and Related Areas* (Washington, D.C.: GPO, 1982), p. 9.

23. James Gilligan, "The Development of Policy and Administration of Forest Service Primitive and Wilderness Areas in the U.S." (Ph.D. dissertation, University of Michigan, Ann Arbor, 1953), quoted in Samuel Dana and Sally Fairfax, *Forest and Range Policy* (New York: McGraw-Hill, 1980), p. 154.

24. Dana and Fairfax, *Forest and Range Policy*, p. 154.

25. Harold Ickes, *The Secret Diary of Harold Ickes*, quoted in Dana and Fairfax, *Forest and Range Policy*, p. 154.

26. U.S. Congress, Senate, *Hearings before Subcommittee on National Parks and Recreation of the Committee on Interior and Insular Affairs on S. 27, "A Bill to Establish Glen Canyon National Recreation Area,"* 92d Congress, 2d session, 1971, p. 44.

27. Ibid., pp. 4, 59, 76, 80, and especially 74 on the access question.

28. Ibid., p. 49.

29. U.S. Congress, Senate, Committee on Interior and Insular Affairs, *Establishing the Glen Canyon National Recreation Area in Arizona and Utah*, 92d Congress, 1st session, 1971, S. Rept. 92-156, pp. 2–3.

30. S. Rept. 92-156, quoted in *Congressional Record*, June 21, 1971, p. 20918.

31. U.S. Congress, House, *Hearings before Subcommittee on National Parks and Recreation of the Committee on Interior and Insular Affairs on HR 15073 and Related Bills*, 93d Congress, 1st session, 1972, p. 36.

32. Ibid., p. 37.

33. Ibid., p. 47.

34. Ibid., p. 42.

35. Ibid., p. 254.

36. Ibid., p. 263.

37. *United States Code* (1982), Title 16, Section 460dd(5).

38. House, *Hearings on HR 15073 and Related Bills* (1972), p. 40.

39. Ibid., p. 245.

40. Ibid., p. 44.

41. Ibid., pp. 87 and 89.
42. Ibid.
43. Ibid., p. 304.
44. See Alfred Runte, *National Parks: The American Experience* (Lincoln: University of Nebraska Press, 1987).
45. House, *Hearings on HR 15073 and Related Bills* (1972), p. 72.
46. Ibid., p. 73.
47. Ibid., p. 258.
48. Ibid., p. 33.
49. U.S. Congress, House, *Establishing the Glen Canyon National Recreation Area in Arizona and Utah*, 92d Congress, 2d session, 1972, H. Rept. 92-1446, p. 8.
50. *Congressional Record*, October 13, 1972, p. 36098.
51. Ibid.
52. *Congressional Record*, October 12, 1972, p. 35292.
53. *Congressional Record*, October 13, 1972, p. 36150.
54. *Congressional Record*, October 14, 1972, pp. 36207-8.
55. *United States Code* (1982), Title 16, Section 1(c)(b).
56. Ibid., Section 460dd(3).
57. Ibid.
58. Ibid., Section 460dd(2).
59. House, *Hearings on HR 15073 and Related Bills* (1972), p. 254.
60. United States, Department of the Interior, National Park Service and Bureau of Land Management, *Tar Sand Triangle* [DEIS] (Denver: NPS, 1984), pp. 1-10.
61. Public Law 94-458, Section 12. Paul Culhane and Paul Friesema note that the Park Service was the first federal land management agency to become involved in land-use planning ("Land Use Planning for the Public Lands," *Natural Resources Journal* 19 [January 1979]: 69).
62. United States, Department of the Interior, National Park Service, *Management Policies* (Denver: NPS, 1975), p. 2-1.
63. Ibid., p. 2-3.
64. United States, Department of the Interior, National Park Service, *Proposed General Management Plan, Wilderness Recommendation, Road Study Alternatives, and Final Environmental Impact Statement, Glen Canyon National Recreation Area, Arizona-Utah* (Washington, D.C.: GPO, 1979), p. 6.
65. Ibid.
66. Ibid., p. 79.
67. Ibid.
68. Ibid., p. 177.
69. Ibid., p. 195.
70. Ibid., p. 179.
71. Ibid., p. 205.
72. Ibid., p. 158.
73. Ibid.
74. Ibid., p. 156.
75. Ibid., p. 229.
76. Ibid.
77. Ibid.
78. See, for example, the *Proposed General Management Plan, Glen Canyon National Recreation Area*, pp. 241-42 (Friends of the Earth) and p. 246 (National Parks and Conservation Association).

79. Ibid., p. 229.
80. Ibid., pp. 267–68.
81. United States, Department of the Interior, National Park Service, *Minerals Management Plan, Glen Canyon National Recreation Area, Arizona-Utah* (Denver: NPS, 1980), p. 14.
82. Francis Rourke, *Bureaucracy, Politics, and Public Policy*, 3d edition (Boston: Little, Brown, 1984), p. 31.
83. Foresta, *America's National Parks*, p. 45.
84. Rourke, *Bureaucracy, Politics, and Public Policy*, p. 43.
85. *Proposed General Management Plan, Glen Canyon National Recreation Area*, p. 246. Contrast the preservationists' opposition to this road with their support for roads in general during the 1972 Senate hearings (Senate, *Hearings to Establish Glen Canyon National Recreation Area*, p. 76).

## CHAPTER FOUR. THE TAR SANDS LEASING CONTROVERSY

1. U.S. Congress, Senate, Committee on Energy and Natural Resources, *Facilitating and Encouraging the Production of Oil from Tar Sand and Other Hydrocarbon Deposits*, 97th Congress, 1st session, 1981, H. Rept. 97-250, p. 23.
2. U.S. Congress, Senate, *Hearings before Subcommittee on Energy Resources and Materials Production of Committee on Energy and Natural Resources on S 2717 and HR 7242*, 96th Congress, 2d session, 1980, p. 84.
3. Public Law 97–78.
4. Senate, *Hearings on S 2717 and HR 7242* (1980), p. 44.
5. Ibid., p. 124.
6. U.S. Congress, Senate, *Hearings before Subcommittee on Energy and Mineral Resources of Committee on Energy and Natural Resources, "Combined Hydrocarbon Leasing Act of 1981,"* 97th Congress, 1st session, 1981, S. 1575, p. 39.
7. Ibid., pp. 2–3.
8. *Congressional Record*, July 14, 1981, p. H15672.
9. United States, Department of Energy, Energy Information Administration, *Annual Energy Review 1988* (Washington, D.C.: Department of Energy, 1989), p. 143.
10. Telephone interview with Reed Ferrel on February 9, 1990. Ferrel has done consulting work for Altex Oil Corporation, one of the tar sands leaseholders.
11. Regina Axelrod, "Energy Policy: Changing the Rules of the Game," in Michael Kraft and Norman Vig, eds., *Environmental Policy in the 1980s* (Washington, D.C.: Congressional Quarterly Press, 1984), p. 208.
12. *Federal Register*, July 18, 1984, p. 29156.
13. 43 *Code of Federal Regulations* 3140.2-3(f).
14. Ibid., 3140.1-4(d) (1).
15. Ibid., 3140.7.
16. Council on Environmental Quality, "Guidance Regarding NEPA Regulations," July 22, 1983, p. 20, contained in United States, Department of the Interior, National Park Service, *NEPA Compliance Guideline*, no. 12 (Denver: NPS, 1982).

17. United States, Department of the Interior, Bureau of Land Management, *Utah Combined Hydrocarbon Leasing Regional Final EIS, Record of Decision* (Denver: NPS, 1984), p. 2.

18. United States, Department of the Interior, National Park Service and Bureau of Land Management, *Tar Sand Triangle* [DEIS] (Denver: NPS, 1984), pp. iv–v.

19. Confidential personnel communication, August 2, 1985.

20. *Federal Register*, May 7, 1984, p. 19439.

21. Ibid., p. 19440.

22. Memo, BLM to Park Service, "Comments on the National Park Service Federal Register Notice on Proposed Procedures for Making a Finding of No Significant Adverse Impact," 1984, Tar Sands File, Park Service Rocky Mountain Regional Office, Denver, pp. 2–3.

23. Ibid., pp. 4–5.

24. Ibid., p. 10.

25. United States, Department of the Interior, Bureau of Land Management, cover sheet notes on "Comments on Park Service Directive for Making a Finding of No Significant Impact," 1984, Tar Sands File, BLM State Office, Salt Lake City, p. 1.

26. Interview with Ronald Bolander, ecologist, BLM, State Office, Salt Lake City, August 19, 1985.

27. Tar sands DEIS, p. 2-55.

28. Ibid., pp. 4-24–4-37, for a discussion of what these models do.

29. Ibid., pp. 4-32–4-33.

30. Ibid.

31. Transcript of public hearing held August 21, 1984, at Hanksville, Utah, on tar sands DEIS, Tar Sands File, BLM State Office, Salt Lake City.

32. Transcript of public hearing held August 23, 1984, at Salt Lake City on tar sands DEIS, Tar Sands File, BLM State Office, Salt Lake City.

33. Ibid., p. 12.

34. Ibid., pp. 18–19 and 21.

35. Ibid., p. 22.

36. Interview with Barbara West, Park Service Water Quality Division, Denver, October 17, 1985.

37. Kirkwood, after the initiation of the DEIS, submitted another lease conversion proposal that was to be analyzed by the BLM. Tar sands DEIS, p. 1-15.

38. Transcript of public hearing held August 28, 1984, at Lakewood, Colorado, Tar Sands File, BLM State Office, Salt Lake City.

39. Ibid., p. 7.

40. NPCA letter contained in Tar Sands File, National Park Service, Rocky Mountain Regional Office, Denver.

41. Ibid., p. 3.

42. Ibid., p. 6.

43. Environmental Defense Fund, Park Service Tar Sands File, Denver.

44. Earth First! Park Service Tar Sands File, Denver. Earth First! was founded in the 1970s as a self-styled radical and anarchistic response to what its members perceived as an overbureaucratization and softening of traditional preservation organizations. No study of preservation groups would be complete without considering this one.

45. EPA, Park Service Tar Sands File, Denver, November 27, 1984.

46. Ibid., p. 4.

47. State of Utah comment, Park Service Tar Sands File, Denver, p. 1.

48. These viewpoints are reported confidentially.

49. Utah comment, Tar Sands File, p. 10.

50. Ibid., p. 11.

51. Ibid., p. 3.

52. The Six County Planning and Economic Development District, Garfield County, and Wayne County all expressed this point of view. Park Service Tar Sands File, Denver, September 5, 1984.

53. See, for example, Garfield County's letter in Park Service Tar Sands File, Denver, October 9, 1984.

54. Santa Fe, Park Service Tar Sands File, Denver, October 15, 1984, p. 2.

55. Ibid.

56. 43 *Code of Federal Regulations* 3140.2-3(f).

57. Ibid.

58. *Federal Register*, May 24, 1982, p. 22474.

59. Santa Fe, Park Service Tar Sands File, Denver, p. 7.

60. Ibid., "Geologic Comments," p. 20.

61. Department of Energy, *Annual Energy Review 1988*, p. 113.

62. Ibid., section 5.

63. 43 *Code of Federal Regulations* 3140.2-3(f).

64. Memo, regional director to BLM State Office director, Salt Lake City, December 5, 1984, Park Service Tar Sands File, Denver.

65. Untitled memo regarding BLM and Park Service preferred alternatives, Park Service Tar Sands File, Denver, pp. 2–3.

66. Memo, chief of Energy, Minerals, and Mining Division, Park Service, to regional director, December 12, 1984, Park Service Tar Sands File, Denver.

67. Memo, acting director of Park Service to regional director, "Directive for Making No Adverse Impacts Determination," March 15, 1985, Park Service Tar Sands File, Denver.

68. Memo, chief of Energy, Minerals, and Mining Division, Park Service, to associate director for natural resources, January 25, 1985, Denver.

69. Ibid.

70. Ibid., as stated by the Park Service in this memo; the actual BLM proposal was not in the Tar Sands File.

71. Memo, associate director to director, Park Service, January 25, 1985, Park Service Tar Sands File, Denver.

72. Ibid., p. 3.

73. Memo, chief of Energy, Minerals, and Mining Division, Park Service, to special assistant to acting assistant secretary, Department of the Interior, February 15, 1985, Park Service Tar Sands File, Denver.

74. Ibid.

75. Ibid.

76. Memo, associate director for natural resources to special assistant to acting assistant secretary, Department of the Interior, February 26, 1985, Park Service Tar Sands File, Denver.

77. Ibid., p. 3.

78. Ibid.

79. Ibid., p. 4.

80. Ibid., p. 5.

81. Ibid.

82. Ibid., p. 7.

83. Message record and BLM briefing statement, April 11, 1985, Park Service Tar Sands File, Denver.

84. Ibid.

85. This discussion stems from three documents in the Park Service Tar Sands File, Denver: a memo from the regional director, Park Service, through the director and assistant secretary to the secretary of the Interior, April 17, 1985; a memo from the superintendent of GCNRA to the regional director, April 15, 1985; and the BLM briefing statement, April 11, 1985.

86. Memo, superintendent of GCNRA to regional director, p. 2.

87. BLM briefing statement, pp. 3 and 4.

88. Memo, superintendent of GCNRA to regional director, p. 2.

89. BLM briefing statement, p. 2.

90. Ibid., p. 4.

91. Memo, regional director, Park Service, to director, April 25, 1985, Park Service Tar Sands File, Denver.

92. Memo, associate director for natural resources to regional director, "Proposed Tar Sand Development in the Tar Sand Triangle" (mimeo), June 11, 1985.

93. Ibid., p. 3.

94. Personal interview with unnamed Park Service official, February 1986, Washington, D.C.

95. United States, Department of the Interior, Bureau of Land Management, *Utah BLM Statewide Wilderness Draft EIS*, 6 vols. (Salt Lake City: BLM State Office, 1986), 5:32 (French Spring–Happy Canyon Study Area).

96. Department of Energy, *Annual Energy Review 1988*, p. 143.

97. Lyle A. Johnson, Jr., *The Second Three-Dimensional Physical Simulation of Forward Combustion in Tar Sand Triangle Material* (Laramie, Wyo.: Western Research Institute, 1986). This report mentions yet another estimate of three billion barrels of bitumen in the tar sands triangle. Jim Burger, a scientist studying the area, noted in a telephone interview on February 8, 1990, that Howard Ritzma, one of the original students of the tar sands triangle, disputes these numbers. Ritzma thinks the area may have more recoverable oil.

98. See, for example, Michael Kraft and Norman Vig, eds., *Environmental Policy in the 1980s* (Washington, D.C.: Congressional Quarterly Press, 1984).

99. All of the BLM officials interviewed expressed some version of this position. Further evidence can be found in a 1988 NPCA newsletter discussing a BLM resource management plan for the San Juan region near the tar sands triangle. According to the NPCA, the Park Service "asked the BLM to designate certain sensitive lands around these parks [Canyonlands, Glen Canyon, and Natural Bridges]—viewshed, watershed, wildlife and archeological areas—as Areas of Critical Environmental Concern and to prohibit activities in these areas which could harm park values. The BLM refused." Also, William Lockhart, "External Park Threats and Interior's Limits: The Need for an Independent Park Service," in David Simon, ed., *Our Common Lands* (Washington, D.C.: Island Press, 1988), p. 28, quotes the BLM as stating that the 1916 NPS Organic Act "does not require the Secretary to leave public lands unimpaired to preserve park values" when dealing with adjacent activities under BLM jurisdiction.

100. J. Douglas Wellman, *Wildland Recreation Policy* (New York: John Wiley and Sons, 1987), p. 223.

101. U.S. Congress, Senate, *Hearings before Subcommittee on National Parks and Recreation of the Committee on Interior and Insular Affairs on S. 27, "A Bill to Establish Glen Canyon National Recreation Area,"* 92d Congress, 2d session, 1971, p. 74.

102. United States, Department of the Interior, National Park Service, *Proposed General Management Plan, Wilderness Recommendation, Road Study Alternatives, and Final Environmental Impact Statement, Glen Canyon National Recreation Area, Arizona-Utah* (Washington, D.C.: GPO, 1979), p. 229 (Sierra Club).

## CHAPTER FIVE. PROTECTING NATIONAL PARKS FROM EXISTING VISIBILITY IMPAIRMENT

1. William Malm, *An Introduction to Visibility* (Fort Collins, Colo.: NPS, 1984), p. 1.
2. Ibid.
3. Ibid., p. 9.
4. Ibid.
5. Ibid., p. 4.
6. R. D. Rowe and L. G. Chestnut, *Managing Air Quality in National Parks and Wilderness Areas* (Boulder, Colo.: Westview Press, 1983), p. 8.
7. An important catalyst was "Smog Alert for Our Southwestern National Parks," *National Parks and Conservation Magazine* 49, 7 (July 1975): 9–15.
8. U.S. Congress, House, *Hearing before the Subcommittee on Health and the Environment of the Committee on Interstate and Foreign Commerce on HR 4151, 4758, and 4444*, 95th Congress, 1st session, 1977.
9. Ibid., p. 457.
10. Ibid., p. 481.
11. U.S. Congress, House Committee on Interstate and Foreign Commerce, *Clean Air Act Amendments of 1977*, 97th Congress, 1st session, 1977, H. Rept. 95-294, p. 204.
12. Ibid.
13. Ibid.
14. Ibid.
15. For a comprehensive account of the role of the courts in shaping clean air policies during the early to mid-1970s, see R. Shep Melnick, *Regulation and the Courts: The Case of the Clean Air Act* (Washington, D.C.: Brookings Institution, 1983).
16. *United States Code* (1982), Title 42, Sections 7472(a) and 7474.
17. H. Rept. 95-294, p. 205. See Jerome Ostrov, "Visibility Protection under the Clean Air Act: Preserving Scenic and Parkland Areas in the Southwest," *Ecology Law Quarterly* 10 (1982): 405–6, on the EPA's difficulty in setting an $NO_2$ standard.
18. *United States Code* (1982), Title 42, Section 7475(d)(2)(B).
19. H. Rept. 95-294, p. 13.
20. *Congressional Record*, May 25, 1977, p. 16203.
21. Ibid.
22. A preliminary list of Park Service class II areas open to class I redesignation by the states appeared in the *Federal Register* on September 7, 1979, with an expanded list appearing on June 25, 1980. The EPA published a list of mandatory class I Park Service areas in the *Federal Register* on November 30, 1979.
23. BART guidelines can be found in the EPA's *Guidelines for Best Available Retrofit Technology for Determining Coal-Fired Power Plants and Other Secondary Sources* (Washington, D.C.: EPA, 1980).

24. Congressional Research Service, *Legislative History of the Clean Air Act Amendments of 1977*, 6 vols. (Washington, D.C.: GPO, 1977–1978), 3:535.

25. William Lewis, "Protection against Visibility Impairment under the Clean Air Act," *Journal of the Air Pollution Control Association* 30, 2 (February 1980): 119.

26. D. H. Nochumson and M. D. Williams, "Copper Smelters and Atmospheric Visibility in the Southwest: A Seasonal Analysis," *Journal of the Air Pollution Control Association* 34, 7 (July 1984): 750–75.

27. Ostrov, "Visibility Protection under the Clean Air Act," pp. 411–27.

28. *Federal Register*, February 15, 1985, p. 6234, and *United States Code* (1980), Title 42, Section 7419 (supplement 4, 1982).

29. Personal communication, Park Service Air Quality Division, March 18, 1986.

30. Congressional Research Service, *Legislative History*, 3:335.

31. Ibid., 3:378.

32. Julie Horne, "Visibility Regulations," *Journal of the Air Pollution Control Association* 30, 2 (February 1980): 121.

33. U.S. Environmental Protection Agency, *Summary of Comments and Responses on the May 22, 1980, Proposed Regulations for Visibility Protection for Federal Class I Areas* (Washington, D.C.: EPA, 1980), p. 1.

34. Ibid.

35. *Federal Register*, December 2, 1980, p. 80091.

36. Ibid., pp. 80085–86.

37. In November 1984, the EPA announced the first meeting of a task force to study and develop strategies for dealing with regional haze. *Federal Register*, November 9, 1984, p. 40770.

38. *Federal Register*, December 2, 1980, p. 80087. This "staged" approach is articulated in the preamble to the actual regulations. Today, some people think that since the regulations themselves only refer to "reasonably attributable" visibility impairment, $SO_2$ impairment can be more immediately addressed.

39. Ibid., p. 80085.

40. Ibid., p. 80091.

41. Ibid., p. 80087.

42. Ibid., p. 80091.

43. Ibid., p. 80087.

44. Ibid., p. 80089.

45. Horne, "Visibility Regulations," p. 121.

46. Ibid.

47. Ibid.

48. Ibid.

49. *Federal Register*, December 2, 1980, p. 80090.

50. Ibid., p. 80091.

51. Ibid., p. 80086.

52. EPA, *Summary of Comments*, p. 165.

53. Ibid., p. 164.

54. See, for example, Hunton and Williams (firm), "Initial Comment of the Utility Air Regulatory Group on Proposed Regulation for Visibility Protection," in EPA, *Summary of Comments*, pp. 24–27.

55. Ostrov, "Visibility Protection under the Clean Air Act," p. 400.

56. *Federal Register*, March 12, 1987, p. 7802.

57. EPA, *Summary of Contents*, p. 160n13.

58. Ibid.

59. Interview with David Joseph, Park Service Air Quality Division, March 12, 1986, Fort Collins, Colo.

60. United States, Department of the Interior, National Park Service, *Air Resources Management Manual* (Denver: NPS, 1985), pp. 37–38.

61. Memo, G. Ray Arnett, assistant secretary of the Interior, to directors of Park Service and Fish and Wildlife Service, July 2, 1981, contained in appendix to Park Service's *Air Resources Management Manual.*

62. Richard Andrews, "Deregulation: The Failure at EPA," in Michael Kraft and Norman Vig, eds., *Environmental Policy in the 1980s* (Washington, D.C.: Congressional Quarterly Press, 1984), p. 168.

63. Richard Harris and Sidney Milkis, *The Politics of Regulatory Change* (New York: Oxford University Press, 1989), p. 258.

64. Paul Culhane, "Sagebrush Rebels in Office: Jim Watt's Land and Water Politics," in Kraft and Vig, eds., *Environmental Policy in the 1980s,* p. 309.

65. Ibid., p. 310.

66. *Environmental Law Reporter,* April 1983, *Environmental Defense Fund v. Gorsuch,* no. C-82-6850, p. 65780.

67. *Federal Register,* May 16, 1984, p. 20647. Some NPS employees questioned the speed with which the EPA anticipated taking over visibility protection from the states that did not revise their SIPs. The EPA could have, they said, prepared its own regulations in case the states did not respond.

68. Ibid.

69. *Federal Register,* October 23, 1984, p. 42671.

70. Ibid.

71. Ibid.

72. Ibid., p. 42672.

73. *Federal Register,* July 12, 1985, pp. 28545–47.

74. Ibid.

75. *Federal Register,* November 13, 1985, pp. 46782–84.

76. *Federal Register,* July 12, 1985, p. 28545.

77. Ibid.

78. Ibid., p. 28546.

79. *Federal Register,* December 2, 1980, p. 80090.

80. *Federal Register,* May 22, 1980, p. 34776.

81. Ibid.

82. Ibid.

83. Ostrov, "Visibility Protection under the Clean Air Act," p. 446.

84. *Federal Register,* December 2, 1980, p. 80090.

85. Ibid., p. 80092.

86. Ibid.

87. Ibid., p. 80093.

88. *Federal Register,* January 15, 1981, p. 3651.

89. Ibid.

90. Ostrov, "Visibility Protection under the Clean Air Act," p. 446.

91. Memo, Park Service director Mott through assistant secretary of the Interior to the under secretary of the Interior, September 9, 1985, Washington, D.C.

92. Ibid.

93. Ibid.

94. Memo, assistant secretary for Fish, Wildlife, and Parks to Park Service director Mott, October 25, 1985, Washington, D.C.

95. Ibid.

96. Remarks by the secretary of the Interior to the National Recreation and Park Association, Congress, Dallas, Texas, October 25, 1985.

97. Ibid.

98. Ibid.

99. Ibid.

100. Ostrov, "Visibility Protection under the Clean Air Act," p. 447(n331) and p. 400(n27).

101. National Parks and Conservation Association, *National Parks* 60, 1–2 (January–February 1986): 38, and National Park Service, Air Quality Division, personal communication. Only the Roosevelt Campobello International Park, which is administered by a commission, identified integral vistas. The EPA is still investigating whether any of these vistas are impaired.

102. For an excellent summary of the hearings, see the report of the Congressional Research Service in U.S. Congress, House, Interior Subcommittee on National Parks and Recreation, *Impacts of Air Pollution on National Park Units*, 99th Congress, 1st session, 1985, pp. 465–81.

103. The 1980 regulations made clear this responsibility of the EPA; see, for example, *Federal Register*, 1980, p. 80085–86.

104. Personal communication, Park Service, Denver, March 1986.

105. Ibid. Also, Robert Yuhnke of the Environmental Defense Fund added that EPA officials in charge of the visibility program told attendees of the 1981 meeting of the Air Pollution Control Association that the EPA did not intend to push visibility protection (telephone interview with Robert Yuhnke, February 10, 1986).

106. House, *Impacts of Air Pollution on National Park Units* (1985), p. 357. The Park Service is certainly not the only research actor on air quality and the parks. See, for example, the statement of Douglas Latimer of Systems Applications in these hearings, pp. 295–302.

107. Personal communication, National Park Service, Air Quality Division, Denver, March 18, 1986.

108. Ibid. The hearings indicate that this was indeed a problem. Cong. Bruce Vento of Minnesota suggested that the EPA administrator in charge of air programs, Charles Elkins, was opposed to a visibility task force's recommendations until more research was done. Paradoxically, one of the task force's recommendations called for more research.

109. Memo from Susan Recce, acting deputy assistant secretary of Department of the Interior, to Charles Elkins, acting assistant administrator for air and radiation, EPA, November 14, 1985, Washington, D.C.

110. Personal communication, National Park Service Air Quality Division, March 18, 1986.

111. House, *Impacts of Air Pollution* (1985), p. 546. This 20 percent figure is partially based on inference by the Park Service. There is, for example, no monitoring of carbon (see ibid., p. 115 and 151).

112. Ibid., p. 469.

113. Ibid., p. 147.

114. Ibid.

115. Ibid., p. 539.

116. Ibid. More specifically, there are fine particulate monitors for visibility at twenty-eight parks, teleradiometers at twenty-nine parks, and cameras at

thirty-five parks (see ibid., p. 29). The teleradiometer was developed by Park Service air-quality personnel.

117. Ibid., p. 411.

118. Ibid., p. 151.

119. See the prepared testimony of George Green of Western Energy Supply and Transmission Associates, ibid., pp. 407–15.

120. Testimony of J. Robert White during the 1985 House air pollution hearings, ibid., p. 319.

121. Ibid., pp. 329–30.

122. Ibid., pp. 466–69.

123. Ibid., pp. 309–10.

124. Recce to Elkins, November 14, 1985, p. 3.

125. Harris and Milkis, *Politics of Regulatory Change*, pp. 265–66.

126. Ibid., p. 269.

127. Recce to Elkins, November 14, 1985, p. 3.

128. *Federal Register*, March 12, 1987, p. 7804.

129. Ibid., p. 7806.

130. Ibid.

131. Ibid.

132. C. V. Mathai, C. D. Allen, and D. V. Giovanni, "Visibility Impairment in the Mesa Verde National Park and $NO_x$ Control Options at the Four Corners Power Plant," in Prem S. Bhardwaja, ed., *Visibility Protection: Research and Policy Aspects* (Pittsburgh: Air Pollution Control Association, 1986), p. 4.

133. Ibid.

134. David Ross, "An Examination of the Relative Importance of Park Attributes at Several National Parks," in Bhardwaja, ed., *Visibility Protection*, pp. 304–19.

135. Charles McDae, "Goals and Initial Findings from SCENES," in Bhardwaja, ed., *Visibility Protection*, pp. 76–86.

136. David Joseph, "Plans for IMPROVE: A Federal Program to Monitor Visibility in Class I Areas," in Bhardwaja, ed., *Visibility Protection*, pp. 113–25.

137. U.S. Environmental Protection Agency, "Developing Long-Term Strategies for Regional Haze: Findings and Recommendations of the Visibility Task Force" (mimeo) 1985, p. 18.

138. Ibid., p. 4.

139. Ibid., p. 18.

140. Ibid.

141. Ibid., pp. 15 and 21.

142. Ibid., p. 17.

143. Ibid.

144. Ibid., p. 21.

145. Ibid.

146. Personal communication from EPA and Park Service air-quality personnel, March 18, 1986, and April 10, 1986.

147. *Federal Register*, July 1, 1987, p. 24670.

148. Memo, Becky Dunlop, deputy chief operating officer of Department of the Interior, to EPA, November 5, 1987, for inclusion in Docket A-86-19, Washington, D.C.

149. Ibid., p. 5.

150. Vermont, "Implementation Plan for the Protection of Visibility in the State of Vermont," Air Pollution Control Program, Department of Water Re-

sources and Environmental Engineering, Vermont Agency of Environmental Conservation, July 1985, p. 5. Hereafter cited as Vermont SIP.

151. Ibid.

152. Personal communications, Park Service officials, March–April 1986.

153. Vermont SIP, p. 89.

154. Ibid., pp. 7–8.

155. This conclusion is documented in chapter 7 of the Vermont plan and in a paper by Richard Poirot, Paul Wishinski, and Richard Valentinetti, "The Origin of Visibility Impairment in Vermont," presented at the Air Pollution Control Association meeting, June 1985, in Detroit.

156. See Vermont SIP for its justification of the sulfate standard.

157. Vermont SIP, "Executive Summary of Vermont SIP" (insertion), pp. 1–2; see also Poirot et al., "Origin of Visibility Impairment."

158. Vermont SIP, pp. 2–3.

159. Ibid., p. 88.

160. Ibid., pp. 2–3.

161. Ibid.

162. Federal Register, July 17, 1987, pp. 26978–81.

163. United States, District Court, District of Maine, "Memorandum of Decision and Order Granting Defendant's and Defendant-Intervenor's Motion to Dismiss," Maine v. Thomas, 87-0204-P (July 27, 1988), p. 12(n20).

164. United States Code (1982), Title 16, Section 7604.

165. As quoted in "Environmental Policy Alert" (mimeo), Washington, D.C., December 2, 1987, p. 5.

166. United States, District Court, District of Maine, "Memorandum of Plaintiffs, State of Maine et al., (1) Replying in Support of Plaintiff's Motion for Summary Judgement, and (2) Opposing Defendant's and Intervenor-Defendant's Motions to Dismiss or for Summary Judgement," 87-0204-P.

167. Ibid., pp. 2–9.

168. United States, District Court, District of Maine, "Memorandum of Law in Support of Defendant's Motion to Dismiss, or, in the Alternative, for Summary Judgement and in Opposition to Plaintiff's Motion for Summary Judgement," 87-0204-P, pp. 21–29.

169. United States, District Court, District of Maine, "Memorandum of Decision," pp. 10–11.

170. Ibid., p. 9.

171. Ibid., p. 12(n20).

172. United States, Court of Appeals, First Circuit, Maine v. Thomas, 88-1983 (May 19, 1989), pp. 19–20.

173. Ibid., p. 16.

174. Utah, "Utah State Implementation Plan," section 16.4 (visibility protection), mimeo, April 15, 1985. Hereafter cited as Utah SIP.

175. Ibid.

176. U.S. Congress, Senate, Committee on Environment and Public Works, The Impact of the Proposed EPA Budget on State and Local Environmental Programs, hearings before the Subcommittee on Toxic Substances and Environmental Oversight, 98th Congress, 1st session, February 16 and March 28, 1983, p. 221.

177. Charles E. Davis and James P. Lester, "Decentralizing Federal Environmental Policy Correlates of Federal Aid Replacement by the American States," paper presented at Southwestern Political Science Association meeting, San Antonio, Texas, March 19–22, 1986.

178. Utah SIP, section 16.6.

179. Ibid., section 16.7.

180. Ibid.

181. Utah Citizens Advisory Committee, *Statement on Visibility*, January 1, 1987, appendix A, p. 1, Office of the Governor, Salt Lake City.

182. Terri Martin, "Utah Decides It Can't Afford to Keep Its Air Clean," *High Country News*, December 21, 1987, p. 14.

183. Letter from Brian Mitchell, Park Service Air Quality Division, to author, January 12, 1988.

184. "Remarks Prepared for Scott Matheson," in Bhardwaja, ed., *Visibility Protection*, pp. 915–17.

185. Telephone interview with Gordon Anderson, August 5, 1988.

186. United States, Department of the Interior, National Park Service, "Effect of Navajo Generating Station on Wintertime Visibility at Grand Canyon National Park: Historical and Supplemental Information," *Draft Final Report* (Denver: Air Quality Division, NPS, 1989), p. 2.

187. National Park Service, "Brief Summary of the Conclusions of the April 7, 1989, Draft Final Report on WHITEX," mimeo, p. 1, Denver.

188. National Park Service, "Effect of Navajo Generating Station," p. 8.

189. Ibid., p. 2.

190. Ellen Hale, "Western Panoramas Threatened," *Idaho Statesman*, July 9, 1989, p. 10A.

191. *Federal Register*, September 5, 1989, p. 36951.

192. Ibid., pp. 36951–52.

193. Barbara Rosewicz, "Air Pollution at Grand Canyon Blamed on Power Plant Partly Owned by U.S.," *Wall Street Journal*, August 30, 1989, p. A20.

194. Letter from Manuel Lujan, secretary of the Interior, to A. J. Pfister, general manager of the Salt River Project, January 5, 1990.

195. Rosewicz, "Air Pollution at Grand Canyon," p. A20.

196. U.S. Environmental Protection Agency, "Approval and Promulgation of Implementation Plans: Revision of the Visibility FIP for Arizona" (draft), pp. 27–34. The other two documents are EPA, "Regulatory Impact Analysis of a Revision of the Federal Implementation Plan for the State of Arizona to Include SO$_2$ Controls for the Navajo Generating Station" (draft), February 5, 1990; and E. H. Pechan and Associates, "Best Available Retrofit (BART) Analysis for the Navajo Generating Station in Page, Arizona" (EPA contract 68-02-4400), January 31, 1990.

197. EPA, "Regulatory Impact Analysis," p. 3.

198. EPA, "Approval and Promulgation," p. 25.

199. EPA, "Regulatory Impact Analysis," p. 23.

200. Ibid.

201. Ibid., p. 3.

202. Ibid.

203. Ibid., p. 40.

204. EPA, "Approval and Promulgation," pp. 12–13.

205. Ronald Foresta, *America's National Parks and Their Keepers* (Baltimore: Johns Hopkins University Press, for Resources for the Future, 1984), p. 121.

206. This is the tone of most of the articles in Kraft and Vig, eds., *Environmental Policy in the 1980s*.

207. Sen. Harry Reid, "Restricted Vision," *National Parks* (May–June 1988): 15; also letter from Denise Scott, EPA, to author, March 13, 1989.

208. Ibid., p. 15.
209. Gordon Anderson interview, August 5, 1988.
210. Ibid.
211. Reid, "Restricted Vision," p. 15.
212. Robert Yuhnke, "Must the West's Air Become an Opaque Shroud," *High Country News*, October 9, 1989, pp. 12–13.

## CHAPTER SIX. CONCLUSION: RESOLVING EXTERNAL THREATS TO NATIONAL PARKS

1. For an introduction to the administrative presidency, see Terry Moe, "The Politicized Presidency," in John Chubb and Paul Peterson, eds., *The New Direction in American Politics* (Washington, D.C.: Brookings Institution, 1985), pp. 235–72; Joel D. Aberbach and Bert A. Rockman, "Mandates or Mandarins? Control and Discretion in the Modern Administrative State," *Public Administration Review* 48 (March-April 1988): 606–12; Charles Levine, "The Federal Government in the Year 2000: Administrative Legacies of the Reagan Years," *Public Administration Review* 46 (May-June 1986): 195–206; Robert Durant, "Towards Assessing the Administrative Presidency: Public Lands, the BLM, and the Reagan Administration," *Public Administration Review* 47 (March-April 1987): 180–89; James Pfiffner, "Political Appointees and Career Executives: The Democracy—Bureaucracy Nexus in the Third Century," *Public Administration Review* 47 (January-February 1987): 57–66; and Patricia Ingraham and Carolyn Ban, "Models of Public Management: Are They Useful to Federal Managers in the 1980s?" *Public Administration Review* 46 (March-April 1986): 152–160.

2. Michael Kraft and Norman Vig, eds., *Environmental Policy in the 1980s* (Washington, D.C.: Congressional Quarterly Press, 1984).

3. National Parks and Conservation Association, *National Park System Plan* (Washington, D.C.: NPCA, 1988), pp. 38–44.

4. Letter from Park Service director Mott to Paul Pritchard, president of NPCA, November 17, 1987, in the comment file on NPCA *National Park System Plan*, Office of Policy, National Park Service, Washington, D.C.; and comments of superintendent of Sequoia and Kings Canyon national parks, March 11, 1988, in same file.

5. Comments of regional director, North Atlantic Region, National Park Service, in ibid.

6. Various comments of Park Service personnel, in ibid.

7. Comments of chief, Science Division, Great Smoky Mountains National Park, National Park Service, in ibid.

8. George B. Hartzog, Jr., *Battling for the National Parks: A Political and Personal Memoir* (Mount Kisco, N.Y.: Moyer Bell, 1988), p. 54.

9. U.S. Congress, House, Committee on Interior and Insular Affairs, *Establishing a National Park System Review Board and for Other Purposes*, 100th Congress, 2d session, 1988, H. Rept. 100-742.

10. Ibid.

11. Peter Steinhart, "The Park Service Feels an Early Chill from Watt's Interior," *Los Angeles Times*, November 8, 1981, part 5, p. 1.

12. William Brown, "Preamble Grist," *George Wright Forum* 5 (Spring 1987): 8.

13. Katharine Collins, "Park Employees Buck Their Boss," *High Country News*, May 12, 1986, p. 4.

14. Ibid.

15. J. Douglas Wellman, *Wildland Recreation Policy* (New York: John Wiley and Sons, 1987), pp. 264–65.

16. Hartzog, *Battling for National Parks*, pp. 273–74.

17. Warren Brown, *Case Studies in Protecting Parks*, Natural Resources Report 87-2 (Washington, D.C.: NPS, 1987), p. 2.

18. Ibid.

19. Barbara Romzek and Melvin Dubnick, "Accountability in the Public Sector: Lessons from the Challenger Tragedy," *Public Administration Review* 46 (May–June 1987): 229.

20. Ibid., p. 227.

21. Wallace Stegner, "The Best Idea We Ever Had," *Wilderness* 46 (Spring 1983): 4 (emphasis added).

22. Romzek and Dubnick, "Accountability in Public Sector," p. 229.

23. United States, Department of the Interior, National Park Service, *Statistical Abstract: 1988* (Denver: Denver Service Center, 1988), p. 4.

24. Joseph Sax, *Mountains without Handrails* (Ann Arbor: University of Michigan Press, 1980), p. 103.

25. "Ban on National Park Hotels Is Urged," *New York Times*, May 25, 1988.

26. National Parks and Conservation Association, *Alert* (June 1988), Salt Lake City.

27. William Lockhart, "External Park Threats and Interior's Limits: The Need for an Independent Park Service," in National Parks and Conservation Association, in David Simon, ed., *Our Common Lands* (Washington, D.C.: Island Press, 1988), p. 45.

28. Ibid., p. 53.

29. For an excellent study of how public policies first become part of various political agendas, see John Kingdon, *Agendas, Alternatives, and Public Policies* (Boston: Little, Brown, 1984).

30. United States, Department of the Interior, National Park Service, *Management Policies* (Washington, D.C.: NPS, 1988), p. 44.

31. Thomas Lucke, "Extraction of Non-Renewable Resources in Biosphere Reserves: An Opportunity to Meet the Needs of Man and Nature," paper presented at the Conference on the Management of Biosphere Reserves, Great Smoky Mountains National Park, November 28, 1984, p. 3. Lucke, in several conversations I had with him, was quite clear about the opportunities he saw for the Park Service in this area.

# NOTE ON THE SOURCES

The extensive endnotes provide a comprehensive list of relevant sources used in this study of the threats to parks issue. The following discussion is designed to highlight some of the more important and interesting works relevant to the national parks, park history and policy, and the threats issue.

Readers interested in the history of the national parks and the national park idea should start with two sources. Alfred Runte's *National Parks: The American Experience* (Lincoln: University of Nebraska Press, 1987) is a superb history of the national park idea in the United States. Roderick Nash's *Wilderness and the American Mind*, rev. ed. (New Haven, Conn.: Yale University Press, 1986), is an intellectual history of the wilderness idea in the United States but contains much useful information on the national parks. Both books also contain good bibliographies of additional works related to national park history.

Comprehensive writing on national park policy begins with John Ise's *Our National Park Policy: A Critical History* (Baltimore: Johns Hopkins University Press, 1960). Ise's work takes park policy up to 1960. Ronald Foresta's *America's National Parks and Their Keepers* (Baltimore: Johns Hopkins University Press, for Resources for the Future, 1984) brings park policy into the early 1980s, as does William C. Everhart's *The National Park Service* (Boulder, Colo.: Westview Press, 1983). J. Douglas Wellman looks, in part, at the Park Service and some of its current problems in his *Wildland Recreation Policy* (New York: John Wiley and Sons, 1987). My own "The National Parks: Political versus Professional Control over Policy," *Public Administration Review* (May/June 1989): 278–86, offers a perspective on the national park policy environment and the difficulties faced by the Park Service in making park policy.

For a more-focused look at park policy, consult the various documents prepared by the National Park Service. These include *Management Policies*, last revised in 1988. These policies provide overall guidance on aspects of park policy. Also, the *Code of Federal Regulations*, especially Title 36, can be helpful. The Park Service has an elaborate planning process that can give insight into how the agency manages individual park units. Park planning begins with a Statement for Management, which guides the planning process. Most units have a General Management Plan. There are also more specific plans used to help implement the General

Management Plan, such as a Resource Management Plan and a Concessions Management Plan. Not all park units will have all of the focused implementing plans. Trends within the Park Service can be followed through three publications: *Ranger*, the journal of the Association of National Park Rangers; *Park Science*, which covers research in the national parks and is published by the Park Service; and *George Wright Forum*, the journal of the George Wright Society, a group whose focus is park protection and research.

The external threats problem can be approached through a variety of sources. Foresta's book has a chapter, "Beyond Park Boundaries," devoted to the threats problem. The Park Service's *State of the Parks, 1980: A Report to the Congress* (Washington, D.C.: GPO, 1980) describes the issue as seen from the agency's perspective at that time. The National Parks and Conservation Association recently published *Our Common Lands* (Washington, D.C.: Island Press, 1988), which examines laws that address selected threats. Some examples are the Clean Air Act Amendments (1977), the Clean Water Act (1977), and the Surface Mining Control and Reclamation Act (1977), as well as the National Environmental Policy Act (1969). In addition, the book presents more general legal perspectives on the 1916 Organic Act and its powers, as well as the public trust doctrine.

There are many external threats issues, and being informed about all of them would be difficult. The Park Service published *Case Studies in Protecting Parks* (Washington, D.C.: National Park Service, 1987), which discusses specific threat problems and agency attempts to deal with them. The major environmental journals, such as *Sierra*, *Wilderness*, and *National Parks*, cover the current issues facing the national parks from an environmental perspective. Another indispensable publication is *High Country News*, which covers a variety of western natural resources issues.

# INTERVIEWS

*Telephone*

Richard Aiken (Department of Energy, formerly with the Bureau of Land Management, Washington, D.C.), February 4, 1986.

John Bachmann (Environmental Protection Agency, Office of Air Quality Planning and Standards, Research Triangle Park, North Carolina), April 10, 1986.

Tim Daugherty (National Park Service, Division of Environmental Compliance, Washington, D.C.), February 3, 1986.

Janet Metsa (Environmental Protection Agency, Office of Air Quality Planning and Standards, Research Triangle Park, North Carolina), April 10, 1986.

Robert Yuhnke (Environmental Defense Fund, Boulder, Colorado), February 10, 1986.

*Personal*

David Joseph (National Park Service, Air Quality Division, Denver) first interview held in Fort Collins, Colorado, March 12 and 18, 1986.

Lorraine Mintzmeyer (National Park Service, regional director, Denver) interview held in Fort Collins, Colorado, October 30, 1985.

Brian Mitchell (National Park Service, Air Quality Division, Denver), March 18, 1986.

William Paleck (superintendent, Saguaro National Monument), November 12, 1988.

Toni Ristau (former project coordinator of tar sands EIS) interview held in Salt Lake City, August 20, 1985.

Thomas Slater and Ronald Bolander (Bureau of Land Management, Salt Lake City state office), August 19, 1986.

Barbara West (National Park Service, formerly with Energy, Minerals, and Mining Division, now with Water Quality Division, Denver), October 10, 1985.

*National Park Service Officials with Whom*
*I Informally Discussed the External Threats Issue*

Robert Barbee (superintendent, Yellowstone National Park)
Thomas Lucke (chief, Water Resources Division, Fort Collins, Colorado)
Molly Ross (Air Quality Division, Washington, D.C.)
William Supernaugh (chief, Resource Management Division, Mid-Atlantic Region, Philadelphia)

# INDEX